THE STRUGGLING STUDENT

THE ACTION PLAN FOR PARENTS TO UNLOCK ACADEMIC POTENTIAL

LISA CROSBY, M.ED.

CONTENTS

FINAL THOUGHTS TO CONSIDER

I dedicate this book to my family.
To my husband, Tim, who has supported me every step of the way.
Also, thank you to my sons who have made me so incredibly proud of their kindness and integrity, along with their personal and professional achievements. My sons allowed me to educate them and still be their mom and friend along the path to high school graduation. After that, they have proven success stories on their own, and a mother could not be prouder. And to my daughter-in-law, who has enriched our family beyond words:
Thank you for being on my team in every way possible.
Lastly, thank you to my parents.
Without their model of hard work and unconditional love,
I know I would not be where I am today.

FOREWORD

As a child and adolescent psychiatrist, you may assume that I have parenting pretty much figured out. Definitely not the case. You may assume that I know all the tricks of the trade on how to raise children to be successful students. This has proven false. You may also suppose that I have a sprawling library and bulging Rolodex full of amazing resources to best accommodate my clients' academic needs (as well as for my own children). That's an unfortunate no.

Working within the traditional school system has been one of my main challenges both professionally and personally. I am not an educator and won't even begin to claim understanding all of the challenges and expectations imposed upon a teacher and school. I gather it goes up much further to the policy makers. However, I can speak as a participant in the system.

Professionally, I have participated in many school mental health programs, attended Individualized Education Program (IEP) meetings, and written countless letters for clients asking for school support. It is also safe to say 80 percent of the kids I see have school concerns. I do my best to piece out and address any mental health issues contributing to academic challenges. For the most part, even with helpful interventions on the mental health side, school support and their interventions are still very much needed. Sadly, save for a few exceptions, my clients and parents consistently voice disappointment in school involvement, or lack thereof.

On a personal level, all three of my boys have had significant bumps in their school experiences. Between the three of them, they have attended nine different schools in two states, including a private religious school, a non-public hybrid model, a mainstream public school, experiential and international baccalaureate schools, and a Waldorf school. I knew that we must have been missing something on our end as every night seemed to result in kid tears, fights, and concerned late night conversations with my husband. Why are they so unmotivated to do their work? Why is their work so clearly below mediocrity? Why are there some obvious gaps in their math and writing? Why do they see such little value in school (besides friendships)? And most importantly: Where are we as parents dropping the ball?

By fourth grade, we were at a loss with my eldest son. He was obviously behind in reading and writing, but school was not concerned enough to initiate an intervention. Each year I could tell he was getting more and more disengaged and sad and did not want to go to school. I could make some stabs in the dark about how to help, but adjustments at home were not resulting in any significant turnaround. Bringing him to therapy was somewhat helpful but did not solve the school issue. I needed some advice, some support, or at least some clues.

After desperately looking for an alternative school option, I came upon a school, Custom Learning Academy (CLA). It was nestled in the woods about one hour away from our home in Nevada. While my son shadowed for a day at CLA, I met with the founder, Lisa Crosby. She was clearly a competent and knowledgeable educator, but she also spoke the language of emotions, motivation, and self-esteem.

For the first time in many years, I felt hopeful for my son. That hope turned into a reality of transformation. She identified important missing building blocks in his reading, language, and math. She also saw he had significant dysgraphia. Ms. Crosby created a program to get him up to speed in all of those areas.

Ms. Crosby also quickly identified that my son had not felt safe learning at school. I knew we were in good hands when, for the first month, she had every student in my son's class put up dividers when test-taking. This was just one stealth intervention she implemented, so my son felt safe doing his work. Her school was therapeutic aside from his specific educational interventions. There were so many intentional facets to her school that primed kids to grow, get out of their comfort zone safely, and love to learn!

Make no mistake though, Lisa was not a pushover. All of her students knew she had high expectations for them both academically and behaviorally. She raised the bar high and was determined to have everyone at his or her potential. She expected respect and kindness and reciprocated those values.

My son moved to grade level in reading and math, and just as important, I could see he was engaged, was confident, and enjoyed going to school. Unfortunately, we moved out of state the next year. We tried more mainstream schools and then a project-based school. Neither was a good fit, and he slipped under everyone's radar again, fading into the *safe* background. To this day, as a senior in high school, he says, "CLA was my best school."

Lisa Crosby was able to answer all those questions my husband and I used to mull over. That is what she does best: answer tough questions and turn everything around. I became fascinated by her understanding of academic roadblocks and how to intervene. What became apparent very early on in our interactions was that Lisa is a part of a bigger paradigm shift of understanding and educating our children. I hope to share, from a psychological perspective, why I believe Lisa's interventions are on target. I also hope to show how incredibly grateful I am as a parent of struggling students to have found this amazing woman.

As a nerdy psychiatrist, I wanted to dissect what was so effective about her ability to transform her students. We are all intrinsically motivated to learn. Learning equals survival and safety if you look at it from a purely biological perspective. On a more emotional level, learning gives us purpose. So, what causes the breakdown of a genetically programmed drive to learn and what causes the shift to apathetic behavior and loss of motivation to learn? And how do Lisa's techniques reboot the instinctual drive to learn?

I am sure there are many different facets to answering those questions. My bias is to see issues and solutions through a lens of relationships. Especially working with children, I am mostly taking stock of the quality of attachment and safety in relationships. If learning is linked to safety and purpose, I knew I was searching for these two ticket items when thinking about the effectiveness of Lisa's work.

Fast forward to my middle son who is working with Lisa now on overcoming his math phobia or aversion. The answer to my query came one day when listening to my son talk to Lisa. He sounded like his best self. Hold on, I know this moment. It is when my kids are not tired, well fed, happy, and respectful, and I realize I pulled off a good parenting day. It is also the moment at work when I can see my clients moving toward health as their parent relationships improve. It was not a complicated piece of insight into my burning question of how Lisa does it, but it made sense. *Best teaching mirrors best parenting!* Teaching and parenting are both creating models for children about learning, exploration, and expectation. They also both have elements of *safety* and *purpose* (or lack thereof). This was satisfying on the mom level but also professionally. By linking an unknown world of education to a known world of parenting, I could now explain her magic. (See Jaime's analysis of parenting styles paralleling positive education for children in Chapter 6: Family Culture.)

What Ms. Crosby was doing at her school, and what she does now with her students, is provide this unicorn-inspired model. You can see it all through the emails about my son as well as already described interactions. She takes struggling students with breaches in school *attachment* and mends them back to health. This style in turn satisfies the two big motivating ticket items to learn: safety and purpose. As a result, the student's genetic drive to learn kicks in, and transformation occurs. To bring this message home, here is a summary of her specific inspired interventions through the view of safety and purpose.

Safety in being seen: Lisa takes the time to listen to the student's education story. Her students learn that they have a place where they can be seen and heard. She discusses the student's needs and how to match them with interventions. This not only includes matching the point of struggle but highlighting the student's strength. There is nothing that feels safer or more valued than when someone knows what you need and strives to match it.

Safety in expectations and limits: Lisa dives in and sets the expectations for performance and behavior. Resistance to her expectations is met with consistent consequences, but also with communication regarding the issue. Lisa will hear them out and adjust accordingly. Most importantly, there is no shame while her students adjust to her limit setting. Performing to expectation is valued and met with praise and encouragement. A student feels safe knowing who the leader is, and respects this. This creates easy alignment with the rules and expectations. There is no one-sided dictatorship or a permissive allowance for low expectations.

Safety in performance: Lisa's definition of expected performance is not getting the answers correct. Her definition of performance is putting in the effort and working to the best of the student's ability. Mistakes and challenges are used for direction of learning, not punishment or shame. The goal is to learn, not to look good or smart. Feedback can be safely accepted for growth and is not internalized as being bad or less than. There is no uninvolved teaching in Lisa's arena. She will not move on until the student can show that the concept is understood.

Purpose in relationship: With safety and respect in place, there is a sense of purpose in following Lisa. Her safe and effective leadership lends to the student's finding purpose in authentic compliance and inspiration versus out of fear or punishment. It also prevents a desire to find purpose in rebellion.

Purpose in performance: Lisa makes sure her students know that effort is rewarded. She helps them to see that effort and challenge lead to accomplishment in something. This is a fundamental ingredient for being a lifelong learner and committing to endless growth. In the end, it is less about math and more about a skill and theme for a life of meaning.

Seeing Lisa's effective inspired parenting style of intervention in contrast to other school experiences answered so many questions about my kids and their cause of struggle. My son is excelling with a combination of inspired parenting and inspired education. What remained to be answered was where my husband and I were falling short on supporting our kids in finding academic success before we found Lisa. I wanted to feel equipped with this answer. The reality is that we will have to integrate back into mainstream schools when my middle son is in high school. I also still have a fifth grader to keep on track.

We are the lucky ones who found Lisa Crosby. Her inspired model of teaching should not be a niche intervention that you can only find in a small city in Nevada. I also understand that homeschooling and having Lisa is not an option for many families. Therefore, reforming our schools to get closer to Lisa's style of teaching should be a guiding light. I am in no place to suggest how, but I know people like Lisa do. I know there is a much-needed shift in our educational systems to find that middle ground where all kids can be seen in some way, feel safe to learn and grow, and rise to their potential. In the meantime, I have at least one name in big bright red letters in my sparse Rolodex for referrals, and that is Lisa Crosby.

— JAIME GARNDER, MD

SETTING THE
GROUNDWORK

1

REAL SOLUTIONS ARE POSSIBLE

Congratulations on beginning the process of helping your child who is struggling in school. You are in the right place. The time for worrying and losing sleep is over. That did not help matters. Now is the time for action. Your child has one chance at childhood. Only you, the parent, can significantly impact how your children will recover from their academic struggles. When offered a lifeline, the drowning person grabs on, and your child will too if you tread lightly on their ego and make it safe and plausible to succeed. To find triumph is the goal, making this journey a valuable life lesson of persistence and resilience.

A child's potential is within them and can emerge at any time. Awaken the strong, active, engaged student within your child or teen. Adults often decide to do this in college – change their ways from minimal effort to truly applying themselves, being strategic and thorough. But this can be done at any age. Parents can be a catalyst of change and the support their child is missing. I am here to guide you every step of the way.

Being a struggling student can actually be an advantage when you view it as an experience in the rearview mirror. This book will guide you to that place of value for a journey you and your child will cherish along the way for countless reasons. Enjoy the process with your child and be their hero. I am here to show you how to do that, one step at a time.

Here, in this book, you will find focus and direction on how to help your child. You may be feeling desperate, or you may be feeling energized and motivated. Either way, you're in good hands, and I understand how you feel. This guide is for parents whose child is currently attending school, anywhere from kindergarten to twelfth grade, and struggling. There is no better time than now to help your children. And no, it is not too late if your child is in middle or high school.

"The devil is in the details" is a favorite phrase of mine regarding my reputation of transforming students into successful, independent learners. In this book, we will focus on those details to help your child thrive. As a parent myself, I know firsthand how it feels to not have my child served in well-intentioned, typical public schools. I was a public high school math teacher when my children were in elementary and middle school. My graduate studies as a literacy specialist led me to focus on neuroscience as it applies to learning. I have been learning about learning, and practicing my skills transforming struggling students to successful students ever since. This book is the culmination of my knowledge and experience in the last twenty-five years, put in one place to help you do the same for your child.

Every parent fears their child might be the worst case, and they might be *unhelpable*. That simply is never true. In a typical academic environment, teachers have a curriculum to follow hinged on the grade or subject they are teaching. That curriculum is currently called the Common Core Standards, and they are national. Students who are ill-equipped cannot keep up with the curriculum or have not figured out how to be a learner, or both.

Learning is a process of self-discovery, and each person's journey to be a confident student is unique. This book will inform, guide, direct, teach how you can influence your child toward increasing their academic self-esteem. Our task is to take an honest look at many aspects of your student to determine what is holding them back. More often than not, there is more than one quality contributing to your child's struggles with a typical curriculum not designed with them in mind. This book will guide you through a comprehensive thought process that will identify where energy should be placed to be most effective. I am sharing the process that I use to find the stopping blocks, and how I resolve them, to bring out the successful student in any child or teen.

Humans are born to learn. An infant must learn to breathe, nurse or feed, and get their mother's attention when needed. All infants are adept at learning: it is programmed biologically. Any student who fits into a public school, who may or may not be on an IEP or 504 Plan, is an excellent candidate for benefitting from this book. When severe handicaps or brain injuries are involved, that complicates matters. However, my method applies to all learners. If the system places your child in a public or private classroom that teaches Common Core Standards, then this book is for you.

As a parent and a passionate educator, I am all in. I am committed to helping students become independent, confident learners in the shortest possible time. The task is to transform quickly and become ready to succeed in school because the curriculum is marching forward with or without your child. Take the time in the short-term to work on what is missing. It is most likely a combination of content and strategies, as well as attitude, but you may be part of the reason your child struggles, and we will address all of this together in this book. Whatever it turns out to be, the most likely causes are in this book. Every student I have helped in my career has had one or more of these issues discussed in one of these chapters. Each chapter identifies fixable aspects I see so frequently in my clients. Experiences with my clients inspired me to write this book to help parents who are seeking real solutions.

Essentially, we need to identify how your child's brain learns best. Keep in mind, what works for you is not necessarily what will work for your child. Parents often feel frustrated when sharing their study habits and giving advice to their children. Their efforts may often fail to bring about a solution. Perhaps this has been your experience.

Possibly you cannot relate to being a struggling student or maybe you were not one yourself. Or it is possible you were a struggling student, and you do not want to see the pattern repeated.

Whatever the case, with each generation the curriculum has compressed and is now very full and rich, and different from when you were there. School moves at a faster pace now than in the past as well. Anyone in education almost thirty years, like myself, can see this occurring. Students who fall behind rarely catch up. Instead, the gap between their skills and grade level usually widens, self-esteem dwindles, and desperation supplants optimism, which is much more painful to watch as a parent. This book is your alternative. Change the trajectory of your child's life and keep reading.

Humans are not all the same, we are the most diverse mammals on the planet. So, why is it a surprise that we do not learn the same way? My three children are entirely different learners from one another. Every student I meet is different from the last. What I love about what I do is encountering new "puzzles." Some cases are relatively straight forward and simple, while others are more complex.

Teachers, talented and well-meaning as they may be, are usually focused on teaching the material assigned to them, instead of your child's individual needs. It is the nature of the current education system, which was modeled from the industrial age. The result is many children struggle, and sadly a majority of students under eighth grade are struggling. We are all individuals with varying points of view and perceptions. The problem is so much effort flowed into Common Core Reform, we lost the baby in the bathwater. Instead, we should focus on meeting all levels of learners' needs, streamline the ones we can, and plan differently for those not in the same place. Time can flex, and the teaching modality can flex. Creativity in school design is beyond overdue. I am a data-driven math teacher and a literacy specialist. I tested my theories on the school I operated for ten years. The proof was in the data. My school tested the theories I could not while I was teaching public school. I also supervised student teachers in many schools and saw how the school culture and data of effectiveness correlated.

From kindergarten onward, the approach presented in this book can yield transformational outcomes in academic achievement, and more importantly, self-esteem. We will learn how to raise a child with a growth mindset that propels them from one accomplishment to another. Everything in this book is research-based and proven to be effective. The professors, scientists, and psychologists who did the research, presented, and taught me are the real heroes that allow me to use their work to transform lives. Now, the trick is to get these ideas into the mainstream to benefit all students in America. (Yes, this is a dream of mine.)

You will achieve what you believe you can, and what you are prepared to achieve. The second part is what is lost in the current American education system. We are not doing a good enough job of preparing our students thoroughly and addressing their unique needs. What I am describing, many will suggest, is impossible. It is not. Your child's teachers are teaching a certain level of curriculum not tailored to your child's unique needs.

Students who receive a diagnosis like dyslexia, learning processing problems, language processing problems, ADD, ADHD, or working memory issues are made to feel that this is a permanent condition, and there is less potential for them to succeed than other students. This is often a misconception. Tests report skills which occur in snapshots of time. Could they be different on another day? Yes! Could these skills be developed or improved? Yes! Humans are born to learn, deficiencies can be addressed, and significant improvements are possible. Every student in kindergarten through twelfth grade has a developing brain. Brains develop uniquely, determined by heredity and environment. What you have thought about, and how you have thought about things, influence your thinking skills. You can learn to think about things differently and seek strategies that make sense to you and improve your performance. Even significantly challenged students improve with the optimism and approach I take. No one wants to be told you are poor at something, and that is the way it is. There is room to grow and learn what works best for your brain. We can capitalize on your strengths and improve weaknesses in thinking.

Increasing confidence is happening all along the way. Basically, do not let any label limit your child's belief that they can grow and improve. Sadly, I see that so often. The label is a way of making students feel they are stuck. I am here to say, no one I have ever met is stuck!

Brains are malleable. Just as stroke victims can relearn how to walk, talk, read, and function after a stroke has damaged the brain, so can students learn new ways to think, study, and generally perceive learning. Some labels become absurd after my work with students. Others are still observable, but much less debilitating to the learning process with improved math skills, literacy skills, and specific coping strategies along with new attitudes. As you read this book, keep in mind how incredibly plastic the brain is, and be open to the research and science I have carefully chosen to include. Each of these chapters has proven very effective in my work with students during my career. Yes, there is always hope for your child. As a parent, it is your job to keep that hope alive so your child can start to believe it themselves.

Schools do a lot of testing. There is testing in each class for each subject. There is unit testing, semester testing, and end-of-the-year testing. Standardized testing and the results are reported and standardized within the state. Some schools use nationally standardized tests to compare their results to other students nationwide. States do benchmark testing. This is testing some random standards that should be mastered at the time of testing in hope of a representative measuring of the school. In all of this testing, parents see grades, and parents see copies of the standardized test results. Teachers look at these test results and report the grades. Teachers do not plan on helping your child to learn what the tests reveal he or she does not know. Unfortunately, that is not their primary goal. Teachers have their hands full teaching the assigned curriculum and attempting to reteach what was missed before the year ends. They do not look back to what was missed in the previous years.

Some schools are using online curriculum to test and assign teaching modules from missing background skills. In my informal inquiries with students, they do not seem to enjoy interacting with a computer learning topics that are stress triggers. Sadly, the strategy is fine on paper to assign learning for missed topics, but this strategy is not proving to be well received or effective for remediating math skills. The data is not good for students to learn from computers which are not interacting with them, but *at* them. Humans do not actively engage as well with a computer as a human being. This is a fact.

What your child does not know is how or where you find the potential to grow and improve. As parents, it is enjoyable to think about what our children are good at and where they shine. This book is encouraging you to discover the areas in which your child may not shine and to show you what you can do as a parent to bring about their growth and development. A good parent knows what their child's needs are, and they remain focused on them. But in the area of education, if it is not clear to a classroom teacher or administrator, why would it be obvious to you?

Until the American educational system renovates, it is your job to use test results to benefit your child. Parents look at test results and discuss them with teachers. Despite what a classroom teacher promises, they rarely provide reteaching opportunities for concepts missed.

I know how frustrating it can feel to sit down and see your son's report card with bad grades. It can also feel frustrating for good grades that do not match poor skills and confidence. Grades are subjective, so you wonder, how is this fair? I understand. A teacher can easily change the grades. They can alter how many points each problem is worth to minimize some commonly missed problems to raise the whole classes' scores. They can add a participation compo-nent to help low scores pass. Teachers make so many decisions about how something is graded, they can control how grades look. Teachers do not want to send the message they are not doing their job by low scores. Teachers can help students during assessments to improve a grade.

I have seen this even in high school math. It is unbelievable watching some teachers guide and give too much help during a test. The results then would not be an accurate measure of the student's knowledge. That would be pushing them through, without integrity. So many variables are involved in grading.

Many of my parents tell me that their child is below grade level but earning a passing grade. What does this mean? Teachers are put in unfair positions with students who are unable to succeed in the level they must teach. Students are put in unfair positions with curriculum that they cannot independently accomplish when their skills are not a match. We pass students along and accommodate the assignments and the tasks all too often to hide the fact that they are behind in skills. If you read the national report card (www.nationsreportcard.gov), a non-profit organization measuring American student performance without bias, you will find that there is not a lot of good news. Sixty-six percent of students in fourth and eighth grades are below proficiency in math and reading. This statistic does not improve between fourth and eighth grade and you can bet it does not get addressed while in the high school curriculum. You are not alone. Sadly, you are the majority. Sixty-six percent of parents in America have a struggling student below eighth grade. That is the sad truth I would like to change. One hundred percent of students I have impacted have beaten all the data and the odds and become successful learners. This requires parent trust and commitment. Trust is hard for some parents; commitment is hard for others. I promise that this book will point you in the right direction for your child's transformation to success.

Grades are a bureaucratic measure of tasks required to earn the points offered. Some of these tasks include testing, completing homework, participating in class, or students presenting to their peers. Savvy students can find clever ways to jump though the hoops and earn a grade when given a more stringent circumstance. Their independent work would not be the same. I caution parents to not see grades in class as the only measure of learning. You will learn what to value over grades. I hope to teach you to value your child's ability to learn and their resilience and determination. Value their confidence and belief in themselves, and value their effort. All of these things are much more important than grades.

Grades are misleading and are not usually relevant to identifying what the problem is with your child's poor academic performance. Parents rely too much on grades to judge their child's progress. I see clients with strong grades who are very behind in school skills. This can happen when a teacher floods their gradebook with points associated with protocols, "effort," discussions, or other points not directly related to academic performance. I was a gradebook trainer for a short time with my public school district in my early career. I was shocked when teachers who used a total points system were unaware of the proportional relationship of grades represented. "Do you want this end-of-the-year exam to only be worth 3 percent of their grade?" I would ask. There are district standards often misunderstood by non-math teachers, often unintentionally, I found. Hence the district sending me as a trainer. They realized this was a problem. Grades are very subjective, and without the details, impossible to make conclusions from.

Welcome to your child's solution to academic confidence! The measure I look for is a student who has a system, has plans for their desired outcome, and can work step by step confidently along the way. Students must understand that all learning begins with confusion, and that the puzzle of finding total understanding is engaging and can even be enjoyable. That is every parent's wish and there is always room for improvement. Set your hopes high for your child to become a confident, independent learner, and keep reading.

Every child can learn. Yes, your child too. If the bureaucracy of turning in homework assignments is your child's challenge, that will be addressed in this book too. Working with students who are struggling is like unpacking the problems that are holding them back. Address the issues that apply to your children one at a time and you will reveal the true students. In due time your kids will emerge feeling unafraid and supported. They will see that they can learn to fly, so to speak, academically with their own sense of how to succeed. Keep reading. There are solutions for your young ones through teens here. This is my promise to you.

RECAP: REAL SOLUTIONS ARE POSSIBLE FOR STRUGGLING STUDENTS

- This book will give you solutions for your struggling kindergartner through twelfth grade student.
- Every brain learns differently, and each person needs to learn how *their* brain learns best.
- Learning how to learn is a unique journey for every person.
- The academic demands on your child are higher than they were for you.
- Students learn best from human interaction, not computers or other screens, based on neuroscience.
- Grades are subjective and only a part of the story; they are not a measure of the topics covered in this book.
- You are not alone: 66 percent of students in America in eighth grade are below grade level in math *and* reading skills.
- Whether your child has a learning processing diagnosis, ADD, ADHD, dyslexia, or bureaucracy issues, the topics and considerations in this book will provide solutions for your child.
- The brain is malleable, and a struggling student can improve when their needs are addressed.
- Potential is relevant any time in life, and always present and waiting to emerge.

2

PARENT'S PURPOSE ON THE PLANET

My adult life began when I became pregnant. I had moved out at seventeen years old, found my own way through college, changed majors three times, and met my husband in third-semester calculus, falling in love on the ski hill. A lot of things led to the moment when I first felt like an adult. I am an adventure seeker, a traveler, and very much a people person. From a very young age I was always told I was like a young adult, though I was the oldest child of three children. My parents raised me around mostly adult family members, who all impacted me during the most developmentally impressionable and emotional times. Adults in my life were involved during the most joyful *and* sorrowful times of my youth.

My parents are self-made people. They both grew up in large midwestern families on working farms. This life demanded long days, working with the whole family, functioning as a team. My parents wanted a different life than their parents. My father joined the military, and for a time, served as a naval fighter pilot. During his lengthy deployments, my mom was forced to become independent. Later, my dad became a commercial pilot for a major airline. My mom formed her own interior design business. She was in charge of many redesigns and new build projects, along with business remodels. They worked hard and played hard. It was the seventies, after all. These were good times, and nothing brings it back more than Creedence Clearwater classics.

I was not the son my dad had hoped for, but I was athletic and interested in how things worked. It was a benefit, in a way, because he taught me to not be complacent, to know how to help myself, and to be prepared. He raised me the way most men were raising their sons in the seventies. I mowed the lawn and could fix many things. I witnessed a lot of car repairs. I felt like if I had to, I could do an oil change, and I knew what a spark plug did. My dad taught me how to change the brushes on an alternator on my Honda Civic. Not many daughters had that privilege. I liked it, and I understood how he explained things. My dad was a pilot, and he owned a small Cessna. Every flight was an adventure and a new perspective. Travel was another privilege I have been lucky enough to experience. Travel has given me the most value for my money, a lifetime of memories that can transport me anytime, as well as learning experiences to broaden my perspectives. I have traveled alone to visit my family and best friends since I was twelve, which was almost like being an adult, but not quite.

I planned a surprise fifteenth-anniversary party for my parents, with their friends' help. I cleaned the house and thoroughly surprised my parents. It was nothing to me at the time, but pretty grown-up, I would say. I imagined living on my own would give me that adult feeling. I felt that my own apartment somehow lacked something. From eighteen to twenty-one years old, I was trying to be a grownup. But not with my own money. I was dependent on my parents. I married at age twenty-five, graduated, and I thought, *I am an adult*. My kitchen was more well-equipped after the wedding, but that did not do it either. It was fun *playing house* with my husband. We lived near his grandparents, who were our main source of social life. We shared many cocktail hours and dinners. They nurtured us with their love and their example, but I still felt young. I was beginning to worry that being an adult was not a feeling I was going to find. Maybe it never came.

When we first learned of our pregnancy, three years into our marriage, suddenly my life was not about me, but about someone else. Who? Who will I meet? Who will I love? The knowledge of your child coming, whether in your tummy or through adoption or surrogacy, the anticipation of the new soul moving into your heart is a powerful emotion. I think it is life changing. I would say it is that moment that changed me. It was the moment I felt like an adult. I guess, being grown up to me is about not thinking of oneself. It is about much more than you. To me, being an adult came when I became responsible for someone else. It fills my heart right now writing about that time and that feeling. The realization that the baby was forming inside me made me prioritize my nutrition. My health was my baby's health. It was a huge shift, and one I welcomed. We lost that first baby, but very soon became pregnant again, with the son who is now expecting his own child and turning thirty later this year. I am writing this book as I await my first grandchild, and I have hopes that the ideas in this book will somehow be incorporated in our education system for my grandchild's educational experience. I am envisioning an educational system that is more advantageous to those who struggle, eliminating the dead end feeling of school being overwhelming.

My husband said I should start this chapter by explaining that I talked to my baby when I was pregnant. I said good morning and goodnight to the baby. I played soft and gentle music for my baby. I went to a concert, eight months pregnant, and we had a glorious time. I graduated with a degree in secondary mathematics education, physical science, and chemistry. I had physics credentials because of my mechanical engineering major, which I nearly finished. Lastly, I had a K–eighth-grade credential, but no real plan to teach in those grades. I wanted to teach high school math. This was where I thought I could really make a difference. I had tutored college athletes struggling with math while I was an engineering major in college. I stumbled upon the opportunity and found I was able to reduce stress while helping someone become lighter, happier, more confident, and independent.

It was very rewarding. I realized what a gift I received while helping others. It really moved me.

I will never forget a pitcher on our college baseball team who was extremely stressed and fearful. He was in what I would refer to as *academic pain.* I helped him find his way out of this pain. Outfielders and a few infielders came after the pitcher. The coach sent them to me to help improve their borderline grades for eligibility. These were intelligent athletes. They qualified to be in college, and yet, they somehow had huge gaps in their understanding of math. I listened to the reasons for their fears and helped them find new ways to feel about math. That emotional work was just as necessary as the factual content I had to explain. If I had not helped them to deal with their emotions, they would likely have given up on themselves, derailed on tests, and fallen apart. They had to learn to manage their emotions and form new confidences. I came to this realization myself. There was no neuroscience or formal instruction from anyone. The tutoring center that hired me thought, *She is in third-semester calculus; she can tutor math.* They were wrong. I was more qualified than that. Neither myself nor those who hired me knew this though. It was life's serendipity, helping me see who I am.

My husband's proposal made me change majors in college, even though I only had one semester left to finish my mechanical engineering degree. It went like this: "Will you marry me, have Samoyed dogs, and have six children?" Wow! Marry him? "Yes." Samoyed dogs? "Yes!" We had one already and I was smitten with the breed. But six kids? I wanted to be a parent, and I thought it was a *loose* commitment. Life is what happens, and we can dream, so sheepishly, about *so* many kids. I said, "Yes." I told myself being a mechanical engineer is a nine-to-five, all-year-long job. Maybe I should spend a decade being a teacher, enjoying summers off and being home earlier than 5:00 p.m. Unfortunately, in reality, this is not usually the case. I would like to debunk that myth about teachers. It is an inaccurate stereotype. But yes, there are the summers off.

I was listening to my heart for those crossroads in my life. I wanted children. I wanted to raise them as much as I could afford, but

I knew we were to be a two-income family with goals of a home, travel, skiing, and an adventurous life. With only student loans to get us started, we were optimistic and educated and off to make our life.

I have an intuition about teaching. There was no formal training at that time. There were no classes on brain development that went beyond a very superficial overview of the development in one class. But I remembered my mother believed in the sing-song way of speaking to a baby. Getting their attention and interacting with them was modeled to me as my mother's hands-on style with us and all the babies she helped raise before and after us. That is a whole other book.

My mother was a working mother her whole life. As one of eleven children, she was *mothering* since she became old enough to babysit her older siblings' children. She got down on the floor and played with us. Even more so with her grandchildren. She has sealed in the practical and medical knowledge a new mother learns with the power of love, attention, happiness, and the connection to intelligence. She valued humor as a measure of intelligence and always stretched my brain to keep up with what the adults were laughing about. Card games and board games were the focus of my free time in childhood. The goal was to keep me thinking, my parents decided. I was raised to respect *thinking* in our home. There was value in vocabulary, and I was complimented when I used complex words. My mother modeled all these values.

I am naturally very empathetic. I care about other people's feelings. There is a general callousness in society which really bothers me. I always noticed when people were hurting, and I could feel their pain if I focused too much on seeing it. I wish I did not feel so many emotions. It took me until my mid-thirties to realize it was my gift. I used to believe that others noticed all that I noticed and felt all that I felt. Eventually, I realized that many people do not allow the feelings of others to burden them. I learned that I am different. Sometimes I need to spend my weekend in solitude to come back to only my feelings. Teaching is a very challenging job, and some children are in pain in their life beyond school. They are not getting what they need. It is very hard to feel the pain of a child. Many times, I have had to call CPS with regard to an abusive or neglectful situation with a student. Teachers are mandatory reporters.

When I began teaching high school math, I was the mother of one son who was two years old. That son is now turning thirty later in the year. Over my career, I have taught math classes from pre-algebra through Calculus BC. I taught at least one at-risk math class every year. My math department chair was a mentor and an inspirational leader. He believed that the students considered *at-risk* needed the most talented teaching. Each math teacher would take one at-risk class to give them our best energy and effort. At our math department meetings, we would discuss our challenging students and share tips and support. His leadership style was effective but, unfortunately, rare. Usually, a new teacher would be stuck with all low-level classes. Most math teachers prefer higher-level classes that allow them to enjoy challenging curriculums and motivated students. During my first decade as a teacher, I was divinely inspired by both my department chair and my principal. Our principal encouraged us to think out of the box and solve problems that most impacted our students. She was also a leader in the social-emotional school culture, and we did many creative things to help each student feel connected, loved, and a sense of belonging. Sadly, this has dissipated with time and her retirement. But it is alive in me, and throughout this book. The neuroscience of emotional safety and belonging is conclusive as to the importance for learning. You cannot separate the human from their heart or emotions. School design has made that crucial error. After my first decade of teaching, I had three sons and earned my graduate degree.

At the beginning of my career, I became a popular math teacher and was considered the "best placement" to send a struggling student. This was just me trying to do a good job caring for students and serving them the best I could. In general, it was not common to put in the effort when a student struggled, and sometimes other staff members criticized me for my efforts. Especially my retake policy, which put pressure on them to do the same, but they were unwilling. I did influence one other teacher to offer retakes on exams, as I recall. There still remained many students I could not help due to my limited time with them. This is a very frustrating feeling most teachers feel at one time or another.

My school began with a thought in 2004, and I took a leap of faith - I did something that was against all common financial sense, but it was the best decision I have ever made. That thought was, *What if I began my own school and really tried to put neuroscience into practice?* My three sons were about to enter the third, fourth, and ninth grades in public school. I was commuting about fifty-five miles to work each way. To say that life was extremely busy is an understatement. I was unable to address all of my students' needs. Did you know the typical high school teacher has one hundred and fifty students? And my sons' academic needs were not being met for reasons I will explain. Their teachers had no time to address their needs, and neither did their mom, a math and literacy specialist. Nothing made sense, and all of a sudden, everyone was losing!

My last straw, so to speak, was my ninth-grade son, who had been frustrated with math since the sixth grade because he desired more learning and more rigor. In seventh grade, my son and a few other students were put in the back of the class and given an algebra book to work from on their own. This group of students had very high test scores that conclusively proved the math being offered was not a match for them. They showed mastery for the year of content about to be taught. There were no classes suitable for this small group of gifted math students, and they had no teacher guiding their learning. Well, not much learning happened. They goofed off together and felt privileged, and it was disappointing. This was a function of the small size of the school and no priority to offer levels of learning, but just a one-size-fits-all education.

Our local high school used an integrated math program, which I had analyzed in textbook adoption committees for my district. This was prior to Common Core National Standards. The program did not meet California nor Nevada state standards at that time and was completely unacceptable to me, for the town, and for my son. That integrated math program also had horrible data of effectiveness. What was I going to do?

My son, who had been bored and frustrated throughout middle school in math, was never going to learn math from this curriculum. I am a data-driven person, and this math program was a big issue for me. I spent my after-school time on many occasions volunteering on textbook adoption committees for a math curriculum for the district in Nevada where I taught. I formed strong opinions on what constituted a well-written, strong math curriculum. What my son was being offered was at the bottom of my list, in the "very unacceptable" category. You get the picture. My math-starved child was headed for a poor curriculum, and I could not bear the thought of another wasted day for his math education at this point. So, I quit my job teaching public school in Reno, Nevada and began my own non-profit private school.

As a backstory, this same son had an incident that I carried much guilt regarding. When he was in fifth grade, he had a colon blockage, which resulted in an embarrassing accident at school. He was in tears when I picked him up. His doctors said I should take him to a colon specialist since colon cancer runs in the family. His colon was stretched out and the cause was unknown. The specialist asked him, after ruling out the worst-case scenarios (cancer and other obstructions) and viewing various test results, "Son, is there anything upsetting you?" My son burst into tears and told us at the UC Davis doctor's office that he wanted his lunch recess back. We had traveled about one hundred miles to learn that he was being denied his recess, which caused him so much stress he had colon blockages that endangered him. Unbelievable! His teacher was unhappy with his handwriting and made him rewrite his work to her satisfaction during lunch recess on most days. He was unable to run around and play for about four months. This was April and this had been happening since January. He was missing the best part of the day; you know how kids feel about recess. He had silently endured this punishment, believing that his teacher must be respected at all costs. I blamed myself for him not telling us. He was shamed into keeping this secret because he was not writing neatly enough, and he did not think it would please us to learn this. His teacher did not ask our permission to penalize our son.

I volunteered during my vacation days each year in each of my sons' classrooms, which allowed me to give my boys the attention other mothers gave their kids, and it informed me to monitor their classroom environment. It means a lot to your child to see you volunteer. I encourage every parent to participate in field trips or classroom needs during their kindergarten through fifth-grade years. It really provides insight and helps you to relate to your child in incalculable ways.

This teacher knew me and had many opportunities to let me know she was keeping my son in at lunch and chose not to mention it to me. I was livid. It had caused my son extreme stress and physical pain and would have resulted in a ruptured colon in the worst-case scenario, which is fatal. When a kid is trying to be good and please his teachers and his parents, this can happen. I have since seen this in some of my clients. Irregularity is a small symptom of this type of stress. This can happen to anyone, including involved and loving parents who talk to their children about their day every day at dinner, as my husband and I did. That was a lesson to me in so many ways. The judgment of this teacher was so wrong. She was insensitive to the stress she caused. A person who cannot read a child's stress level should not be in charge of children. My son was emotionally unsafe.

A child's desire to please their parents is strong. This is true even if it means hiding or being deceptive. There is a private place in us all. My son's only fault was trying to please everyone and respect the adults around him. Those four years, between fifth and ninth grade, he battled through without the math education he desperately needed. My being unavailable was the final straw. I knew it was time to quit my career as a teacher.

I decided to start a school and get "accredited" to teach him math myself and transfer the credits. That became my dream and drive. I knew I wanted to teach him the chapters that were not required in the state curriculum but would provide a thorough and complete math education. Most teachers skipped or did not have the time for these chapters. The probability and statistics chapter was not required in several courses, but there was a focus in Algebra 2, for example. I loved teaching AP Statistics, and without the strength of the background years, it was more difficult for kids to get through it. Yes, a math-rich education would surely serve my son, and I was determined to provide that.

I decided to quit my job, but we needed my income. We figured out the required minimum income after my commuting costs and after-school care costs for the kids. I had begun fantasizing about "my dream school" four years prior. Now, I was ready and motivated.

I had earned my master's degree in literacy with an emphasis on neuroscience as it applies to learning in 1999. By the time I graduated, I went from two to three children in our family. I was teaching high school math, and I had a baby under one year old when I entered into an exclusive cohort literacy specialist graduate program. It was a three-year commitment that meant going to school every Tuesday and Thursday night for three years and attending summer school for two summers. There was no stopping, the classes were offered just for us, and we all moved through the curriculum as a group. The cohort was filled with exceptional teachers of all disciplines and grade levels.

During the first year of the program, my oldest son was five years old and we had a baby boy. It was a busy time. But I was so motivated to learn about reading problems. It was a stumbling block for so many of my math students as a high school math teacher. We found out I was pregnant after the first semester of my master's degree. How can I have another baby, work, and go to graduate school? Somehow, we managed, and my mother was a big part of why I survived that challenge. She babysat my two boys, then three boys, two nights a week during my classes for three years. They did not suffer, but loved their very fun grandmother, which helped me focus on school. I remain very grateful to my mother for this support.

Fast-forward to my next catalyst to open a school. It was 2005, when my middle son was in the fourth grade, the year I quit my teaching job. He was reading four-plus years above grade level. Yes, he is a "gifted" student, who has his own frustrations. He was adorable, a living "Hummel" as a toddler. If you know those German porcelain collectible figurines, you get the picture. We were complimented many times by older folks who saw him. Such a handsome little boy with those big blue eyes, they would say. He was quiet, mischievous, and way too smart for his own good. When we caught him on the roof at my sister's house at four years old, he said, "I was just looking." Athletic, bright, and a natural leader, he liked to be challenged. I wanted to broaden the curriculum, not necessarily to move him through faster, but to challenge and engage him. He did not experience any particular academic crisis, except that middle school was not challenging enough for him and boredom was something he coped with. He had been coasting. His fourth-grade teacher actually bullied him, and his classmates supported him. This was a strange situation. I think he was too smart for the class and that threatened his teacher somehow. She retired after that year. But there were a few meetings that spring about her treatment of my son in her classroom. Fast-forward, he had a knife pulled on him in middle school in seventh grade. Then he was accused of something he did not do. As a big kid, he was not emotionally safe. It was a fiasco. The school was not serving him. In eighth grade, he transferred to my school full time, by his own choice. He knew staying meant nothing new, and he was tired of it all.

Then came my youngest son, a blond-curly-topped cheerful dancing boy. He was funny, soft-spoken, and sensitive. He would often get carsick on our RV journeys. He was also musical and artistic. He kept up athletically and enjoyed sports like his brothers. We were the "Crosby family ski team" on the weekends. Our marriage began with ski hill dates, and we passed our love of skiing on to our boys. My husband is a graceful former ski team racer. He skied his whole childhood. My youngest son was one of those kids who lost something every week. He struggled to turn in homework and manage all the bureaucracy of being a student. He exasperated his teachers. He was bright and passed every test he took. He was often in trouble for not completing assignments on time. He lost privileges. We had many conferences about his issues. There were attention and focus challenges and some anxiety with trying to do all that was expected of him. I am not sure if that anxiety had to be there, or if he was pushed to develop it, but we will never know for sure. Brains are patternistic. Once a pattern of behavior is established, it takes effort to break the automatic cycle.

My youngest son was passing tests and reading at grade level. He was doing fine academically but feeling constantly frustrated with the protocols of school. He was finding a way to learn, despite all his stress and focus issues. He wanted to do everything right but really could not focus long enough to do so on command. Somehow, I could drop him off with the paper in his hand, and it would not make it to the homework box. He would lose his lunchbox weekly and regularly visited Lost and Found. He was a kind person, compliant in class, and sincerely trying to do his best. Most teachers saw the goodness in him, but failed to find a way to make him feel successful. He was in a constant state of worry and fear. How sad was that? I do not think of the ADD or ADHD brain as having a problem. I do think it is labeled as such just because it does not fit into our narrow education system with requires much sitting and listening, opposed to active kinesthetic learning. There is another way, other than labeling these kids as having "a problem." I think the system is the issue, and we need to make room for all types of learners without the negative connotations. Full transparency here.

My youngest son would want to stop by and check Lost and Found frequently. I would ask, "What are you missing?"

He would say, "I don't know, but maybe I will find something of mine."

He was aware of his forgetfulness, and we tried many strategies to help him keep track of his things. The transitions in school were too fast-paced with too many details, but the learning was fine for him. Yet, he still felt like a failure. We minimized the mistakes and moved on each time, the best we could. I tried to offer strategies and hope on a daily basis. I would buy four coats per school year because it was easier to plan on the loss of it than to panic about what he would wear to be warm the next day. We lived in a snow country at about 6,800 feet in the Sierra Nevada Mountains, so my son needed a coat each day. School was not the same for him as it was for the other two. Same teachers, same approach, but he was suffering and made to feel bad every day. He wasn't scared of learning, but he was losing his confidence in the classroom. Doctors might have labeled him ADD had I sought to have the label, but I saw no advantage to him. He was very academically capable each year of his learning. He was not behind. He kept trying, and so did we. And no one in our house was allowed to tease him for his forgetfulness.

I did not want to label my son. I saw what happened to kids with that label. They had "accommodations." Teachers "expected less" of them. I did not want that for him, nor did he need that. Asking for some flexibility for deadlines or turning in things was not ever approved. Rules were rules. The reason is the measure of responsibility these tasks were measuring, and why allow him to take full advantage of the rules? This was hard to watch, and we decided to end the cycle of self-criticism when I pulled him out of school. He was my first full-time student. I was intending to be a supplemental school for our community. There was a need. But for my youngest son, I became his full-time school. By the end of the year, eight other parents asked me to take their children on full time. I did, and the next year we offered all grades.

I wonder if my youngest son could have been a gifted student in a subject or two if had he not been under constant stress and feeling like a failure with the bureaucracy of school. My dream school would accommodate him and help him form strategies to grow where he needed to grow while challenging him academically. I watched his academic self-esteem be reborn. My youngest son taught me an important lesson about the concept of self that students have. "Academic self-esteem" is everything. It is the underlying fabric upon which learning relies.

My school, Custom Learning Academy, was in business from January 2005 to June 2015. It was a non-profit private kindergarten through twelfth-grade school that became fully accredited in 2007. It was NCAA approved in 2009. I was so proud to see its name on the pull-down menu of college applications and on the CommonApp. I was on "the map," as my dad used to say. My school was respected and serving my community in so many ways. I offered courses for credit if students wanted just one class, or full-time school. Local students took high school classes to make up grades or improve their GPA with us.

Our maximum class size was ten. Our teachers were excellent, compassionate, and gifted communicators who connected with students. I offered an academic after-school care that the kids considered more fun than learning, but we snuck in amazing literacy work.

The principal of the local high school sent his daughter to my school for math because she was math-phobic, and I had a reputation for turning kids into math superstars. My students played sports at the local public school if they would take two electives there. We worked out all the kinks. I was so proud of what I accomplished, and serving my sons' needs along with other students in the community made me feel as though I had made the right choice.

My goal was to put neuroscience research into practice and see if I really could improve education. To me, that meant going back to the data each year to measure my theory. I gathered data by doing a nationally standardized complete math and literacy assessment on all entering students. This way, I knew them as learners and their skill levels in all pertinent skills. Additionally, I found out where their fears were and their confidences. The students trusted me to help them overcome their fears, and together we did just that, one student at a time. I would note every trigger when a student was unsure or self-deprecating or stressed. We addressed every student's needs, like a checklist.

At the end of each school year, I would administer the ITBS test (the Iowa Test of Basic Skills), a very reputable, also nationally standardized test. I would get a detailed report to use for my planning next year for each returning student. Parents loved the data too. We could all see the data going up, and we also saw the kids walk with more confidence and have higher test scores. I was able to move literacy up to three grade levels up in one year, commonly. I could take anxious learners and turn them into capable learners. I planned it, and it happened.

My oldest son graduated from the public school and only took his high school math classes with me. When he arrived in college, we learned another lesson about grades. Each of my two younger sons took fifteen credits of AP classes and all their core subjects and some electives. My focus-challenged son was never shamed. He was able to accomplish the same as his gifted older brother with a slight modification of due dates and times. My youngest son is the best writer among them. My oldest son took all his math classes from my school and studied for the SAT with my staff. When we realized his writing skills were behind grade level in his junior year, he was tutored in English by my team. He was earning top grades in Honors English classes, but I realized that did not mean he was proficient. Of course, he had slipped through my very vigilant efforts. Again, I felt like I'd failed him.

My oldest son was accepted into Willamette University, a private college in Salem, Oregon. He was excited to play D3 football. His GPA was 3.75, and after a lot of preparation, his SAT score was over 1,400. He earned an academic scholarship but failed his English placement test for English 101. Talk about pulling the rug out from under him with confidence as he tried to go to college. His grades in high school English at the public school in our town did not really matter; his skills were still not up to par.

Literacy skills matter, and this is yet another case where the grades were misleading. All students enrolling in college must take a math and English placement test, and that is where the rubber meets the road, so to speak. Your child is aiming for this competency. Really, we want to have your child ready for their best future, no matter if college is in the picture or not.

The public high school my oldest son attended only read two books per year. My school read a novel a month from sixth through twelfth grade. My older son missed the beauty of literature and did not learn how to enjoy it. He missed growing his vocabulary and writing skills naturally. He had to cram and remediate his skills in one semester of college, under stress to perform and keep playing football. That remediation cost quite a bit at a $50,000-a-year college and did not earn him college credit. Which way would you prefer your child grow these literacy skills? Before they go or while they are there trying to acclimate? This is a lesson clearly learned I hope saves you time and money and saves your child the struggle.

My other two boys could play football, wrestle, and play lacrosse for the local high school while attending my school full time. They were required to take weightlifting for the football team, and one more elective there to play sports but all their academics were taken at my school. All four cores especially were taken at my school, including math, English, history, science, and foreign language. Sports gave them positive social lives full of teamwork and people skills. My younger two boys read ten books each year in English at my school. My two younger sons were well prepared for college and my older son persevered and now holds two college degrees.

At the time I write this book, my oldest son is twenty-nine years old, making a good salary as a facilities director for a hospital. He has a civil engineering degree, has experience as a project manager, and has earned his master's degree in finance. My second son is twenty-four years old, working as a civil engineer like his brother and father. He is a project engineer in an airport division of his company supervising the construction of an airport in California and another one in Montana. He manages men twice his age. He has one class left before completing the same finance degree his brother earned and has hopes of entering into real estate development. I am proud of how hard they are working and that they both earned master's degrees.

These days the bachelor's degree is like the old high school diploma. It is required for most jobs that have benefits and upward mobility. Entrepreneurs always have opportunity in America too, and college promotes the critical thinking required of being a business owner. I know this firsthand after running two businesses. It is learning on the go! Apprentices require hands-on learning, but learning is learning. Confidence in learning will serve your child no matter what their path is in life. So, this book is not explicitly focused on the college-bound student, but just a goal of your child living to their potential. Every well-meaning parent has this wish for their child.

Sadly, many of my sons' peers from high school and their football team minimized education efforts and found out that being "sponsored" on ski teams did not pan out as they had hoped. Without confidence in learning, math, or literacy skills, their education halted. They struggle with the limited options for well-paying employment. Unfortunately, the culture of the public high school they attended was not promoting academic excellence, but rather mediocrity. The kids were rowdy on campus and rowdy in class. Boundary pushing was a town culture, which carried into the school. My suspicions were confirmed when I supervised a student teacher there. The adults were not in control of the school but reacting to the rowdy permitted behaviors that the students found so entertaining. All too common a culture to observe. Teachers can be overwhelmed in classroom management. Did you know that the average week of instruction wastes seven hours of time on low-level classroom disruptions? It is a task in and of itself to manage large groups of students so learning can happen, and that was the issue with the public high school my kids attended when they were involved. There were changes in principals and many reasons for this lost culture. A story I hear about all too often.

My youngest son aspires to be a dentist. He is finishing his business degree and enjoys the freedom of online learning. The COVID-19 pandemic did not change his life much, and he is also working at Starbucks as a supervisor. He loves the freedom of learning online. He can take breaks as needed and learn at his own pace. He loves the people part of his barista job and takes pride in his barista skills. He has risen to management level and has shown his loyalty to Starbucks.

Coffee is not a problem for a focus-challenged person. Rather, it mellows their brain and has the opposite effect. He has no trouble sleeping after coffee. It is an over-the-counter version of the meds given to students. Coffee is not good for developing bones and brains. As Toby Amidor, MS, RD reminds us: "Too much caffeine can lead to insomnia, jitteriness, upset stomach, headaches, difficulty concentrating, and increased heart rate. In younger children, these symptoms occur after just a small amount. Further, childhood and adolescence are the most important times for bone strengthening. Too much caffeine can interfere with calcium absorption, which negatively affects proper growth. Additionally, adding cream and loads of sugar, or drinking high calorie specialty coffees, can lead to weight gain and cavities. So, when is it okay for kids to start drinking coffee? A few sips here and there are no big deal. However, when sips turn into daily cups, that's a whole other story. Coffee is addictive and withdrawal symptoms are real, so the later you start, the better. I recommend starting toward the end of adolescence at a minimum, when growth and development is slowing down."

My youngest son is now twenty-three, and he loves his coffee. It serves him productively. He used Adderall his senior year of high school and at times in college. Eating pure, exercising, and coffee are the best combinations for his best focus. He has learned how to hack his brain and be in charge of habits and strategies that get him to the results he desires with his given focus challenges. At my school, we honored his spirit and soul. We knew he was trying. We just helped him try to find ways that worked for him and it has proven successful in college for him. His positive self-esteem and creative approach along with perseverance is paying off. He is a confident person with big goals for his future. He aspires to be a dentist after he completes his business degree.

There were many reasons for me closing my school. Mainly, I was tired. My youngest son was graduating, and collecting tuition was stressful and harder than it should be. We wanted to sell our home in the mountains and move to Reno for less maintenance. It was time to escape the snow and the need for chopping firewood. Our "woodchoppers" were away to college, and my husband is not capable of such physical labor anymore without pain. We love our new life near the mountains. My goal is still to live my life's purpose, helping struggling students and changing lives, one at a time. I feel so blessed to be able to do what I do.

I formed Academic Transformations as the next phase of my

career in 2016. It is a for-profit corporation where I offer student advocate services, learning coach services, and public speaking. I spend most of my time with students, changing some aspect of their strategies. Often, I repair literacy skills. Other times I repair math skills or number sense or all of the above. Sometimes I am helping students test strong, or cope with something they cannot independently learn. I am preparing them for ACT and SAT tests, or GRE tests for graduate students. I help people of all ages, from preschool through college students. I have helped adults who need to not fear fractions or pass a nursing exam. I have helped a fireman pass his exam on the last try! So many educational issues and the solutions are all not as complicated as one would think. But I guess I have been observing, learning, and following the many leading neuroscience researchers, and I have a long list to thank when it comes to the answer of why I can help so many. I like to discriminate between what is research based and what is a theory in practice with no evidence of effectiveness as of yet. Sadly, education is flooded with both elements and I can see how teachers get lost in using techniques that get results verses techniques that feel fun or manage a group well. I know how hard the job of a teacher is firsthand. I did it for twelve years as a public high school teacher. Learning with a purpose verses engaging in busywork are two different things.

I believe that nothing happens by accident. There is a reason for every person in your life. I am amazed at the miracles I have been fortunate enough to experience. I sometimes feel divine intervention when I am working with students or attending a neuroscience conference. I may be worried about a particular student when a session will bring me to tears, and somehow, what I need to help that student is given to me by the brilliant person who did the work that proves a solution. That happens to me at most conferences I attend. But I do have many students on my mind. It is where I have learned the most about how to direct students toward a positive direction. Every student has taught me something to help the next student. And each student I meet is unique, and so is your student. Together, we will solve some hidden stopping blocks.

The lead cohort professor of my graduate degree led my first trip to a neuroscience conference for educators with all of us during the last year of our graduate program in 1999. Little did I know, I would find a new lifetime interest and fascination in learning directly from neuroscientists and neuropsychologists. I see the hard work firsthand from researchers personally sharing their studies, results, and data from the best universities in the world. It is something to meet these people and see their excellent intentions to move education forward. I am impatient at the rate at which this wealth of knowledge is trickling into the American education system.

I am very perplexed at what is known about learning and its deficit in the American public education system. I have favorite neuroscientists and neuropsychologists I follow, and I meet more each year. You will hear about a few of them who directly apply to the chapter topics I have included in this book.

Thank you for reading about my parenting story, my career, and my life. I am excited to impact your parenting and your child's education. With this book, I aim to share with parents what I have learned about helping struggling students succeed. Parents are children's first and most important teachers. The task is handed to you, and if education is a weakness for your child, I am here to help both you and your child.

My hope is that parents will find a way to help their child directly or know who to involve if a specialist is required. This book is a sort of "academic wellness check" for any parent to consider for each of their children. Thank you for reading and I hope you find what you are looking for within this book. All the best to you for your commitment to your child's education. I applaud you for taking the time to read this book for your child, their success, and future learning confidence.

3

ACTION PLAN

When a parent knows their child is struggling in school, sending them back each day becomes a painful routine. The stress your child feels is played out in many ways: a sassy reply, a missing smile, a temper tantrum, and tears. Oh, yes, there are usually tears. If your child is not sharing what they are excited about at school, then that is a problem in and of itself. Is your child among the majority of the students in America behind grade level and struggling? You are not alone, and there are solutions for your child.

Do they fake feeling sick to stay home? Do you witness Academy Award-winning descriptions of feeling unwell? A child learns to please others to avoid restrictions, limitations, and punishment, and to control adults' positive perceptions. Kids need to decide how they will please their teacher, please their parents, please a nanny or after-school caregivers. It becomes exhausting and impossible to be sincere. Some kids try to fly under the radar, and others are elaborate pleasers and enjoy the attention. It is hard to realize that depression sometimes looks very cheerful and always wears a smile. The real trick for struggling students is to somehow get through all the moments where someone might know they are unable to read out loud, comprehend, do the math, or take tests – whatever it is that they are weak at, maybe taking notes or knowing how to study. Often, these kids focus on the perception of those around them. It distracts from learning that feels too far out of reach. Maybe what you mistake as *lazy* is hiding a more serious problem, intentional avoidance or "learned helplessness" which is more unconscious avoidance.

Whatever the case, something is going on that you should address. There are times when teachers can re-engage a capable student. I wrote this book for the unmotivated student rather than the motivated one. The goal is to help parents see the missing components in their child's skills and strategies. Your child should focus on learning during his school day rather than surviving it.

Speaking of motivation, that is a common question. How do I motivate my child? Let's start there, as this is the action plan chapter. Maybe motivation is your child's only problem. To understand motivation, I recommend you refer to the Color Code Test, from Cornell University (https://www.colorcode.com/choose_personality_test/). This test classifies personalities by how they are motivated. Very interesting to connect with your child in a new way and understand what generally motivates him or her. Most of us are combinations of two or three types but the percentages indicate the strongest for us. This process helps grow your child's emotional intelligence by discussing ways for them to get along with those not motivated by the same thing. By doing this with your child, you begin the connection and conversations to begin the process in this book. Connect and reassure your child you are here for them with their struggles in school. You are going to figure it out together. This is laying the foundation for the relationship that is possible.

As you read this book, you will learn the possible causes of often invisible learning problems, and solutions to obvious learning problems that typically go unaddressed in most schools. Each chapter covers a topic and includes descriptions, warning signs, behaviors, and methods to assess levels of skills to identify what is hampering academic achievement. Behaviors and attitudes are both symptoms and sometimes cause further issues. Humans are complex beings, and everyone's story is unique.

Following each chapter, you will find a recap of the main ideas. Additionally, you will find the online chapter recaps and a more detailed checklist for those who prefer to print the workbook associated with this book and work with the ideas printed in a hard copy format. The workbook provides space for your notes about your student and a checklist of traits discussed in each chapter.

As you read beyond Chapter 4, you can keep track of each chapter and make some notes and check for what applies to your child. Reading this book is meant to give you a productive direction toward solutions that are efficient, long-lasting, and life changing. This might be the most valuable parenting book you will ever read, because your child's "academic self-esteem" is what either limits them or propels them into being a learner. Academic confidence translates to many types of learning in life and on the job. If you try to avoid math, you also are limited from many trades, for example. Think about what you avoid and how it affects you.

Do not get "academic self-esteem" confused with other aspects of self-esteem. There are many. There is social self-esteem, athletic self-esteem, technology self-esteem, creative/artistic self-esteem, musical self-esteem, and body image self-esteem, to name a few. Students can break down their feelings about themselves into compartments. Some students may think if they have low self-esteem in one area, they will have low self-esteem across the board. This is a conversation to have with your child. Where do they feel confident, and where do they feel insecure? Do you know how your child would respond to these inquiries? If not, it is time to ask. If you assume these stay fixed, you would be incorrect. These may change weekly for young children or monthly for older students, in my findings. If your child has a fragile area, this is an opportunity for you to offer some training, experience, lessons, exposure, or simple conversations to positively impact or cause them to rethink these feelings.

Worrying about those we love when we see them struggling is natural. Feeling helpless to help solve a child's problem costs you by taking energy. There are emotional damages and costs from the loss of universal parenting goals - the desire for your child's success and happiness. That also means you must work on helping them achieve confidence in order to live a free life in pursuit of their dreams and desires.

My hope for every student I work with is that their academic confidence translates to pursuing a career of their choice, even if that career is parenthood and not in the workforce. We need educated parents for the next generation. A child's dreams and desires should not be restricted with avoidance, but the opposite. Those dreams can be reached with the skills to choose college, trades, parenthood, or any career of their dreams. The ability to be a good citizen involves literacy, math, and critical thinking skills.

Taking action in several directions is something you will feel confident about when you finish this guide. I promise you that the energy you spend will feel like love and support to your child. They will feel as though you are taking a detailed but gentle interest in them. One step at a time, with strategies and support. It is always a multifaceted issue. Your focus is to find the missing skills and strategies, and often emotional healing accompanies academic strengthening. Ask them what stresses them out. They will tell you. Believe me, they know and worry about it. They must redefine who they are to themselves in a more positive light. Let go of the negative, being stuck, excuses, and stories. This chapter will help you organize your thoughts and see the big picture that can support you in helping your child.

At the least, this chapter will be a tool for future teacher meetings and requests of professionals that will surely save them time and let them know you are a knowledgeable and involved parent. As you will begin to understand, many issues are not solvable by the typical classroom teacher. You will see why 66 percent of America's students are below grade level with the methodologies currently commonly used. Because many of these issues go unchecked and unaddressed, students need to survive in ways they conceive. Long-term ramifications are not always considered. It is more about your adolescent's short-term survival. As adults in their life, we must help them make choices that serve them and build strong habits using the resources around them and common sense.

I want to ask every parent to talk with their children. Take a neutral stance. Hide your opinion and discuss all aspects of this issue with your child. Try to understand their point of view and their motivation for that viewpoint. Decide how to base your opinion on a thorough investigation of the best information available to you. It's also important to teach your child to evaluate the marketing that consumes so many young people and that there are often pitfalls in advertising. Remind them that their consciousness is for sale. Teach them to seek a balanced life, using technology, but still living their real life.

I wish there were a curriculum strand from kindergarten through twelfth grade that focused on critical thinking. This is the missing link we as parents can try to insert as much as we can in conversations and our family culture to help raise children savvy enough for the pitfalls of those trying to take advantage of them or sell them something. Let's not indoctrinate our children but teach them to analyze and think critically for long-term desired outcomes. That is my wish for curriculum: to shift to critical thinking at the forefront of our knowledge, expanding it and motivating the next generation to become the next generation of experts.

Can we hope to raise a generation to make thoughtful choices, from a loving perspective for humanity and our planet, if we do not show them compassion while society educates them? If they are suffering, being shamed, feeling inadequate and less than, how can they begin to become positive members of society with that much pain? It is a simple thought. Serve students where they are. Give them what they are missing. Nurture them back into an appropriate grade level by maintaining high expectations and designing their curriculum with current research-based pathways back to grade level.

After working one-on-one with clients with various levels of deficient skills in math and/or literacy skills, I can tell you what is possible. I can move reading ability up to three grade levels in one year. I can replace number sense in students who have none at any age. I can diminish or eliminate the dyslexic symptoms in a reader by moving where reading is processed in the brain. I learned by listening to and reading neuroscientists and neuropsychologists who share their research at conferences I have attended. I give them full credit and wonder why the brilliant information available to educators on learning, memory, and language acquisition has not matriculated into the education system. We can do better in support of our students, so we must.

My favorite cases are the largest challenges. The information you learn in this book will serve your child's transformation well. Plan on committing three to eight hours per week, applying what you learn, and getting involved, or getting certain specialists involved. I will advise and guide you along the way, and you will learn a new way to look at your child with the insight you are seeking.

Be ready to think, notice, and prepare some questions for your child or teen as you go through the book. I will provide a summary checklist with the necessary information you can take with you to their next teacher conference, or the next IEP meeting, or 504 Plan meeting, where you will be able to contribute helpful information. Be prepared to make a change in the educational decisions you have made.

As a supplement to this book, I have created a workbook for you at no cost. To reference the workbook, go to the secret back page of my website: www.AcademicTransformations.com/TheStrugglingStudent/more and enter STUDENTSUCCESS. There, you will find a series of videos from me to you along with a downloadable version to use as a note-taking guide for your thoughts about your student.

RECAP: ACTION PLAN

- You have a reason to be reading this book. Your child is struggling in school.
- Does your child avoid learning or seem to be ill on test days?
- Does your child have avoidance strategies for school, indicating how uncomfortable or painful it might be for them?
- Consider all aspects of your child's self-esteem and decide if your child relates their academic self-esteem to any of them. Or is it isolated in their mind?
- Implementing information in this book will feel like love to your child when gently communicated.
- Information gathered in this book will give you the vocabulary and details about your child that will make future teacher meetings and IEP or 504 Plan meetings dramatically more productive.
- Your child's attention is a commodity, and in this day and age, they should be cautioned about giving it away willingly.
- Critical thinking is learned at home and exercised at school. Students without home support of this skill are at a disadvantage in school.

4

UNDERSTAND THE STATE OF AFFAIRS

In Chapter 4, we will begin by analyzing the systematic approach to education to create the foundation for what we will learn throughout this book. Public school takes a systematic approach to education. I want to explain the elementary, then middle school, then high school approach separately. I am not going to focus on physical education or arts education because this book is about academic struggles, and these subjects are secondary concerns to parents whose kids cannot keep up with the four core subjects. But while we are on the subject of physical education, may I comment that no subject is more important for brain development, body health, and, one could also say, for the soul. The evidence is conclusive to the connection between brain health and movement. Parents need to understand that all exercise, fine and gross motor exercise, is essential to healthy brains. There will be more about this in Chapter 13. So, I am in no way minimizing that component of a developing brain's healthy regime by focusing on the four core subjects. But this book is focused on helping struggling students in academic performance, not artistic or physical performance.

Kindergarten through fifth grade is where every child's educational journey begins. Each grade is a product in terms of the curriculum delivered to the students. There is one level of the curriculum offered per grade. Level refers to the reading ability of each grade curriculum. The elementary school curriculum is aligned to the common core curriculum, which was established in 2010. Prior to that, each state had its defined standards. Without going into the controversy associated with the establishment of a national common core versus state standards, the past and the present have something in common. Both clearly define what teachers are required to teach for any given subject or grade for which they are hired. For the last ten years, the United States of America has adopted a National Common Core Curriculum, which I am not analyzing here in this book.

Common Core allows schools to align their offerings to the students. And for students who change schools, anywhere in the nation, theoretically, there is continuity to education received in different places. Most parents understand that the reading ability for language arts, social studies, and science aims to be the same for each grade. The reading level is a calculation of the complexity of a sentence, and also correlates with the size and how the text is written. This is more thoroughly discussed in Chapter 15: Reading and Comprehension. There is a rigid expectation of skill for each grade. The mathematics curriculum also attempts to align with the reading level of the grade within the word problems and directions given. Math includes more words than ever since Common Core Curriculum. As a math teacher myself, math is useful in real-world situations outside of school, so I understand the intention. But students behind in literacy skills, especially reading, will also struggle desperately with math. The common core has rewritten computational-focused curriculum to a more concept-based curriculum intended to teach a richer mathematical understanding. This has exasperated the frustration of struggling learners in elementary grades with reading struggles. Math has an extensive vocabulary. Some may say it has its own language. Reading and math are not separate subjects. Better said, reading is in every subject, especially math. Reading skills in math are unique, and I will address that in Chapter 15.

Math generally tests logical thinking using quantities. Each logical thought creates or strengthens neuron connections, making you smarter. You need the math from time to time, and different careers and hobbies require it. Math changes how we think about everything, improving our logic and patterns. Math has an essential purpose in a developing mind. Parents need to support math effort and encourage patience in figuring out why errors occur. Practice and repetitions are necessary until accuracy is achieved. That process is the intended outcome of learning computational skills. It is a valuable process to learn the strategies of deducing where errors occur and how to improve. To explain and give counterexamples in sentence form for a math concept is expected within each grade level in the elementary years. The language arts component of math intentionally attempts to exercise language arts skills. Mathematics is aligned each year to the reading ability of that grade level for this reason. Mathematical thinking creates new neuron connections in the brain that improves overall intellectual ability.

Middle school math offers a variety of tracks. You can take pre-algebra in seventh grade, or you can have another year of the sixth-grade review again in seventh grade and begin pre-algebra in eighth grade. If you take pre-algebra in seventh grade, you can take Algebra 1 in eighth grade, which is considered grade level currently. In the past, Algebra 1 was a ninth-grade course, and now a majority of grade-level kids are taking geometry in ninth grade. This is considered behind European, Japanese, and Chinese standards. Some districts have their ninth graders take Algebra 1 again. Exceptions happen, and these two levels are generally available. Larger schools and districts can sometimes allow students to get ahead and begin ninth grade with Algebra 2, the course following geometry. This usually occurs in metropolitan cities, like the San Francisco Bay Area. My clients who live there seem to have more of an opportunity for advanced math courses due to demand from an educated population and large schools that can offer more choices. Course offerings are a factor in the size of the school. Success in computational skills in elementary school is not a predictor for algebraic mathematics of high school, which requires the use of a calculator. Keep students' mathematical self-esteem alive through the computational years and explain that brain development is not complete until age twenty-one. Calculators are also allowed after Algebra 1, which is a great equalizer for many students. You can get better at math after high school when your brain develops further. Math skills are not determined at any grade, so get that notion out of your mind and stay open to your child's potential being strong. We should never falsely label students and shortchange their potential, which is commonly done by the system and often by parents. Parents speak from fear, forgetting the impact their view has on the child. If you are one of those math haters, please keep that to yourself because that will negatively influence your child in the short and long run.

In middle school, science includes three years that cover three general foundational ideas in physical science, life science, and Earth science. The concepts taught in these classes are precursors to physics, biology, chemistry, and other science offerings in high school. Social studies content is an area I do not want to dissect, but the reading ability and writing skills required to participate in the course require the ability to analyze and infer comprehension concepts to show mastery. I am passionate about these subjects and teaching them to promote analytical thinking. The scientific process trains people on how to make sound conclusions that are repeatable. Science is critical in promoting and using the logic mathematics teaches in ways that reveal our world to the students in a new and intelligent way. Social studies content is another controversial topic. I am not writing a book about that. But who can argue that the study of history is not a valuable way to understand our place in a changing landscape? All the topics covered in middle school social studies will be retaught in a high school social studies curriculum.

From kindergarten through eighth grade, literacy alignment makes it possible to plan for the expected literacy skills. The language arts curriculum is designed for that purpose. It teaches reading comprehension, writing skills, punctuation, grammar, and fluency. Teachers are obligated to stick to these standards in kindergarten through fifth grade and trained to teach these formative skills. Once students are in sixth grade, they need to be proficient grade-level readers. After sixth grade, students will not receive reading instruction directly, but rather will have language arts classes that expect reading skills. Elementary school is the ideal place to become proficient in reading and computational skills required in upper-level grades.

Testing measures to these same Common Core standards. This sounds like a very solid and sound plan for education. Here is one reason why this well-planned system is not working. It begins with children entering kindergarten with varying experiences in their prekindergarten education and home life stimulation and interaction, entering with a wide range of abilities to learn to read and count.

The number of conversational turns with a child determines how developed their language center of the brain is. The frequent use of screens does not develop the brain in the same way, as research has shown. The human brain is diverse, with varying talents, perceptions, and thoughts. We know that the amount of enrichment experienced also impacts the readiness for learning. Ask any kindergarten teacher if they can tell what parents speak to their child a lot and what children have confidence in what areas. For a kindergarten readiness test on my web page for parents, see www.AcademicTransformations. com/TheStrugglingStudent/more. (Password: STUDENTSUCCESS) Learning can be measured in the retention of ideas and ability to grow in literacy and math skills. Equipped with these skills, the science teacher can teach, and the social studies teacher can ask you to read and discuss it in class with those who could comprehend it. Everything hinges on math and literacy skills in school, along with the student's approach and attitude to the learning process.

For the 66 percent of eighth-grade students in America who are below grade level in math *and* reading, they cannot grow using the product assigned to their grade. (Again, I refer you to the data in the National Report Card, 2019, link provided in Action List on my web page.) We can surmise that the American education system works for about 33 percent of our elementary and middle school students. High school teachers are not qualified to remediate students' skills when they arrive in ninth grade. It is not a part of their training, nor is it their goal. This is a shocking reality that explains the trends economically and socially in our country. America has lost its education ranking in the world. It matches what I have seen in my career over the last twenty-five years in education.

I meet students and tell them what I do for a living: I tell them I'm a learning coach and reading and math specialist and ask them what I can help them with. And I create a safe space for them to let me know how I can help them. Almost every student I meet has something they wish they could change, something they fear, or something they feel inadequate at. Students hide this secret and cover it up, avoid it and get somebody else's help, or cheat their way through what it is they cannot figure out on their own. The system expects that they get on the escalator of increasing levels and keep up. If they cannot, then there are labels given and accommodations made. This means lowering standards. And there is no plan to help your student catch up. There is not a remediation plan, but there is an effort to make them not feel bad about how far behind they are. Special education teachers are helping kids cope with schools that are too hard for them. They usually have to prioritize doing the schoolwork and not remediating skills. I have known many talented special education teachers who provide a safe place in the school for help which feels like lifesavers every week to struggling students.

The SPED (Special Education) teachers and students are surviving impossible situations. Students should not be wasting their time in a curriculum that does not fit their skills. Reading specialists say they are not working within their independent level. They require support to accomplish the learning objectives within the curriculum. But the support and dependence do not help the struggling student in the long term. They feel incapable and begin to expect to fail. This is the birth of the fixed mindset you will learn about in Chapter 7: Your Child's Belief in Self. Kids drop out because of academic levels forced on them by a system that has overtaken their abilities. The shame and humiliation are unbearable. I find this unacceptable as a parent and math literacy specialist.

In general, high school curriculum requires four years of English, three years of math, three years of history, and three years of science to graduate if we focus on the core subjects. English is offered at remedial levels for those unable to continue the tiered curriculum of increasing expectations. This means the reading is more complex, the writing more analytical, the vocabulary is about 3,000-5,000 words per year, and the sentence length grows along with the demands of comprehension. It is essential to fix reading issues before the eighth grade, if at all possible, because high school is the bridge from reading and interacting with childhood texts to learning complex concepts and preparing for college-level texts. This does not happen with the remedial class beyond an eighth-grade level. Students stuck in these courses have such great literacy holes, and their skills are so out of concordance that they are stuck. The teachers do not have the knowledge that a reading specialist knows, and they do their best. I think COVID has pulled the curtain back and revealed to parents in America how their child interacts with the expectation of their grade level. Maybe that is why you purchased this book?

"By age three, when many children enter early preschool, youngsters from well-to-do families have a working vocabulary of 1,116 words, compared to 749 words for children in working-class families and 525 words for children on welfare," according to a 2003 study by Betty Hart and Todd R. Risley, in their book *Meaningful Differences in the Everyday Experience of Young American Children*. Vocabulary is something we teach as parents to our children from their first word and throughout their lives. Students need to acquire new vocabulary through listening, talking, and reading. By the time students graduate from high school, if they are grade level, they should have a total of seventy-five thousand to one hundred thousand words in their vocabulary.

You finally see what you know you need to fix. In a way, I am glad. Because as parents, we need to take control of and be responsible for our children's journey in education. We cannot delegate it all to the system. I agree the system needs to be reformed to become more student-centered and not so product centered. In the meantime, you, as the parent, need to take matters into your own hands and find solutions to assist and benefit your child's smooth progress in skills. Some you will be able to do. Others may be among the most difficult challenges you have faced. I am here to encourage you to do what will matter most in the long run. There is nothing more rewarding than seeing your child excel and achieve as an adult on the wings of their education. I am enjoying that with my three sons as I write this book. I think it sets up a lifetime of happiness and possibility, which is a mother's dream come true. In the long run, we want a student who feels capable and able to be independent. Is your child in elementary school? Maybe hope to get them there by middle school. Possibly your child is in middle school, and you are hoping to get them there by high school. Perhaps your child is in high school, and you are hoping to make college possible. Whatever the case, it is always possible. Humans are born to learn. Time is the solution and there is no better time to start than now. It does not matter if your child's journey is "typical" or "on track," but it is *their* journey. Honor each part of it, have creative solutions and hard work. Be their pathway to becoming a stronger student, and you have taught a pretty valuable life lesson. Creativity, strategy, and effort solve a lot of things in life. Model that for your child.

I gave up the priority of living up to the iconic high school culture expectation in America for my sons. They participated on football teams and attended an occasional prom, but not a lot of the other aspects. There are toxic hallway interactions around these events. And do not get me started about the Valentine's Day popularity contests, which were brutal for most. I have asked parents in my thousands of consultations in the last twenty years, "Why do you want that stereotypical high school culture for your child?" Most say that they want their child's experience to be different than theirs was. Therein lies the heart of why parents are so invested in this unrealistic experience. It is sadly a harsh social environment for the majority, and it is fair to say the minority enjoys the social scene as positive.

The response I value the most is athletics. I completely agree that team sports teach workplace ethics in skills such as working together toward a common goal, teamwork, and communication. This is a valuable asset in society. Those without that shared experience stand out in jobs that require a team mentality. But the king and queen naming at prom, and the traditional Valentine's Day popularity contest of who receives roses from their admirers, often just points out who *did not receive* a rose from their admirer. It is a lot to cope with when the schools are as large as they are in America. High schools are generally between 2,500 and 5,000 students. The objectification of girls in cheerleading tradition is a difficult reality for me. I appreciate some schools that choose to wear a more conservative outfit and make the cheers athletic and inspirational. This is not always the case, though.

The damage from rejection and judgment on the teenage psyche is devastatingly painful to watch. I have been spending every year with high school kids for the past thirty years. Your kids may come home and pretend that culture is not hurting them and that it doesn't matter. But I want you to know, in many cases, there is damage to their self-esteem. Academic excellence far outweighs the value of the large school culture, which can be cruel and judgmental – the positives in a school environment heavily criticized for not being emotionally safe. Something to think about and consider on a case-by-case basis. This is the appeal of homeschooling. If someone is an introvert, the sheer number of people can be very stressful in general. I offer these as thoughts to consider.

No matter how you feel about testing, my focus is not on testing. Testing is a tool to measure a student's ability to handle the level of the content and to give some insight into what is lacking in their performance skills. I more value the enjoyment a student can have while learning, and the potential for their future to learn what their heart desires, to find their place in the twenty-first century, and to not be hindered by their reading or math skills. My goal is for students to grow into adults capable of financial independence. Education is a predictor of financial success and we can all agree it improves your choices in life. I am a fan of tiny-house living and living from your organic garden and keeping life simple, but I do not garden, full disclosure. Earning a lot of money is a common life goal. But our students must be literate critical thinkers who are able to read and understand mathematical concepts to access the knowledge they want in this world. And most importantly, being a voter requires critical thinking, and is essential to the future of our democratic freedom. Education for the youth of America is of national importance in my opinion.

Professor Buckley, education specialist Diane Ravitch, and others have talked about how private schools may play a greater role in the solution. And they are right. Even in West Georgia, where I live, the region spends a lot on building bigger schools, even though not-for-profit private institutions have space that could be filled by the growth in student population for a fraction of the construction costs.

Private schools, which were exempt from the maniacal obsession with testing (according to Ravitch), have adopted the creativity that students really need to succeed in the global market. This is more about innovation and free thinking than memorization of material that can be easily accessed by a computer. And testing reflects more of the latter than the former.

Another point of view about standards and thinking about raising the bar: "The problem with that is if you had hard tests or hard standards you made your schools look bad. So, there was a real, kind of perverse incentive baked into NCLB," Hess says. The desire to correct that mistake, Hess says, led to the creation of what became the Common Core. The numbers game and misleading statistics is not a game I want to play. This book promises to focus on the student who is struggling and in a system that is essentially not helping them change that.

RECAP: UNDERSTAND THE STATE OF AFFAIRS

- Physical education is paramount for brain health, learning, and stress management for students.
- We have a product-centered education system in America, where each year we teach a product to students who may or may not be compatible with that curriculum.
- I propose that American education needs to move to a student-centered education system.
- Reading and vocabulary are skills needed in every core subject, including mathematics.
- By thinking logically and mathematically you improve your overall intelligence by creating new neuron connections.
- Level options for students in the mathematics curriculum begins in middle school typically.
- Science in middle school covers life science, physical science, and Earth science, all precursors to high school topics.
- Kindergarten through fifth-grade teachers are reading teachers.
- Conversations with your child increase the ability of the language center of the brain and will influence their ability to read.
- Currently, the American education system is working for only 33 percent of students as measured by the National Report Card.
- If students fall behind the levels of the curriculum, usually they acquire a label, "accommodations" are made, and the gap between grade levels will grow.
- Vocabulary development each year in school expects that students grow to a 75,000 word vocabulary by twelfth grade.
- High school culture is not emotionally safe for the majority of students.

- Athletics and participation in sports, or other team endeavors, promote social skills needed in most occupations.
- High school curriculum has a fixed expectation in the four core subjects.
- Testing is a very subjective tool – to your child's ability to test that day and how it is delivered with respect to their skill sets.
- Testing results should be used to benefit the child and teach what is not learned yet, with pointed efforts.

FAMILY MATTERS

5

PARENT RESPONSIBILITIES TO INFLUENCE

We've learned more about the basics of our education system in Chapter 4. Now, we can focus on the power and responsibility we have as parents to influence our kids at home. By being the parent, you are poised to be the most influential person in your child's life.

That is the power we have as parents, accept this, and do not shy away. It is a sweeping force, stronger and more effective from you than from any teacher due to the love your child has for you. My hope for this book is to channel the powerful bond and relationship you have with your child and give you the tools to foster your child's healthy, strong, and positive academic self-esteem. No one is more committed than a parent who loves and desires a positive and fulfilling life for their child. This book joins that intense bond with the jewels of my thirty-year career focused on highly effective teaching for those who need it most.

Did you know that most behavior patterns are learned at home? Our brain has mirror neurons that imitate our parents. We are the most powerful influence on our children. It may seem that your child is telling you of their many other influences if they are a teen, but the reaction and conversation from you trump what they are telling you.

Remember this. Your child is born loving you the most in all the world, and this gives you the power of influence if you are a continued source of love. This continuity of love throughout one's life cannot be undervalued as it builds the foundation for self-worth.

SELF-WORTH IS THE LAUNCHING PAD OF DREAMS AND GOALS

Learning is the requirement to achieve all dreams and goals, so we are at the essence and meaning of human life when we consider this chapter. Giving life to another person comes with great responsibility, and growing the brain until adulthood is the lengthiest process involved. Let's do this right, as their life depends upon it.

We are all different people and unmatched in our own ways. We all, in turn, parent differently, and there is a beauty to the idea that we are all unique individuals, parenting our child to the best of our ability and with our own preferences and priorities. We do not get a manual of what is important to do when raising our children. It is baffling that we get to take that new, fragile, yet amazingly resilient infant home to rear as we see fit. What we do and what we prioritize to our children affects how they perceive themselves and the world. I am not here to tell you how to parent, but I do want to help you lay the foundation for a brain that can excel in a learning environment. Everything in this chapter promotes an academically successful brain. I think of my mother, my aunts, my grandmothers, and my great grandmother and realize that I had stunning examples in my life, but I do not believe they knew the neuroscience of their efforts.

Caring for a child involves basic premises, providing love, food, shelter, warmth, and a sense of belonging, safety, and security. Sounds pretty simple. But it is actually very complex, especially in the fast-paced world in which we live. The responsibilities of family, work, and home management are primary to the parent providing love, food, shelter, warmth, and security. Parents need to have an attuned executive function (see Chapter 11), or the ability to set goals, outline the needed tasks, plan, and then execute the tasks they choose are important for parenting. With all of these choices happening within every parent, it is no wonder we all do this job differently. The purpose of this chapter is to review and remind you what parent responsibilities directly affect the academic performance and success of your child.

When we look at the basic list, they seem so short and simple. To care for and raise a child, we agree that love, food, shelter, warmth, and security are reasonable. Let's take each one and discuss what impacts learning directly.

We can begin with love. Love is a basic human need and is received with attention, touch, words, and gesture and behaviors. You can tell children they are loved, but more important is to show them they are loved. Love is measured in time spent together, attention, and conversations. By conversations, I mean one-on-one conversations, going back and forth, or "conversational turns." When someone is included in a respectful and calm conversation, they feel safe, important, and loved. You will hear more about "conversational turns" and their importance later, but in this chapter, I think we can all agree it does mean love when you receive someone's attention from a conversation. But when someone is engaged in one-on-one exchanges, that validation is much more powerful, intense, and absolute. The number of conversations directly impacts your child's feeling of self-worth and the idea that they are lovable. Increase the conversations you have with your child, no matter the age. As their parent, you hold immense power to influence your child's sense of self-worth and feeling of being loved. The whole world does not need to love them, but children need to feel the love and validation of their parents, or at least one parent, or a parent figure in their life.

Children form perceptions and then make conclusions based on those perceptions. Children's perceptions begin as literal, through sensation and stimulation. Then they learn organization and the ability to identify and recognize objects. People use rules to organize. To form these rules, they have schemata and scripts learned from you and vicarious daily experiences that include television, reading, or hearsay from peers or family members. Categories are formed and perception errors are corrected as they become apparent. A script is a form of schema that focuses on action, event, or procedure.

Then we have a process of how we behave, and how we organize it with our actions, which are organized by a pattern. Perception then develops to interpret and evaluate. Perception is influenced by a complex combination of experiences, needs, wants, values, expectations, physical state, emotional state, and gender, to name a few. These are influences of perception and behavior. Next, the brain adds the faculty of memory, which is a storage of both perception and interpretation-evaluation. Then, recall information decides if it is consistent with schemas or not. In psychology and cognitive science, a schema describes a pattern of thought or behavior that organizes categories of information. There are many types of schemas, including object, person, social event, role, and self-schema. In psychology and cognitive science, a schema describes a pattern of thought or behavior that organizes categories of information. Schemas are modified as we gain more information. This process can occur through assimilation or accommodation. This is a way of saying, you can influence how your child interprets things by giving them more information. Analyze your child's schema systems in their world. Where are they strong, and where do they need to grow?

If not, the rethinking of the schemas occurs, and a new perception is formed. Uncertainty in a perception leads to a person feeling stifled. A person analyzes their own logic and critical thinking through an emotional state.

Analyze your child's perceptions and consider their world and their situation within your family and life. Teach your child not to make assumptions and how to add to the information they need to make a good conclusion. Help them realize that we choose what we perceive, and that perceptions change and evolve as new information occurs.

When you focus on learning, which requires a brain rich in neuron connections (or synapses) making highways of logic, experience, and information references, the important thing is to lay a wealthy groundwork of neuron connections. You make a new neuron connection when you hear a new word, see something new, or have a different experience.

A baby's brain begins to develop in utero and does not finish developing until early adulthood. This process can happen in a "starved" environment, resulting in the lowest cognitive function, or in a "rich" environment where the brain reaches its potential. When you think of the extreme possibilities, you realize the responsibility a parent has to raise a child and help them achieve their optimal brain. A baby ignored or untended will not create as many neuron connections as the baby who is spoken to, held, and attended to by a loving caregiver. Just changing a diaper and returning them to their solitude is not the same as being playful, talking, or singing to the child, touching them, showing them objects, naming them, finding humor, and laughing with them. When the diaper change brings parent and child together, there is a choice every time to make it one that improves their brain and hence their academic potential. The difference of "care" that includes loving interaction versus the fundamental needs of a diaper change and then returning to a crib or safe position is quite different. When a neuron connection is made the brain is forever smarter. Most parents intuitively understand this by creating a rich experience for their children. Rich in experience and rich in interaction with the world around them, this does impact brain development in the most positive of ways. Taking this idea through life and growing your child's range of experiences as they become older is a delicate dance of judgment, time, money, and priorities. But nature is free, and taking a walk and having a conversation with your child is simple, free, and effective. Time is really the commodity we all realize is limited. Make time for your child because their brain depends upon it. Time equals love. Try not to get caught up in the expenses or complexity of what you think you need to give them. Being creative with your child, accomplishing a project together, reading together, or just experiencing nature together is a gift you are giving their brain in the measurable way of love and neuron connections. Create that "superhighway" from the road.

What communication should you have with your child? Any

conversation "counts" for language development in the brain, but I recommend you delve into understanding your child's perceptions. Adults forget that a child perceives things very differently, and children commonly make false assumptions. Conversations that begin with you asking a question, then moving to why they feel the way they do and listening to their names for things and rationale can be very productive. You are refining and understanding their views and building vocabulary, memory, and experiences. Parents show love by listening.

Since neuroscience is so conclusive on the ideas that conversations enrich learning and engagement with a loving parent is so powerful, I sent a "Weekly Report" for each student at my school every Friday. I intended to inform parents about what their child was specifically learning in each class to promote those conversations. We all know that it is so hard to get the full story from our children at the end of the week. How many of us have asked our children, "What did you do this week in school?" and heard, "Nothing." We are posing a general question, and we need to be specific. I recommend at open house to get the teacher's syllabus or curriculum plan for this purpose, so you can talk to your child about what is happening in class. What an amazing parent you would be if you tried to talk about math, English, history, and social studies learning each week. Model reveling in the information, find wonder, and help enrich and give more context to the topic for your child's deeper appreciation and engagement. My hint is to involve emotions to make learning memorable and active.

Neuron connections in the brain look like an oak tree. Imagine a big sturdy old oak tree, with its many branches reaching to the sky, the branches getting smaller and smaller the farther up you go until you have the newest shoots and leaves reaching up to the sun. This is how a neuron looks in the brain at the microscopic level. The base of the tree is the cell body, with the branches are the dendrites reaching out like a vein branching into smaller capillaries. When a neuron connects to another neuron, we call that a synapse between the two neural receptors. This is the way a thought travels in the brain via synapses. The speed at which ideas travel is about 223 miles per hour, faster than the fastest land mammal. The cheetah can run about sixty-five miles per hour.

Brains can be thought of as "wired" and when you realize that these connections do not form on their own but from experiences and conversations, which reframes why you spend time with your children. This reframes how important your child's time is and how it is spent. Additionally, reconsider what they are doing when they are not with you. Focus on them feeling safe, loved, and stimulated with new experiences. Reading can provide "new experiences" in repetitive situations. Do not discount the power of reading for language and literacy development. Use these ideas as considerations for care, after-school care, and time spent away from you, and prioritize making new neuron connections. We are different in culture, beliefs, knowledge, and experience. Our diversity makes this world interesting.

HOW PROPER NUTRITION AFFECTS YOUR CHILD'S ACADEMIC PERFORMANCE

When it comes to food, there are rules for giving your child what is needed for learning. I must say I am often appalled at the control some parents give to the child for food preferences. By modeling eating various foods and also trying new foods with an open mind, you are teaching your child to do the same. If you are finicky, then your child would be too. It is not that you share this trait; it is that your child is modeling after you. The most important thing about food is that it fuels the body and the brain. Your child needs nutrition that promotes brain health and development.

Your child's body needs a protein-rich breakfast to optimally start their brain for the day. Yes, a cut of oatmeal has six grams of protein and so it can be eggs, beans, bacon, sausage, ham, or oatmeal. Please do not start their day with sugar! The American diet is full of sugar. Processed sugar is an evil that we should generally avoid. It is calorie-dense, destabilizes our blood sugar, and causes weight gain. The natural sugar in fruits like apples and in the addictive high fructose corn syrup are both sugar to your brain.

In large quantities, all sugars are dangerous to the brain. The nerve cells in your brain use sugar, or glucose, for fuel. A developing child or adolescent should consume no more than twenty-five grams per day of sugar. There are twelve grams of sugar in three-fourths of a cup of Cocoa Puffs cereal. An average morning cereal bowl contains double that and then you are at your daily max at breakfast. But the milk has sugar – there are twelve grams of sugar in cow's milk (skim, 1 percent, or whole is all the same sugars for cow's milk), or ten grams of sugar for rice milk. If your child drinks soy milk, almond milk, or coconut milk with their Cocoa Puffs, then there are little to no added sugars. Processed breakfast cereals, bars, and snacks are loaded with sugar. This is not what your child needs. How much sugar does your child eat? Track it and become aware of what their diet is doing to their brain and their academic performance.

When there is too much sugar in the brain, your child's reward center is activated. One result is your child craves more sugar, which creates distractions. Eating sugary foods causes the desire for more sugar, an addictive cycle. The addiction comes with symptoms of withdrawal. Physical symptoms include shaking and teeth chattering for sugar cravings.

Sugar also contributes to depression. Sugar impedes the body's ability to produce serotonin, which can lead to depression. Most of your body's serotonin is produced in the gut and if the function of your gut is compromised by too much sugar, then the result is low serotonin and low immune cell formation, which is another problem altogether. Staying healthy is directly related to our immune cell formation, so you can deduce that sugar reduces our immune system.

Sugar contributes to anxiety. We feel the "high" from sugar, but the crash after that initial burst of energy is a form of hunger, which falsely creates a feeling of desperation for food. This is a hypoglycemic state that causes weakness, anxiety, and confusion. The brain reacts by sending out a panic adrenaline alarm. There is a protein in the brain called BDNF (Brain-derived neurotropic factor) which decreases when you eat too much sugar. This decrease happens because BDNF is essential in reducing anxiety, panic, and stress reactions. A deficiency in this protein can worsen anxiety and depression. Students who struggle with panic attacks or test anxiety (or any school-related anxiety) should be weaned from sugar as a component of treatment. Sugar causes insulin resistance. This is how the blood regulates sugar and it is needed to be managed for healthy brain cells. People with high blood sugar have a faster rate of cognitive decline. The higher the sugar, the swifter the decline. People with type 2 diabetes are twice as likely to develop dementia, which is why Alzheimer's disease is now referred to as type 3 diabetes. If you have minimized the sugar warnings in the past, I hope this overview gives you more "food for thought" about sugar in your child's diet and your diet, too.

Your child needs oily fish in their diet for learning. They need omega-3s to help build the membranes around each cell in their body, including the brain. Eating fish improves the neuron structure within the brain. It also increases blood flow to the brain which explains the correlation between cognition and eating oily fish. The best fish to eat are salmon, mackerel, tuna, herring, and sardines. But you can get omega-3s from soybeans, nuts, flaxseed, and other seeds.

Enjoy dark chocolate for the flavonoids in the brain. Flavonoids are a type of antioxidant essential for brain health. Eating dark chocolate for the flavonoid-rich cacao is proven to increase the brain's plasticity, which is the ability to learn, remember, and repair itself. So, chocolate is really brain food and probably my favorite advice in this book. I learned so much about chocolate, which also has a positive effect when you study with it and then eat it before a test, which can improve your ability to retrieve information.

Berries also contain flavonoids, and they reduce inflammation. The antioxidants in berries include anthocyanin, caffeic acid, catechin, and quercetin. These are great for the brain's ability to communicate between brain cells (neuron synapses), reduce inflammation in the brain and body, boost learning and memory, and reduce age-related neurodegenerative diseases and cognitive decline. Pack those strawberries, blackberries, blueberries, blackcurrants, and mulberries into your child's diet (and dipping them in real, low-sugar chocolate is a brain-healthy treat).

THE IMPORTANCE OF SAFETY AND SHELTER

Shelter for your child is a home, however that looks. A home needs to provide safety, warmth, and love. That can happen in a studio apartment, a tiny house, an RV, or a large palatial mansion. Time together is harder to manage in a mansion, but it happens more naturally in smaller spaces. So, think about your home and if it affords you the relationship with your child that you desire.

Safety is more than physical security; it is also emotional security. Both are equally important for students. Be careful if you are a single parent and your home has household members changing or coming and going. This can be stressful to a child's sense of security. Also, if new members do not respectfully honor the child, then you are trading a fundamental need of your child for the right to have someone else in your home. Whatever that reason is, consider how your child perceives this visitor and whether the disruption to their routine is worth it. What do you need to do to keep your child in emotional safety? We cannot force our understanding or perceptions on children. Some children are very receptive, while others are seemingly stubborn. Whichever inclination your child exhibits, you have the largest influence in their life.

If you child worries about any of the basic needs, educators commonly refer to Maslow's hierarchy of needs. This is a widely accepted theory that explains that our brains are wired to worry about survival and food/ water, warmth/ shelter, and physical and emotional safety as primary needs that, if not met, will prevent the brain from learning. Learning is a higher order thought process and requires safety to occur. This chapter addressed the lowest two levels. Chapter 9: Primal Reflexes will address the next two levels of this hierarchy.

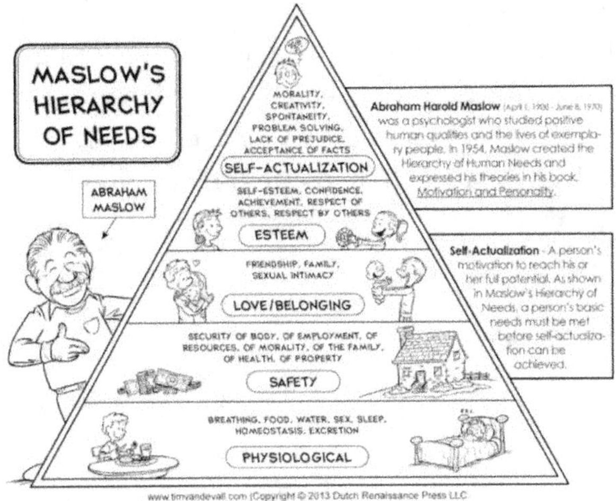

Mirror neurons are the key to understanding how human beings survive and thrive in a complex social world, according to neuroscientist Vittorio Gallese, MD, PhD, at the University of Parma. "This neural mechanism is involuntary and automatic," he says, "with it, we don't have to *think* about what other people are doing or feeling, we simply know." Furthermore, he asserts that, "It seems we're wired to see other people as similar to us, rather than different . . . At the root, as humans, we identify the person we're facing as someone like ourselves."

Children will mirror those in their environment. Those they love and depend upon are not only consciously mirrored but also subconsciously imitated. Recently, on a chiropractic visit, the chiropractor saw me waiting and standing on one leg, leaning. He told me, "Your hip would be happier if you stood evenly on both feet." I was unaware I was standing that way. He asked me to stand, and it was just a few moments. I naturally, out of habit, began to lean on one leg more than the other. He said someone in your family must do that. And sure enough, my dad stands that way, his brothers stand that way, and I remember my grandfather, my father's father, stood that way! I had not consciously realized that my standing habit was just mimicking what I observed. It has been a battle to change that in my fifties after a lifetime habit, because of how unconscious it is for me. But where awareness goes, change can happen. My hip is happier, and I figured out a small solution for myself. Be willing to see things in yourself that might be mirrored in your child that could improve. Model identifying something that needs addressing and then plan for a step-by-step way to change it. Most importantly, follow through.

RECAP OF CHAPTER 5: PARENT RESPONSIBILITIES TO INFLUENCE

- Love is a human need and a priority for a developmental brain.
- By being the parent, you are poised to be the most influential person in your child's life.
- Be open to your child's unique learning journey. It is probably very different from yours.
- Love, food, shelter, warmth, and a sense of safety and security are primary parental responsibilities.
- Parents can influence their child's perceptions to then influence their decisions they make on their own.
- Talk to your children about what they are learning.
- The food you feed your children affects their thinking and learning.
- Emotional safety is a parent's responsibility for their child.
- Give your teens a curfew: "Nothing good ever happens after midnight."

6

FAMILY CULTURE

A child's academic success correlates with aspects of the child's family culture. What aspects of family culture are the most telling? Family education, family income, parents' criminal activity, family structure, parents reading, mathematics aptitude, decision-making style, and the family communication style.

LET'S BEGIN WITH COMMUNICATION STYLE

Is your family the *Reactive Type* of communicator? This type tends to only talk about things when they are confronted directly with the situation or action, at the moment. There is a general angry tone when dealing with the child's behavior. Often a child or teen will test boundaries and initiate some type of communication. For example, teens may want a later curfew or a child a later bedtime. The Reactive Type communicator might react with frustration and impatience. Emotions may run high, and no one seems to be able to stop the communication chaos. Peaceful times are few and far between. This communication style teaches your child to negotiate limits. It also teaches family members to avoid the reaction of the person delegated to discipline.

Is your family the *Wavering Type* of communicator? This communication style has set clear boundaries but is inconsistent. There is a lot of talking and not a lot of action when it comes to discipline. Children will push the limits to see if, this time, the boundary is being honored or not. "Caving in" when you are tired will leave you a large price to pay. As a parent, we need to anticipate our child's behaviors and set safe and clear boundaries. This is a skill, do not get me wrong! The consequences must be reasonable and consistent for the child to respect the system. This style of parenting encourages testing limits because your child must keep engaging to learn what the rules are at this moment.

Is your family the *Proactive Type* of communicator? This style establishes firm boundaries. There are age-appropriate rules that foster and encourage decision-making by the children and growing independence skills. When misbehavior occurs, words are followed by appropriate action. The child learns how to accept limits and act in acceptable ways which will help them handle life's challenges.

Parents may struggle with adjusting the boundaries to the developing child in all of the communication styles. It takes intuition, knowing your child, and anticipation of events and situations to properly prepare your child for appropriate behaviors. You hear parents tell their child to "be good." This is a concept and not direct, specific instruction. When you are taking a four-year-old to the library, you might have a talk with them in the car and say, "This is a quiet place, and we are going to use our whisper voices. Do you understand? What did Mommy say?" See if your child can show your *shhh* symbol or some cognition of your explanation of what is to come. Reward it and let them know how long you plan on staying. Then you bring something quiet for your child to play with between engagement with the books. This is teaching your child about library culture, letting them know what to expect ahead of time, and defining what "being good" means in the library. You are setting them up for success and are very proactive in communication. The reward is pleasing you, verbal praise, and a hug. This is a healthy exchange of teamwork, respect, and positive communication.

That same scenario by a Wavering communicator would say to the child before entering the library, "This is a quiet place, so you must be good, OK? You can have this candy if you are quiet in the library!" Then the library experience is too stimulating, and the child is excited by the seeing-eye dog and the other children, and begins to run, laugh, and scream with excitement. The child cries at the hampering of their exuberance and asks for the candy, then asks again with tears. Then begins to cry loudly and insists on the candy. The mother gives the candy to stop the four-year-old from crying to restore the library's silence. This preschooler just learned that they could have the reward no matter what, and they can get it faster with tears. You can bet tears are coming next time they do not get what they want. A Reactive style would not talk to their child ahead of time and would respond with frustration to the child while the event is happening, spreading stress and frustration to all who are in earshot.

You can think of teens and their boundary-pushing the same way as the preschoolers. Parents need to be adjusting their parenting techniques as they age to be appropriate. Let's consider another scenario. Your eleventh grader wants to use the car to go with a friend to Disneyland for the day and you live within an hour of the park. As a Proactive style parent you ask your teen, "Now that you have your driver's license, is there anything special you have been looking forward to doing? This is an exciting time; you are a driver!" Your teen explains, yes, they want to go with their friend to Disneyland for the day. You explain that you think they are ready for the drive and for being on the freeway, based on their driving experience, but you are not sure they are ready for the responsibility of a friend in the car. You caution them about the dangers of distracted driving and remind them that the driver has all the responsibility. You ask your child what would happen in every possible scenario you can imagine discussing. You ask your child how they will avoid their phone distracting them. You would ask who would be in charge of the music. You would agree if they left and came home in the daylight for this first trip. It wouldn't be dark until 8:00 p.m., so that would be a long, fun day with an early start. You allow the responsibility and keep it appropriate. If something goes wrong, you let them know that there will be a mandatory "four-month parental driving class" before an independent trip again. You agree to the choice of friend, someone who shares the same values of fun and compliance to safety, whom you know well. Then you wish them well as they leave the driveway with all the plans in place. You are teaching independence and rewarding a responsible child who was willing to thoroughly discuss the trip ahead of time. Are you guaranteed a teen who complies 100 percent? Heck no! But I say, permit them while they think it is yours to give, and you build a bond during the transition to adulthood. Be on their team but loving enough to go through the trouble of assuring their safety.

The same parent who has a Wavering communication style might say, "Yes, you may. How fun!" to the trip. Then the next morn, the parent would say, "You know, I was thinking . . . and I am not sure that I am ready, no, I am not sure that *you* are ready to take the car on the freeway that far just yet." Then off it goes: "Oh, Mom, why not? I already asked Kim, and we are all set to go, and now you are ruining it! *No!* I am going!" Walk away, door slams.

Teens are in an egocentric brain development stage, and they cannot see other people's points of view often. They are overly concerned with their friends and cultivating a positive impression with them that yields more social engagements. The social connections are directly linked to their concept of self often, and excessive emotions surround this shift from the family being the center of the teen's life to the friends being either also in the center of their life or replacing the center of their life. This does not end well. The teen goes anyway, but the other parent allows an older sibling to drive them, and they stay until midnight, and the teen comes home with alcohol on their breath after 1:00 a.m. The Wavering parent is left to decide how to punish a teen already distant and upset. It is an uphill road from there. The truth is the teen does not feel loved or respected in the way they need in this case. The good-intentioned parent who said yes prematurely just needed to predict what would eliminate the worries for this first trip.

If the same scenario happened in a household where the parents had a Reactive style, the teen would ask on the morning of their Disneyland day, "Hey, Mom, can I have the car keys, because I have the day off and I want to take Kim to Disneyland. Can I? I told her I would pick her up in twenty minutes! I am so excited to celebrate getting my license! *Please?*" The mother would say, "Hey, what are you talking about? Honey, I am not awake yet. Why are you asking me this so early in the morning? You never get up this early. You want to do *what?* Jeez, cannot we have a relaxing Saturday? I was hoping to have your help today in the yard. No, I do not want you to go. You are not ready for the freeway! Also, how can I trust you will come home early? I do not want to have to come and find you at midnight! Remember when you did not listen to me last summer and came home at 3:00 a.m.?"

"*Mom!* That is *not* fair. I have got to go. I have the keys right here, I am going . . . OK! Please, why are you so *mean?*"

"Can I get a cup of coffee, please? You woke me up with this *big* thing and you are not being fair to me."

"Bye, Mom, I am going! *If I do not leave now*, I won't be able to go! Casey's mom let him go last week, and I am going. You can kick me out, but I am out of here."

Teen storms out with the keys as the mother's first cup of coffee is brewing. That sounds horrible, doesn't it?

INHERITED ACADEMIC ATTITUDES

If you hated math: You refer to it as the "torture of your childhood" and recount your fears of the math "mad minutes" where the timed tests freaked you out. You are planting a seed of how to perceive math and your child's potential to find joy in their math abilities is severely affected and limited if not ruined. Parents who model pencil and paper calculations or estimates to solve real-world problems with ease and confidence are modeling math in the world and the usefulness of math along with the rewarding challenge and puzzle it can be. Logic can be a game in the house that is fun or a reference to something unpleasant and hard. Math attitudes need to be positive from the parents in the home. Kids who come to school with a predisposition from their parents are almost hating math on their behalf. They have decided they are like their parent and that is it. They subconsciously feel that their home culture needs to be honored by adopting this attitude.

I have taught math for so many years. When this strong parent influence was there, it was very near impossible to move them beyond feeling capable and neutral about math. Math can be fascinating and something kids learn to "count on." Sorry for the pun, I could not help myself. Parents, please help their teacher with at least hiding your hatred of math until they are already feeling competent, or until after they graduate from high school. From math teachers across America, we thank you, in advance.

PARENTING STYLE AND LINKS TO SUCCESSFUL LEARNING MODELS

Here is an enlightened analysis from Jaime Gardner, MD, (author of the forward to this book and mother) regarding parenting styles and positive education she observes in my work with her children's academic transformations. Jaime is a current client, and mother of three sons. She is a practicing psychiatrist who also enrolled her two older sons in my school for a time when I was running that. She is a friend and respected professional, but mostly she is an insightful mother who has had an academically struggling child.

Jaime says, "For simplicity's sake, the easiest model for parenting styles are four categories first described in the 1960s by Diana Baumrind: Authoritarian, Permissive, Uninvolved, and Authoritative. Understanding these parenting styles and applying them to education models should shine some light on why Lisa's work is so effective . . . and why it's a rare find in our education systems.

"Authoritarian parenting styles are focused on implementing strict rules and discipline. This is mostly a one-sided *do as I say* interaction between parent and child. As far as safety, making mistakes can feel shameful and unsafe. Similarly, it can feel unsafe to show messy feelings or struggles in general. Purpose can often turn to avoiding rejection vs. navigating how to be authentic and human. Similarly, seeing school in this light, a primarily authoritarian school can also lead to inauthentic learning. Some students may strive for perfection and mostly regurgitate information vs. critical thinking. Others may rebel and self-sabotage: 'I will reject you first before you can reject me.'

"On the other side of the parenting spectrum is the permissive style. Here, parents are involved with their children but have very few rules and/or inconsistently reinforce them. This is the *do as you want* parenting narrative. Shifting this model to schools, some school systems saw the harm in authoritarian education. Unfortunately, this reaction has produced educational systems that have swung too far to the other side and become permissive. A permissive school model may give their students too much say in their learning and expectations.

"This can result in rules and expectations for performance being set too low and/or expectations just not consistently enforced. Kids will figure out pretty quickly how to work the system, like *Lord of the Flies*. Ironically, instead of trying to instill creativity and freedom, it can actually feel unsafe. It is developmentally inappropriate to have a child and even a teenager feel in charge. It is too much pressure to have that much control when neurologically they are not ready to take over.

"Regarding purpose in a permissive school system, it can get lost. Purpose is often a result of facing a challenge. We do not often find purpose in things that do not create some type of growth or push. It would not be an accomplishment if it were easy. If the expectation is low, and the challenge is minimal, the purpose starts to dwindle. There can also be a lack of respect for the teachers that are following the permissive style of the school. This too can cause a lack of buy-in into the work as well as behavioral challenges. In some cases, students will find motivation and purpose in these systems but often linked to non-academic motivations such as peers or sports.

"The third parenting style is uninvolved. Parents are indifferent, unengaged, and neglectful. There is a lack of communication and nurturing in this style. Children are not *seen* and their needs are not acknowledged or met. They do not feel they have a place in the family and feel insignificant. The lack of safety is obvious here if a child is unable to rely on caregivers for protection, nurturing, and support. Imagining this style in school, a comparable example may be if students are not seen. For the most part, in traditional schools, the students who are seen are those who are gifted and talented, those who perform below grade level, or kids with behavioral challenges. Besides those main categories, there are students who find it is safe to just do the minimum and stay under the radar.

"Although this may be the easiest way, it does not foster self-esteem or confidence in learning. Instead, it can promote learned helplessness. Here, kids can learn that efforts to get their needs met are unsafe or ineffective. This can result in just giving up. Looking at purpose in this style, a student's performance in an uninvolved education will likely depend on the expectations of the student's parents. In other words, the parenting style at home determines the performance of the student. This can be problematic when both systems are operating in the ineffective territory. For example, a student with authoritarian caregivers under a neglectful system may still look successful as the motivation is driven by performing for his/her parents. Permissive parenting styles may chug along, assuming all is well, if there are minimal school concerns with their kids' education. Or permissive parents may assume the school will satisfy the student's academic needs without checks and balances.

"Finally, there is the authoritative model of parenting which is the best parenting model and can be presumed the best school model as well. Authoritative parenting promotes secure attachment, where there is a back and forward between parent and child. Parents are attuned to what their children's needs are and match them consistently. Parents with this style also set clear limits and rules. What is different about this vs. the authoritarian model (dictatorship style) is that time is taken to explain the rules and adjust if needed. Explaining rules and expectations, like all good leadership, shows that the person expected to follow the rules is respected and valued. It also highlights why the rules and expectations are important and have a purpose. This leads to more buy-in and compliance.

"The rules are then enforced with non-shaming consequences and positive rewards for compliance. Children who have been raised with this type of parenting result in the best outcomes. To name a few, they are more responsible, secure, have better self-esteem, healthier relationships, and can self-regulate. An authoritative education model would be a hybrid of setting rules and high expectations but meeting the individual needs of the student. Students would feel safe to make mistakes and could navigate challenges while developing a stronger sense of self and accomplishment. They would also feel secure with the fair and adequately explained rules of the school. Purpose would come from moving through the challenge in a supportive and nurturing environment.

"I like to call authoritative parenting *inspired parenting*. First, I always confuse it with authoritarian parenting (dictator style). Also, I think this better captures the goal of a child's growth. *Inspire* is from the Latin root meaning *inflame* or to blow into something. Something that has been inspired is as if breath (life) has been added to a spark that grows into a full flame.

"Of course, in a messy world, there is a spectrum to all of the parenting styles, some more pronounced than others. Also, there can be a combination of all styles both in parenting and school systems. For the most part, in my experience, it has been very hard to find education systems that mirror the inspired (authoritative) model.

"This led to an enlightening discussion with my husband. After abandoning authoritarian education early on, my kids' school experiences have been a combination of predominantly permissive and/or uninvolved systems. The kids knew there were expectations to get their work done at home, but were more motivated by avoiding consequences vs. a desire to learn. They were also motivated by peer interactions. But as mentioned above, it appears that a child's purpose of learning in a permissive or uninvolved school will fall heavily to the parents. In our case, we were being permissive parents when it came to school.

"Both my husband and I were educated mostly by authoritarian education systems. This was especially the case in our medical education. We both felt the message we got was that our performance was tied to our worth. And performance here was not effort and working through challenges like Lisa's. Rather, it was getting everything correct. We did not want our kids to attribute their worth to perfect performance. In an effort to avoid this, we overshot it by lowering our standards for their education. We relied on just making sure there were no concerns from the school. Left unseen by the system, this was not a good marker of their potential or relationship with learning in general. My poor older son will suffer the consequences of this. However, I feel confident this time that, with Lisa's interventions and learning from her teaching style, we will be better prepared."

I loved Dr. Gardner's analysis and observations so much that I asked for her permission to quote her directly here for you, which she granted. We are all parenting the best we can, and often small shifts produce huge outcomes. Educational models are one to question right now when your child is not being served. The rights of the individual learner are very real to me and should be addressed with some systemic developments moving forward in education. I hope to be a part of that revolution that is available to those who open their minds and consider the best we can do.

Let's talk about the reading culture in your home. This is another hot topic within family culture attributes that determines a child's success in school. There are obvious correlations between parents who model pleasure reading in front of their children, not only after they have gone to bed! Modeling enjoying reading and talking about your books in front of your child, models that reading is worthwhile. This is a simple thing to do at home that provides an internal motivation to learn to read as well as, "My mom and/ or dad enjoys it." With this one act, you will give your child what every teacher works so hard to do: motivate them to read. The parent will likely take their child to a bookstore for hot cocoa and enjoy the experience like a special treat. They will also go to the library to research something or get books to entertain themselves at home for short-term periods.

They will explore a new interest by getting a good book on the topic. All of these experiences shape their attitude to the teacher saying, "We are going to read this book today."

When a family is only hardworking and there is no time for enjoyment of books perceived as leisure and enjoyment, that is in a way "literary deprivation." Reading is a major focus in K- grade five, and you have the opportunity to impact this experience by supporting the love and enjoyment of books. Or you can be the family that is very active and fun but does little to zero modeling of any pleasure reading. This also makes an impact. Suddenly, there is the elementary child who views reading as a task that is "too much work" and does not see the potential pleasure component of reading and learning. Ideas and thinking are not generated by books in this child's mind. They might see reading as not worth the effort if they have not seen a parent enjoy reading. Their parent may exercise in their free time or do crafts, fix engines, travel, ski, or hike, but not read. No visits to the library or bookstores, no love around the experience of books. This means their teacher has to create all the love of books and experience with books with the challenge of changing what you have set up in their mind already by not reading to them, in front of them, or for yourself.

Please, help the process of reading instruction, vocabulary development, writing skills, and fluency skills by being a reader in front of your child. Express excitement to finish a book, to read the next chapter, or in what happened as you read last night at breakfast. Make it part of the family culture, and your child will read to just fit in. Especially if you share tender loving moments with your child with books. Love and reading can go together and children who experience this are at a huge advantage.

Research shows us, according to the *Learning and the Brain* 2019 presentation by Joanna A. Christodoulou, that, "If there is family bonding in the home and members are loving, supportive, and connected emotionally, there is a less academic risk for that child in general." Another protective factor is strong parental attachment. They have a parent to go home and talk to about their feelings of the day and feel supported. They have a cheerleader for their accomplishments and someone who holds fair and consistent boundaries. Boundaries equal love to the child, which seems counterintuitive to some parents who fear following through, but it is true. Kids feel safe to blame a strict parent for a rule or boundary and the reality is they are kept in appropriate situations for their age and moral development.

The next topic is one I cannot overemphasize as being a predictor of academic success. And that is whether your child has a "fixed mindset" or a "growth mindset." A child with a fixed mindset will view failure as a permanent poor skill. The growth mindset child will view failure as a learning opportunity and be curious about what he does not know or understand and start to work through the details of his confusion with a positive productive attitude. The growth mindset is positive and optimistic about one's ability to succeed. They believe that if they work hard, they can change the outcome and achieve their goal. The fixed mindset child will have negative self-talk about being stupid or feel shamed when they fail and perceive it as a permanent measure of themselves. They will feel overwhelmed by focusing on the negative aspect of a poor grade or score and feel bad about it. Shame is usually generated by the child themselves or the parent at the disappointment of the grade.

Holding high expectations is tricky when your child is struggling. Many parents I work with struggle with how to parent their child into a better outcome. Parents influence which mindset kids have by how they praise them. This topic is covered in Chapter 6 with regard to how to help your child develop a growth mindset. In this chapter, I want to talk about how to parent to instill an approach to life that handles challenges positively. Life is not easy, or clear, or fair many times. Tragedy and adversity are sure to be in your child's future. These academic challenges are actually opportunities to teach resilience and fortitude for life's challenges. Having a growth mindset embodies that optimism.

Here are some specific parenting tips to help your child develop a growth mindset. Do not praise your child's general intelligence, like:

"You are so smart!" or, "You are a math genius," or "You are a natural at this!" It is much better to praise the effort by saying, "I can see you put a lot of time and effort into this. Great job!" or, "You are doing a great job studying." If your child has hit a bump in their progress and, say, gets a poor science grade, you should not say, "I guess you are not too good at science, are you?" This implies a permanence to the grade and their potential. How silly, of course. They were not good at it here, but that does not mean they cannot learn to be better next time. You should not say, "Maybe you are not going to be a scientist?" No, no, no! If your child fails a big science test, better to say, "What can we do differently next time?" or "Is there another strategy you can try?" If your child is swimming, and definitely not ready for the Olympics, do not say, "You are a natural at swimming!" Better to say, "I love watching you swim." No one is a natural at anything. You get to the Olympics through hard work and dedication. We need to teach our kids that they too can achieve anything with perseverance and hard work. Praise the work, not the result! You will help your child's internal talk to be encouraging of themselves to problem-solve and persevere.

If something is too easy for your child and not challenging, to instill a growth mindset, you should say something like, "That looks too simple for you. Let's find something more challenging." If you praise the accomplishment when it was obviously easy, you are giving a reward for not too much effort, and the praise is not earned. It promotes them to seek the praise of other small efforts, which is unrealistic.

If your child shines in an area, like they wrote a great paper, and this can be any grade first to twelfth graders, praise them like this, "You have worked hard at writing this so beautifully and it really shows!" This is better than saying, "You have a real talent for writing!"

Having a talent implies that they are just capable without any effort. That is not the case in life usually. To accomplish things, you need to practice and learn from your mistakes. This requires a belief in yourself, and the ability to take on the work required to get yourself to the goal. You need to persevere and be willing to put the effort in.

Students need to learn that the harder the task, the greater the reward. Not that they earn rewards for little to no work. That is not how life is or skill-building of any kind. Athletics requires practice, the trades require practice, academics requires practice. Life requires a growth mindset, so praise appropriately and your child will learn that hard work and perseverance leads toward their achievements.

RECAP: FAMILY CULTURE

- Reactive Type of communicator: one who typically expresses emotions, and loudly reacts to situations.
- Wavering Type of communicator: one who sets boundaries but does not hold them firmly, which gives children a sense of insecurity.
- Boundaries equal love.
- Proactive Type of communicator: establishes firm and reasonable boundaries, discusses infractions to help their child understand, and gives appropriate consequences.
- Parenting Styles: Authoritarian, Permissive, Uninvolved, and Authoritative (Jaime Gardner, MD), and children respond best to authoritative for the safety within the boundaries.
- View academic challenges as an opportunity for self-discovery and self-growth.
- Remove all comparisons, stigma, and judgment.
- Celebrate each step toward each goal along the journey of remediating your student.
- Never praise grades; praise studying and put in the effort to encourage the increasing learning efforts required as students progress to high school.
- Encourage your child to embrace new and unknown challenges.
- Emotionally connect and bond with your child because there is a direct correlation to less academic risk for your child.

7

YOUR CHILD'S BELIEF IN SELF

As we discussed in Chapter 6, boundaries equal love. Many other experiences form a child's perception if they are valued and cherished. This belief by their caregivers or parents is essential to one's foundational belief in themselves.

The external pressures are influential, no doubt about it, but the internal beliefs determine everything. We began to discuss your child's mindset and how they view the process of learning and challenges presented to them. We will discuss this further in this chapter and explore ways for parents to influence their child's belief in themselves.

External pressures are what people expect from you and what society expects from you. There are unique expectations in every family culture that may be positive or negative. The same culture can affect different people uniquely. I am all for positive pressures and influence. Having high expectations is saying you believe in someone, and really is a message of love, when expressed with sincerity.

Any sarcasm delivered with high expectations can be a devastating blow to self-esteem. Self-confidence is formed by a blend of the perceptions of those we love and a combination of what we choose to believe. Children form large conclusions with their limited world experience. Some moments count more than others. Emotions play a big role in what is memorable. You can give a straightforward compliment such as, "Honey, you look beautiful tonight." Or you can give a sarcastic statement like, "You were such an ugly little girl! What happened?" and the intent may be the same, but the sarcasm only inflicted injury to their sense of self despite the intention. You cannot claim your style is "sarcastic," because that is a cop out. Say what you mean and mean what you say, is a good rule to abide by with children. Remember, sarcasm is poison in families and especially to children. Damaging sarcasm can never be retracted and can have long-lasting effects. "That will happen when you maintain your 4.0." is a cruel statement when responding to a request your child may have that is unrealistic, knowing that might be above his or her abilities. You are further insulting them and saying no to the request. This is very harmful to the child's sense of self. Sarcasm might only have a place when a parent wants to make fun of themself. Only then can it be appropriate from a parent to a child. Never at the child's expense, please, parents. Think about your tone and how you speak to your child. Build up your child instead of tearing them down. Again, as the parent, you hold so much power, and you can use it for growth.

"Stress kills" is a statement accepted as an unfortunate medical statistic with regard to cardiovascular health. We know stress raises our blood pressure and is unhealthy in general for us. High blood pressure and cardiovascular damage are measurable proof of this statement. Cardiovascular issues are attributed to a shocking number of deaths each year. According to the American Heart Association (AHA), nearly half of all adults in the United States have cardiovascular disease. It caused more deaths in 2016 than in previous years, despite rates of cardiovascular deaths declining worldwide. Recently, a loved one of mine was diagnosed with gliosis which caused a brain injury. This is damage to the microscopic capillaries in the brain that can be described as an old, cracked hose that leaks. There was a warning from the many years of fluctuating blood pressure and highly emotional reactions. The body is not indestructible. Stress can have devastating effects.

Stress kills also our ability to learn. This is proven in so many studies, beyond a doubt. We must change the fundamental pressure cooker built into schools and transform it into achievement ladders where hard work and support will get you to your goals. "Stress kills learning" is also suggested in neuroscientific research. The brain is wired for survival. When threatened, the brain will respond quicker than the visual process takes to process the event. Even in just a stressful situation, like worrying about a bully at recess, worrying about your parents divorcing, or being fearful of an upcoming math test, the amygdala (which contributes to emotional processing) sends a signal to the hypothalamus, which operates like a command center. The hypothalamus uses the nervous system to communicate to the body, which is why the "flight or fight" response is so reactive. The autonomic nervous system engages your blood pressure, heartbeat, and breathing. The two parts of the nervous system are the sympathetic nervous system and the parasympathetic nervous system. The sympathetic nervous system is reactive and uses energy to respond. Then the parasympathetic nervous system uses reason and logic to think and reconsider the perception of stress. The initial hormone involved in this stress response is epinephrine, also called adrenaline, which causes the heart to increase and blood pressure to increase. Breathing increases and then a release of blood sugar and fats happens to fuel the rush of energy required for the flight or fight response. These feelings creep into a student's experience when they do not have adequate skills to manage a relaxed state. No wonder, in our typical school setting with twenty-three to thirty-five students per classroom and one adult to give emotional support to them, classroom management becomes a priority over emotional support and relationship with students. After sixth grade, teachers typically have between a hundred-fifty and two hundred thirty students which prevents relationships that some students may need in their learning process.

Stress is exasperated if the curriculum is not within a student's ability or is far below a challenging level. Stress is present after a death or family tragedy. Divorce is statistically proven to lower academic achievement for one to three years. Please do not minimize the seriousness of stress in your child's life and the impact on their ability to learn.

Stress symptoms such as sweating, stomach cramps, and your mind going blank are common. I have also witnessed students faint and throw up from stress. Panic attacks or loss of control of emotions is also a common adolescent stress reaction. Stress for elementary students commonly initially presents with students regressing in milestones. There are strategies we can use when the fight or flight response tries to take over, to help us learn.

Meditation is the best skill to teach to fight stress and improve self-esteem. Being worthy of relaxation time and encouraging chosen positive thoughts to focus on is very healthy for any age person. Taking control of one's state of being through breath control is a powerful life skill. Your child will monitor and regulate their emotions better if they have skills in the art of meditation. This can be a family pursuit. You can use this as a tool for challenges like going to the dentist or having patience. The art of clearing one's mind and relaxing with intention is a skill that is easy to learn and extremely useful in many life moments.

I do not want to lightly mention suicide and school violence. They are the ultimate fear of the worst kind of stress for every person or parent. Over the last twenty-five years of my career, as the incidents happen nationally and locally, I was personally impacted by too many losses. There was a freshman girl, who I will call Sadie. She loved riding horses, competing in jumping horses, and being very involved in her high school. She struggled with math and I was her algebra teacher and her geometry teacher in her sophomore year. What a pleasure it was to help her become a confident math student. In her junior year, she was brutally murdered by her ex-high school boyfriend, who lured her out of class and to a local park, where he stabbed her over eighty times. He was struggling in school, came from a prominent family, and was not coping well with school or the loss of his girlfriend. I had several ski athletes years later who suffered learning problems from concussions from ski jumping. One was a dyslexic reader whose working memory was severely hampered, making school even harder than the reading problems that shamed him every year since first grade. He hit the wall in middle school and again in high school - he was not motivated to go to school. He was a creative person whose talent on the snow marveled all who saw him ski. He suffered humiliation and failure at school until his eighteenth birthday and then hung himself. He did not want to live life as a failure (school made him feel he could not succeed) in life. These are two that never leave me. Despite my involvement – they happened. Shocking losses. No one saw either tragedy coming, but learning stress played a role in both.

Watch for warning signs for suicidal thoughts in children to include changes in eating or sleeping habits, unexplained severe or violent behaviors, withdrawal from family and friends, sexual promiscuity, truancy, or vandalism which are out of character. These are all warning signs. Drastic personality changes or distress or panicky behavior are also warning signs. Giving away prized possessions or a sudden drop in school achievement are all warning signs of suicidal thoughts in children and should be taken seriously. Seek help from a mental health professional immediately.

The reality is that human hearts and self-esteem are fragile. Children's formation of their belief in themselves is something to construct. Parents, teachers, and schools need to be involved in the work of building each child's self-esteem. This competition culture in school, which rewards the few and frustrates the majority, is an unnecessary pressure for kids. Some schools have a culture where everyone who shines is honored for their gifts, and thus they are allowed to explore and express them during their learning journey.

According to the National Report Card in 2019, 66 percent of eighth graders in America are below grade level in math and language arts. Our system is "working" for 33 percent of students. Not only are students' self-belief in themselves impacted by learning stress but there are other threats that also distract from learning. School bullying, school violence, sexual assault, and fights at school are not discussed enough. The CDC reports in 2019 that one in five high school students reported being bullied on school property, and more than one in twelve have been cyberbullied in the last year. Eight percent of students were involved in a physical fight on school property one or more times during the twelve months before the survey. More than 7 percent of high school students had been threatened or injured with a weapon on school property during the twelve months before the survey in 2019. The most disturbing fact is that about 9 percent of the high school students had not gone to school at least one day during the thirty days prior to the survey because they felt they would be unsafe at school or on their way to or from school. A brain fearing for its safety cannot learn. One of my sons was threatened with a knife. The other witnessed students shooting up drugs and was threatened by the needle. The third son was bullied. All these incidents motivated me to provide a learning environment that promoted learning in safety. No child needs to feel threatened at school, period. This is a reason to take your child out of a particular school setting and find an alternative.

The worst statistic on the CDC web page is that 48 percent of students in middle or high school experienced some form of sexual violence at school during the 2010-2011 school year. These are alarming statistics. We have a long way to go to serve our youth. It is time to wake up and address these issues in a more proactive manner. I now know this is possible. It is out there for all to read. But it has not found its way into our system with consistency as of yet. Warning signs this may be happening to your child include nightmares or other sleep problems, seeming distracted or distant at times, sudden changes in eating habits, or sudden mood swings. Another sign is if suddenly your child has money or expensive toys or gifts without reason. If your child exhibits adult-like sexual behaviors, language, or knowledge, then you have reason to suspect abuse and should get a mental health professional involved.

We all need love, acceptance, support, and patience. We can address students' needs by utilizing specialists and creative solutions that are respectfully delivered. The best lesson to teach is the one that hard work and perseverance make a difference. Progress is progress, and slow and steady wins the race. Aesop's fable about the hare and the tortoise was right. Recalling Maslow's hierarchy of needs, we need to feel safe and we need sleep, food, and love to be a learner. We need to have positive beliefs in ourselves.

Suicide is on the rise among the youth in America. From a PBS Newshour article titled "Youth Suicide Rates Are on the Rise in the U.S.," here are some shocking recent statistics: "While suicide was the 10th most common cause of death among Americans of all ages in 2017, it was the second leading cause of death among young Americans age fifteen to twenty-four, according to data from the National Center for Health Statistics and the Centers for Disease Control and Prevention. And no racial or ethnic group has been spared in this rising rate, said Sally Curtin, a statistician with the National Center for Health Statistics who has studied these suicide trends for years and served as the report's lead author." See link to this article in the Action Plan online.

Some parents say, "I love you" often. Other parents do not but save that phrase to punctuate life in other ways. Some parents give compliments generously, sometimes even undeserved. Other parents rarely compliment. Are compliments earned in your parenting style, or are they given out lightly? This is a very influential factor in your child's academic success. Does your child have a "fixed" or "growth" mindset? Do they have the belief in themselves to work hard and earn each accomplishment? Or does your child complain about hard work, wish everything were easy, or avoid challenges? Have you made their life too challenging or too easy? There is a sweet spot. To do too much for your child is very enabling. They need time for some chores, time to read for pleasure, time to talk to adults and peers that care about them enough to discuss opinions and topics, and they need time to play and organize their own imagination. All these factors contribute to the growth of the brain. The brain is malleable and moldable and you can construct a positive self-belief in a child with a growth mindset. It is never too late, but it does get harder the older you are because changing patterns of belief is hard work. It's best to start from the beginning, and it's best to start now.

One of the most important life lessons is to realize that mistakes are learning opportunities. That used to be the slogan of my school. I posted this sign in every classroom: "Every mistake is a learning opportunity. At Custom Learning Academy, we skip the 'feel bad' part." So many students lament the shame of mistakes and deplete their energy by associating self-criticism or "not being good enough" with making a mistake. If the perception of a mistake is so negative, then school is associated with fear. After a while, not trying is much less painful than really trying. It becomes the inability to really put effort into learning, instead just skating through with minimalistic effort. Educators have a term called "learned helplessness" that becomes the habit and mindset of students who feel that their efforts are pointless. It is a severely "fixed" mindset that gives up on sincere effort to feel less. Less criticism, less personal about their grades, and less invested in the school. It is a detachment strategy to hurt less. One can understand how it must feel to be unable to succeed when you try, really try, over and over again, watching those who seem to live in the zone at school and score top grades with admiration at being "smart," thinking it must mean you are "dumb." How long can the human ego take the pain? That depends on one's personality. Do you quietly wither inside, counting the days to be done? Or do you get angry? The reaction can be as individual as the person experiencing it.

To grow in our world with curiosity, wonder, and a positive belief in ourselves is what we would call a "growth mindset." We need to learn as we go, and how better to learn what we need to know than through our mistakes? Working through your mistakes is the point of homework. As a high school math teacher, I had to assign homework. And then grading it was a challenge for one hundred and fifty students with daily homework. I used to do a visual check for effort, then as we graded it in the class, it was expected that students correct their work and learn from their mistakes.

Students were encouraged to ask about errors. Some regularly did the task and made the efforts to understand their errors and some did not. They would not try to figure out why they were wrong, but would just feel bad or mad about being wrong. How is your child doing on grading their math homework? If you do not work through your errors in the homework, they will happen on the test. Some sort of hope or prayer is used as a strategy by those kids who just assume, "I cannot understand." That will lead them nowhere good and is not an acceptable attitude. Being a learner is about attitude and the belief that your hard work will make a difference in the future.

When one strategy fails, try another. Learn what works when. This is easier said than done and obvious to some and invisible to others. Do not assume that children and teens are strategic thinkers. Metacognition, the ability to think about one's thinking, is a learned skill. When failures occur, the best growth mindset conversation to have is thinking about the lesson, what you learned from that mistake, and what you can try differently, which is the next logical thought if the first two are allowed to marinate. Some students make a self-critical conclusion like "I cannot" instead of "What did I do wrong?" and "What can I do differently?" But you can teach that thought process. Encourage each effort. It is a perseverance game that needs strategies. Strategies on how to study. Tell your child that you don't read math like you read a novel. Math needs to be read slowly. Teach your child to pause and think, and form questions they can ask their teacher as they go. Have your child decide what makes sense and what is unclear. Reading strategies, study strategies, time management strategies, sleep strategies, and practice strategies are all factors that influence the student's learning journey.

Strategies for new vocabulary are important. Research indicates that there exists a correlation between vocabulary learning and reading ability, comprehension, and general skills. Students need to capture new words in three ways: they need to notice the structure (for spelling), meaning(s) (sometimes multiple meanings are diverse), and lastly annunciation (how you say the word properly). That takes thinking and relating what you learn to what you already know. There are three ways to keep up with the yearly expectation of students growing their vocabulary by 1,000-5,500 words each year. By the eighth grade, students are expected to know 50,000 vocabulary words. Just slowing down to notice that these three things can be taught, maybe is all that is needed. Permission and purpose with a strategy is a powerful thing to teach. Success can improve self-esteem. The harder the task, the more the reward.

Parenting can be trying to be very positive and still inadvertently promote a fixed mindset. Some examples can be how you compliment your child or teen:

Do you say, "You are so smart!" or name another trait: beautiful, talented, etc.? This is something that they did not really earn but were just given by a parent who loves them too much. Then it becomes a burden to keep up, and the risk of challenging things to change the perception of that trait turns out to promote a fixed mindset. One that avoids challenges. All from a compliment that most parents think will inspire greatness. The opposite occurs. Better to compliment the effort. "You worked so hard on that! Wow." Compliment taking the time to do such a high-quality job or excellent attention to detail. Do not give traits away lightly, but encourage the journey to earning a trait.

If you practice mindfulness, take time for quiet, meditate, and pray or just be still in nature, you may be aware of what thoughts are swimming around in your head. The quiet beliefs that exist. Now, when you focus on those beliefs about learning you can feel the answers almost more than knowing what you might say in words. How do you feel about learning math? How about science? History? English? When you ask yourself these things, you realize you have a specific belief about yourself. You get these beliefs from your experiences. Those specific moments had a large, lasting impact. Helping your child through a limiting belief to a growth mindset about a subject they may be weak in is a journey of love, trust, and incredible life impact. It helps if you can know what they feel about themselves being able to succeed or not. Can those beliefs change? Not if we are not aware of them. What we don't know that we don't know is the most dangerous. We can only change what we identify.

To see what I am talking about you may want to stop as you read this chapter, and take some deep breaths, try to relax, and allow yourself to answer the questions I am about to pose to you about your child who is struggling, and consider the same ones for yourself. You can change the questions to the ones that apply to you, shifting the focus to the dark corners of your feelings and beliefs that you feel about yourself. No one is finished learning and growing. Carl Jung called it living life being self-actualized. Life is the path of continual growth. It is a humbling stance to take, and one that attempts to keep your perspective open to the new possibilities: open to curiosity, learning, and hope. It is a belief in oneself that helps anyone stay positive.

Let us take an emotional measure of the feelings in each situation. By doing so, the emotional response is an excellent indicator of where work needs to be done. The most anxious feelings associated indicated a large need for intervention. Each of these circumstances can feel positive, stimulating, and exciting to experience.

I can promise you that this journey of your child's self-belief is the beginning of the content issues with your child. Begin with any small success; it is analogous to building a snowman. You need to begin with that first snowball. But remember, your child does not know all the reasons for their inability to succeed. It is rare that a student can succeed and does not by choice, and if that is the case, it is an alarming attention-seeking effort. Typically, it is a process like peeling an onion. It takes layers and revelations, but you get there, and once a student realizes that what is happening is their lifeline, they do grab on. When students meet me and I tell them I can help them be better at what they are wanting so badly to improve in, they will trust me and work with me immediately. Students really do want help, but they are mostly asked to cope and perform in school. Be a lifeline to your child and provide a growth mindset for them to take to school with them.

RECAP: YOUR CHILD'S BELIEF IN SELF

- How do you feel after a verbal lecture in history or science? Did you follow and understand?
- How do you feel after a math lesson on a new topic? Do you like following mathematical ideas?
- Are you able to grab parts and work out other parts you find challenging in learning math?
- Do you pursue understanding or do you give up on math?
- Do you read your math book? All the information is right there.
- Or do you go right to the problems and try to get them done as quickly as you can?
- Does your school give you textbooks or "packets" or is it all online? (Every parent should know.)
- Do you mind reading out loud if a teacher asks you to?
- Do you feel like you understand what you read well enough?
- What things do you say inside your head when you are at school and feeling challenged? Do you encourage yourself or put yourself down?
- Can you write your thoughts in a good sentence (first grade), paragraph (third grade), or page (high school)?
- Can you properly punctuate and capitalize your sentences? (After fourth grade, this should be solid.)
- Do you have a talent in school? What would that be?

SOMETIMES HIDDEN FOUNDATIONS

8

UNDERLYING FOUNDATION

What are your child's core math and literacy skills? Now you are thinking about each grade as the product of learning which is a large awareness to what your child is aiming to be able to accomplish. Each grade has its own graduated literacy expectation throughout the year to bridge the prior grade to the next grade in incremental reading and math standards. It changes over the year intentionally inching toward the next grade level. Now you are thinking like a teacher, and you are closer to understanding how you can help your child function within these expectations.

This chapter is going to give you a few tasks to undertake utilizing this year's curriculum (if you are reading this during the school year) and what to do if you are reading this during summer break without access to curriculum. These next steps with your child will immensely help you understand if the data you are receiving matches the performance you witness. It will also be a first-hand experience seeing your student interacting with grade-level text. You will be given some things to look for, and that might be new or something you regularly do.

Let's tackle spelling, reading, comprehension, grammar, writing, orthographic knowledge, and phoneme knowledge. That sounds complicated, right? Well, we can get a general idea by checking fluency. Fluency is the critical bridge between two key elements of reading: decoding and comprehension. In a 2000 report, the National Reading Panel defined it as "the ability to read text quickly, accurately, and with proper expression." Fluency has several dimensions. Successful readers must decode words accurately. But they must move beyond decoding and recognize words in the connected text quickly and automatically. They must also read with expression to bring meaningful interpretation to the text. All three dimensions, accurate decoding, automaticity, and ability to read expressively, work together to create effective comprehension and overall success in reading.

Step one for the fluency check would be to find a leveled passage with a word count in your student's current grade. It is not too big a deal to count words or estimate by a line of text and count lines. If it is summer, then use the level they just completed. That would be a good place to begin. You need to obtain a grade-level passage and know the count of words for at least fifty words for first graders, one hundred words for second and third graders, and two hundred for fourth through eighth graders as a minimum. This can be done by utilizing a textbook issued this current school year in any subject: a social studies (one to eight)/ history (nine to twelve), science (one to twelve), or language arts (K-grade eight)/ English text (nine to twelve) book passage will be fine. You can try one of each if you suspect a particularly at-risk subject area. If you suspect that, then by all means check a passage of each core subject. If you cannot get your hands on a labeled, grade-level textbook (not a random handout or passage a teacher may have assigned), then I will suggest a plan B. There are online resources of leveled passages by grade level. When I search, I see several.

For elementary passages, another option if you want a resource that is handy online and for printable resources, I recommend a subscription to ReadingA-Z.com, especially if you think your child may need kindergarten through sixth-grade level (even if older, up to seventh graders who are below grade level) reading growth. At

ReadingA-Z you will find high interest, older students with respected leveled reading passages, printable books with comprehension tests, and other language arts worksheets in the areas of social studies, fiction, nonfiction, and science printable book topics. The ReadingA-Z site offers fluency passages that include a word of their fluency passages, but they only go through sixth grade, or Level Z in their system. Both the grade level and the letter level are used in their system which keeps where a student actually is hidden from them for the benefit of older students. This resource has about six levels per grade for younger grades and a bit less as they near middle school. Don't let that confuse you. Choose a passage in the middle range for that grade for this first step.

If you have a kindergarten through sixth grader, you have the leveled passage for the fluency test. If your child is older, a middle school or high school student, then may I recommend again turning to a textbook. Your local library or Amazon would be a resource for this also. Older student reading passages exist, and typically a reading specialist tool. From a textbook, we will need you to choose an interesting chapter in the book. I suggest the first section to any chapter of interest. This section will include some initial teaching (with no prior knowledge expectations) and then questions following the section for comprehension. Suggestions are a biology passage or US history for tenth graders. Count the words in the passage, if you do not have a word count included in your resource.

In order to administer the fluency test, get a timer ready and explain to your student that we are going to read, and the goal is to make the least number of errors. Make a copy of the section you have counted. Sometimes with a nervous reader, you may want to count a section in the middle and let them get going and time the section that is planned. They can keep reading if it goes longer, of course, even if they are reading more. You want to read each word, use proper voice inflection for punctuation, and think as you read so you can discuss it after you finish. It is not about speed! It is about accuracy and understanding of what you read. Time the planned short passage as they read. While timing, you should also note exactly what they say, if different from the printed words. Do not assist or say anything. If they self-correct after saying something wrong, write "SC." If they repeat a word three times in an effort to say a word, for example, make three tally marks, and then if they get it right write "SC" (self-correct). If they get it wrong, just the tally marks. The idea is that we are going to count the errors.

If they read over a period and it does not sound like the end of a sentence, that is an error. If they repeat a whole phrase and fix it, then that is one error. If they track to the next line and skip a line, that is an error. We do not need to worry about anything exactly but get a sense of the number of errors in a passage. When they are done reading, start engaging in questions about what they read, or just ask them about it in a conversation. Ask basic questions about it and then ask a few details. Lastly, ask something more inferential or abstract about the passage. Dismiss your student, and when you are alone, do a few basic calculations.

The goal is to count the errors. Subtract "Errors" from "Words Read" to arrive at your student's number of "Words Correct," and then divide it by the number of minutes it took them to read the passage. (To convert seconds into minutes, take the seconds and divide them by sixty. The decimal should be added to the whole number of minutes for seconds and minutes represented all in minutes accurately.) Take the Words Correct and divide it by the time in minutes, and you will have your child's Words Correct Per Minute (WCPM) score.

Now, what we are looking for here can be looked up on this chart, in Figure 1.

From kindergarten through grade eight, we can interpret a lot about the reading ability of your student through their fluency. Even if you feel your child is a "good reader," I recommend that you continue to read about the details to see if your assumptions are valid. Reading issues can be subtle, so please keep reading. We can look up your child's Words Correct Per Minute Score (WCPM). First, go to the grade level (if K-grade eight) and then look for your child's score and follow that row to the left. When you correlate it to the percentile, the percentile for the grade level helps you know where your child is compared to other kids in his or her grade nationwide. Ninetieth percentile means that only 10 percent of the kids in your child's grade generally will do better than your child. He or she is scoring near the top of their grade. The tenth percentile score would mean that 90 percent of kids in your child's grade would place ahead of your child's skill, and they are grade level but at the bottom of the group of grade-level kids. The tenth percentile is saying that your child is academically independent but on the low end.

The goal for our children and your student is to be within ten WCPM above or below the fiftieth percentile score for your child's grade to be able to function confidently in that grade.

Now, if your child's score is at or above the fiftieth percentile score, you can assume that your child is functioning in their grade level with reading ability. It tells us that in addition to their reading ability, their spelling and literacy skills are in line.

To measure comprehension, you need to assess if your child was able to discuss and understand what they read. You may have felt that they correctly comprehended some of what they read, but not all. This is a common reading problem. The brain is so busy decoding and dealing with the words involved that making meaning is not possible too. That is another sign that the student is not at the top end of their reading ability, when fluency is there, and comprehension is not. I have seen students with amazing fluency but no comprehension. This is a more complex situation. Usually, the reading speed should be around seventy words per minute, and often comprehension cannot occur due to a reading speed too fast. Students often need to learn how to slow the reading speed down to seventy-to-eighty wpm.

If your child was below the 50th percentile line, then repeat the fluency check with grade-level passages one year below their grade level until they score above the 50th percentile line. This will give you a general idea of where their reading ability is, which is also an indicator of the other literacy issues.

If your child is two years or more below grade level, I recommend you get a literacy specialist involved. It takes an expert to find the necessary skills to work on to improve reading skills. This exercise is helping you see a functional literacy level.

Find the last standardized test that your child took. Usually, these are end-of-the-year exams unless your child took assessments as a part of a 504 Plan or IEP testing process additionally. In 2020, not many students took these end-of-the-year tests with the move to distance learning. So, many of you will turn back to 2019. On these standardized tests, you will find the reading grade level equivalence to see where they were at that time. This will tell you if they are on the incline or decline. All of this information tells you how your child is reading. If you think a passage is unfair for any reason, repeat with another passage.

No matter the results, please refrain from having an emotional reaction. You are not doing this to upset yourself, you are doing this to help your child. You cannot fix what you do not identify. This is why you bought this book. Let's rejoice at every step to knowing *what* to do. Skills not mastered on a standardized test are a road map of where to begin helping your child. If you just learned that your child is below reading ability for their grade, remember what that means to you. Your child is trying but it is too hard. Your child's grades are *not* a measure of their effort. Being in school with significant areas of weakness is *hard*.

If your child is anywhere between kindergarten through sixth grade, begin working through the ReadingA-Z.com materials at their independent level. You can find this by the fluency passages and the scores that you have just learned for placement levels. This reading journey, inching up levels, will be fun for both of you. I recommend all the worksheets and comprehension tests along the way, under-standing all errors. Mistakes are learning opportunities. Make it a goal to be curious about errors.

This process may be one you two can tackle. It is common for your child not to want to be transparent with you about their reading. This is because they feel so strongly about trying to make you proud. The shame they feel is a sign of their expectations of themselves. Try to be stoic about this process. If you cannot, then you may need to plan on hiring a literacy specialist.

Make notes about your findings. Does your child's reading ability match the standardized testing results, or has your child made changes in how they compare to their peers? What has your child experienced since the last result? Divorce or death of a close person can derail students for up to two years. Adolescents cannot manage to learn when their emotional state is not stable. Whether that is truly their safety or their perception of emotional safety, which divorce is classic for destabilizing, learning is secondary to survival for the brain. There is a lot of daydreaming and refiguring out life when something rocks a child's stability.

Your child's reading problem may be caused by other factors. Keep reading. Keep going through the checklist to find the source of how to best help your child whose reading ability is below grade level.

If your child is fearful, shamed, and stressed about going to school and facing the reading challenges they are asked to do, and they have angst, it is time for a major change. There is *no need* for shaming a student. If your child can express to you how reading in school feels to them, please listen. We can make goals to move up. But this moment is about being in the reality of the task that is not being addressed in school.

I want to say that it is not an impossible task to move grade levels of skill. It is achievable. A skilled reading specialist can move up most students easily, systematically, and positively. It is a very empowering journey that opens up life's possibilities. Struggling readers do not think they can change. They cannot see or know what is holding them back. The child's brain makes all sorts of inappropriate conclusions about their own potential and what to expect from themselves in the future. Your job is to support your child in this transformation. It will give them the most joy and optimism once achieved.

Every brain is teachable. I have not encountered one that isn't. So have faith. You will achieve goals with perseverance, patience, and belief. What better way to heal your child? You can do this. Find resources that are in your area. Check with your local university and see if they have a literacy center to assist you.

My recommendation for planning is that you need to devote about two hours per week per year they are below grade level to reading remediation. This is something to gear up for. This means reading at their independent level, going slowly through comprehension errors. I recommend taking time to write written responses and correct those to upgrade them. Ease your child into this plan and see if they can feel good about the process and embrace it. This may take weeks to align.

Plan and set this weekly time up when your child has the setting that best suits them and the energy to put toward the project. You will enjoy the process more than you think. I have done this with adults and really any job that needs to happen just needs to begin. Take baby steps toward the goal and then you realize you are there. If your progress does not flow from reading at their independent level after four weeks, you will get a sense of whether you might need a more trained eye on the process. But the love and attention to be with your child in their effort to build up their skills by reading and thinking and reading where they can succeed is a reward in itself. Remember that they seek your love and approval more than any other person in their life.

Working on sight words is also recommended. Fry sight words are organized by more frequently occurring words and often they are exceptions to the rules, so they are recommended to memorize. There are one hundred per grade level up to the fifth grade. If your child's reading level turns out to be in that range, you can help them by printing the Fry signs list and testing if they can accurately say the word instantly. Spell the word out, look at it, and say it. Write it and notice the spelling, until they know it. These can be conversations and syllable by syllable spelling analysis. Work through all six hundred words in order and promote reading remediation. Many of these words are considered oddballs in spelling patterns. Noticing when a word follows the rules and does not is notable. For example, the word "faith" uses the "ai" to make the long "a" sound, which is following the rule. But the word "said" sounds like "sed" with a short "e" but is spelled unexpectedly.

If spelling is severely below reading ability, then there is a reason to get a reading specialist involved from the beginning. Spelling is the leading literacy indicator and reading will not grow, as I have described if orthographic (or spelling) knowledge is lacking. Spelling must be fixed first, and to remediate spelling is beyond the scope of this book. It is important to teach spelling systematically and thoroughly, with a chronological order known to dictate language development. If you are a parent wanting to have a program to learn to use, please read *Words Their Way* by Dr. Bear, Dr. Templeton, and Dr. Invernizzi. This program is not a weekend read but a long commitment. It's not for every person. See the data of effectiveness on this program and know that my bias comes from learning from these authors directly in my master's program. They have given me the foundation of knowledge that has made me successful at remediating students.

I also recommend www.TalkingFingers.com which is a phonics and spelling program of twenty lessons that can reteach the foundations of orthographic (spelling) lessons in kindergarten through third grade and also move where reading is processed in the brains closer to the reading center of the brain. Poor readers process reading in inefficient parts of the brain causing slow processing speeds due to all the neuron connections to travel to read. The program is created by Dr. Jeannine Herron and her work has changed my effectiveness and helped me with all types of poor readers often labeled dyslexic or language processing challenged. I recommend this for all reading challenged students placing in first through fourth-grade levels. These topics will help solve the hidden issues and also improve how the brain thinks while reading.

Read with your child at a level they can perform with confidence. Collect the words they have trouble with into a notebook. But give them the words one at a time, at the time they stumble. Study the words you have collected. Have them spell each word and notice the structure. Ask them to write the words in a sentence and make flashcards to practice recognizing them. After they learn these words, they can post them to see them as accomplishments. As this "word wall" grows, you accomplish several things. You produce a rewarding visual of their growth. This fuels their confidence. You perform repetitions of the word, which also solidifies each new word in their vocabulary. Words that were once unknown become known. We have discussed half of the foundation of learning, very loosely, reading. Writing, which follows reading, is the last growth area of literacy. Your child should be writing as they go in response to questions about the text. If they get feedback and learn how to improve their writing, their reading skills will come naturally. If it does not, hire a reading specialist.

Except for the math phenom student, every student I have assessed in the last twenty years has *something* they are not proficient in from their past. I find this to be true with grade-level kids with no problems in school. Math is full of details. Absent or sick days can create a hole in the learning process.

This is why I checked my own three boys each summer for math knowledge. I also asked them to race me across the pool every June. If they did not beat me swimming, they had to take swimming lessons. That made sense to them all and it took until they were eleven or twelve to beat me and I lived up to my word. It is not about earning the right to stop swimming lessons because of a certain age; it was their swimming skill. We live by lakes and have a boat, and swimming proficiency was important for their safety. I took lessons through middle school including diving lessons since I lived near a junior college with an Olympic pool and lessons every summer to advanced levels. I swam in college for fun for PE credit. I like to swim, and I am a good swimmer. My boys learned that age is not a qualifier. Skill is. Teach your children that age does not earn you anything. Skills do. You do not get your license to drive by being sixteen. You need to be sixteen and pass a driver's test.

Where they did not master from this year in math is a good place to begin thinking about your child's math skills. Use a textbook from this year and use the *pretest* in the front of the book. Or you can buy a math textbook of your child's grade level. I recommend looking into publishers like McGraw Hill or Prentice Hall. If you have last year's book, use the *year-end review* to test your child. There is no need to reinvent the wheel. This does not have to be complicated. You can purchase a math text and matching teacher's edition on Amazon and use it to begin. If your child fails the pretest, go back a year and do the same and gather topics to study. You can also look at the last standardized test score. See the results and compare it to what you find.

Math needs to be explained by a math-confident person, preferably a math major who can correctly answer why to any process or step. If you cannot answer why then you are not the right person. Math is not memorizing a sequence of steps. Your child needs someone who can explain the theory along with the process. That is the number one priority. Find a person willing to work through math concepts and practice with them. When raising my boys, I always found weaknesses in their grasp of math concepts. They were not remedial in math. They were typical kids who were missing things here and there. Because I knew what my boys needed, I could make choices in their summer practice where they used those concepts. In delegating a little time each summer, on the RV trips we took, or on local camping trips, we found time to work on learning, usually after breakfast, before the day of summer fun commenced.

Buying each level of math textbook below your child is a plan. Work your way through and up to where they need to be. Do it in order and be systematic. Practice until they master a topic. Mastery may be quick or long, depending on the topic. It is not about doing ten problems of each skill needed. It is about mastering the topic. How many practice problems will it take for your brain to master a concept? That depends on who you are, and the answer is different for different brains. There is no right answer. Teachers guess at how much homework to assign. Your child needs to learn ASAP that their job as a student is not about getting the assignment done. It is about mastering the concept. Maybe you will need a bit more practice than assigned. That is fine. Learn the goal and teach them that not mastering things equals falling behind.

Kids need to learn how to ask questions. Some students cannot even form questions when they are with their favorite teacher. Kids need to learn how to ask a critical question that is specific enough to get them further along the path to full understanding. Forming a specific question is a skill that requires them to identify where they are lost or confused. It requires some analytical skills and inspection. It is essential to nurture and grow the ability to form these essential specific questions. Is your child able to control their emotions when confused? If not, this is another sign it is urgent to grow the ability to form critical questions.

Learning is a journey that looks the same for everyone in one noteworthy way. It begins with confusion. And the path is unique for everyone, and the goal is to work through all of your uncertainty and end up in complete understanding. I find that students think they understand long before they actually do. Teaching someone when they arrive at total understanding and what that feels like, is a worthwhile lesson.

Your goal is to obtain concordance for your child's math and literacy skills. This means that if the reading, writing, spelling, and fluency skills are all at the same level, then they will move up together with ease. Has your child ever experienced this? If not, it is not about IQ and is more about concordance. If your child is three years below grade level (or more), I recommend you design a year of math and literacy remediation and nothing else. I would suggest no science or social studies classes with testing. Instead, push reading passages on these subjects with a focus on spelling, comprehension, and learning new vocabulary skills.

Math skills require a different premise. You need to be able to estimate and expect a ballpark idea of what answers should be. That number sense needs to happen with the awareness of the size of numbers. Cook and measure to begin or grow this awareness in a fun way. Cut a recipe in half and talk about what to expect. See Chapter 17 on math and number sense for more on this topic.

Math also requires working memory to put ideas together. Math requires creativity, reading skills, vocabulary, understanding, and working memory to think computationally and logically. If your child lacks working memory skills, writing more steps down can be a simple strategy that helps the process improve. Do not try to hold math ideas in your head when your working memory is weak. Maybe calculators are a requirement, and logical thinking is the focus. Elementary computational skills are not mandatory, but they make life, money, and numbers easier. If your student is in high school, begin with Algebra 1, and you or a math teacher work through each chapter review until the student has mastered each chapter. As for geometry, be sure to master the area, volume, and surface area computational skills with formulas. Learn about triangles and study the theorems with pictures.

Maybe you notice that your child is not properly reading graphs or geometric figures. Dysgraphia is a visual perception issue that makes details in graphical figures hard to interpret clearly. If you suspect this, outline what is to be noticed in highlighters, changing colors to emphasize what should be seen. This often solves the problem or helps significantly.

Use cumulative reviews of the year to sort out their weaknesses, beginning back as far as necessary for the review to be effortless and easily completed with little to no errors. These are the areas to learn, practice, and master before moving forward. This systematic approach, moving forward until you are at the current grade, is my recommendation to guide math remediation. Reading to learn math as you go with a good resource is possible. It takes commitment and effort, but I encourage you to do it! Math confidence comes with patient learning and learning how to learn from one's mistakes. All the lessons needed are in one's mistakes. Do not be afraid to look and have a math person who can explain the "why" to any step that is being thought of as "monkey see, monkey do" math memorization. A math person can be a parent with a math background, like an engi-neer or architect. Maybe this "math person" is an older student who is strong in math. Someone with math confidence to assist your student with positive strategies and attitude is a good start. This is not enough in math. Keep a math notebook of the newly learned topics in case old anxieties creep in. Your child has a resource to remind them that they do know it and understand it. Convince the brain of mastery by doing in math.

High school kids using calculators should only go back to Algebra 1. All prior concepts will happen and can be addressed within the algebra concepts. You need a good algebra book with excellent examples and rigorous word problems in each section.

If math anxiety or math testing is an issue, there is a separate chapter dedicated to that contagious idea. But teaching content is content. Math and stress do not have to go together.

Are they within the independent range of the product offered for their grade? If they are not, then plan to get them there. Be systematic about it. Start slowly and work at a mastery level. Do not prepare what to learn each day, but plan time to devote to learning and take whatever time is needed on each topic. Some will be long and others short, and your child can have the luxury of learning as they need in this process. School is generally at a set pace, which has nothing to do with your child's brain or rate of learning. This remediation plan we are talking about is something that should happen at your child's pace. Give them that and reward the hard work. Do not focus on the pace.

I hope this chapter has given you a strategy to determine where your child is in their foundational skills and how to orchestrate the plan to get back on track. If your child is more than two-to-three years behind grade level in either math or literacy skills, I address that in the chapter titled "Drastic Times Call for Drastic Measures."

RECAP: UNDERLYING FOUNDATION

- Spelling trouble indicates a reading problem because spelling is the leading literacy indicator.
- Fluency when reading is a good indicator of independent reading. If there are more than ten errors in one hundred words, then the student is at frustration level.
- If spelling is a challenge, I recommend www. TalkingFingers.com, written by a neuropsychologist to not only teach spelling and typing but move where reading is processed in the brain to improve reading ability.
- To improve cognitive function, the only computer program with data of effectiveness, written by scientists, proven to grow and improve focus, decision-making skills, and other brain functions is www.BrainHQ.com.
- Math review should happen each summer to keep skills sharp and catch missing concepts from the year.
- Concordance with math and literacy skills, which means solid skills in each, is a goal for all students.

9

PRIMAL REFLEXES

Every person is born with primal reflexes that assist in the actual birth process and are the first neurologic skills babies' brains begin with. A part of brain development is to grow out of these reflexes and into other neurological skills along the path of brain development. When a primal reflex is not "resolved" by the age of one year old, they are considered a "neuro-developmental delay." An unresolved primal reflex could explain reading problems, motion sickness, visual-perception problems, photosensitivity, or many more solvable issues.

Brain development begins in utero and continues until a person is in their early twenties. This is a complex process. This chapter is going to examine the essential infant reflexes that aid survival and also ensure that the new shocking world that the infant is born into is one that they can interact with. The initial reflexes are intended for a limited amount of time to serve their purpose and then more sophisticated brain processes are to take their place. If you think about it, an infant is reacting to their environment. As we mature, we choose how to react to our environment to get the responses we need. Savvy parents come to realize very quickly that their infant is doing what they need to do to get what they want and need from their parents.

This chapter could get very scientific to explain this phenomenon, but I am not going to get too technical. If you want to learn more about this topic from respected founders and experts in this area, then read more from David McGlown, Peter Blyth, and Sally Goddard. These are the pioneers who applied the science of reflexes in brain to development stages in children who struggle in school. Thanks to their amazing work, educators like myself can use tools to move children past seemingly permanent stopping blocks in achievement. This may sound fantastical, and really the brain is an amazing set of neural connections that is fantastical and mysterious.

When we have new thoughts and learn new connections about information, our brain must store it in a way that we can access the information the next time we need it. We know from stroke patients that they can relearn how to talk, walk, feed themselves, and even read, despite the damaged areas of the brain needed for the task. Somehow the human brain can reform neuron connections and work around the damaged area to compensate.

If a person can rebuild the knowledge lost in a brain injury such as a stroke, then why can we not teach some kids to read, write, and compute as well as other kids? The answer in this chapter is sometimes there are infant primal reflexes that did not disappear and resolve into a pathway of higher brain functions and this is preventing the learning. This is a very simplified statement of the power of investigating this information. The good news is that you can "test" or check for physical signs in your child to rule out or consider whether this is involved. Each of the reflexes has purpose. If one or more is still present in your child, then the solution is to obtain some physical therapy to teach the brain how to move past it and onto high order thinking needed for learning.

There are seven primal reflexes I want to introduce to you with some general information about how to identify each reflex. These reflexes form in utero and are present at birth. Over the first year of life, all of these reflexes should disappear, except one (Landau reflex) which I will explain further. There are degrees to which these reflexes can be present in a child. It can be severe to mild, so keep that in mind. Maybe something is slightly present or significantly present, and that is something to note on your Action Item sheet if you are tracking ideas for your child using that comprehensive checklist for this book.

The first reflex is the Moro reflex. This reflex forms at nine to twelve weeks after conception and is used as a diagnostic sign of development of the central nervous system. The baby will retract or withdraw from stimuli. This reflex acts for the infant as an early form of "flight or fight" instinct. This reflex should transform into an "adult startle reflex," which is much less reactive. This reflex helps the baby gasp their first breath because of reacting to the new, cold environment in the air once born and forms in utero.

Moro reflex is triggered by any sudden, unexpected occurrence or stimulation of the labyrinth, which is the complex structure in the inner ear which contains the organs of hearing and balance (vestibular system). It consists of bony cavities (the *bony labyrinth*) filled with fluid and lined with sensitive membranes (the *membranous labyrinth*). Other triggers are noise, sudden movements, or change in light. Lastly, the Moro reflex can be triggered if there is pain, temperature change, or rough handling or touch.

The Moro reflex causes physical responses which include freezing in place, startled response, then a cry, and activation of the fight or flight response. This response automatically alerts the sympathetic nervous system and results in a release of adrenaline and cortisol into the system. These are stress hormones, and they produce an alert reaction with a large energetic surge. There is also an increase in breathing, which can cause hyperventilation, increased heart rate, rise in blood pressure, reddening of the skin, and a possible emotional outburst with anger or tears. If this is present in teens or adults, there is a possible long-term effect of poorly developed CO_2. An ongoing CO_2 problem could be explained by this reflex being unresolved. The Moro-present child is basically living in fight or flight during every waking moment, caught up in a cycle of reactions, then hormones, then anxiety, typically. The Moro reflex is an involuntary response to a threat being triggered over and over.

Any of the following may be a sign that this has not been resolved: an overreaction or hypersensitivity to one or several sensory stimuli, like sudden noise, light, movement, or alteration in position or balance. If your child seems constantly "on alert" and cannot relax appropriately, that is a sign of this reflex still being present in some form. If your child is perceived as one who "overreacts" to perceived or imagined threats, he/ she may be a "fearful" child or an overactive, aggressive child who is highly excitable. Often this overexcited version cannot read body language and seems to need to dominate situations. In both versions, the fearful or the overactive child will try to manipulate situations to lower their responses as a way of coping.

Other signs of the Moro reflex present are motion sickness, poor balance, and poor coordination. These are from the vestibular system involved in the inner ear. Take notice if your child is physically timid and does not seem to trust their balance as other children or teens do. The inability to ignore irrelevant visual information often results in teachers commenting that your student is watching other students instead of doing their work, or they are "easily distracted." Other signs include possible auditory confusion due to specific sounds or difficulty discriminating between sounds or shutting out background noise. Allergies and lowered immunity are also symptoms because of the constant release of adrenaline and cortisol overtaxing the immune system over time. If your child picks up every cold and cough or if they are oversensitive to their environment with allergies, this is something to notice. The child may also generally dislike changes or surprises in general, maybe to the point of anger that is perplexing.

The Moro reflex is usually very noticeable in the emotional profile of a child. Here is a list of psychological symptoms to consider: anxiety seemingly unrelated to reality, mood swings, and tense muscle tone that is called "body armoring," difficulty accepting criticism (since this is impossible for them to change without intervention), the cycle of hyperactivity followed by fatigue, difficulty making decisions, low self-esteem with insecurity or dependency and a need to control or manipulate events to avoid the reactions they feel. As you can see, this reflex is very connected to the senses, and the hypersensitivity would be very uncomfortable if you experienced this constant bombardment of feelings and hormone reactions. This makes you wonder, how many diagnosed ADD or ADHD cases are just unresolved Moro reflexes? Professional therapy can resolve and provide much-needed solution parents may be unaware is necessary for cognitive development.

Now, let's discuss the Palmar reflex. This reflex forms eleven weeks after conception and should resolve between two and three months after birth. The response is to grasp with the hand. If your palm is touched, a baby will have a gripping response. To hold and let go is a skill learned when this response is resolved and then forms into the skill of being able to pinch an object between your thumb and pointer finger. The sucking movement also causes the Palmar reflex to grip in infants. The primate babies who need to hang onto their mothers exhibit the purpose of the Palmar reflex for safety. The link between gripping and sucking in this reflex is noticeable (if present) when a student is writing. Their tongue movements match the movement of their hand and protrude from the lips from left to right. Maybe you have seen adults who also do this. Very possible it is an unresolved Palmar reflex.

The long-term effects of an unresolved Palmar reflex can be seen in poor manual dexterity. This is because the reflex will prevent independent thumb and finger movements. Lack of ability to pinch objects might affect pencil grip when writing, speech difficulties with sounds in the front of the mouth, and hypersensitivity to tactile stimulation. This may be seen in requiring only very soft clothing preferences or fabrics that touch the skin. I have seen this present in children with negative attitudes about seat belts, wearing jeans, waist bands which are too tight, or certain fabrics that "bother" them. It is an obvious quality when this is a top priority on a daily basis, not just an occasional preference.

The next reflex to explore is the Asymmetrical Tonic Neck reflex (ATNR). This reflex develops at eighteen weeks after conception and is present until the baby is six months old. The reflex causes the head to turn, along with the arm and leg on that side to extend. This is the kicking sensation that happens in utero and the cause of why newborn babies commonly kick their covers off. As they are looking around, their arms and legs naturally extend and move. This reflex also assists in the birth process to move the baby through the birth canal causing the mother and baby to be acting together in the birth process as cooperative partners. Conversely, the birth process activates or reinforces the ATNR so that it is firmly established for the first few months of life. This reflex should cause a baby to move their head to one side when lying on their tummy and prevent suffocation. It is considered a possible cause of SIDS (sudden infant death syndrome) for a reason for infant suffocation. It is the first eye-hand coordination with which a human baby is born.

By six months of age, a baby is reaching and touching objects. Now, the baby is making higher-level decisions about their hands independent of the head. Manipulating objects with the hand such as early toys and rattles help to develop this resolution. If this is not resolved by this time, then it will inhibit the development of several other functions. This will include crawling with a fluid movement if the head is not independent of the arm movements in crawling. Crawling and creeping are very important in the development of hand-eye coordination and other central nervous system skills. This one reflex can cause a domino effect on other skills developing to include the connection with the inner ear and movement.

An unresolved ATNR will cause difficulty in a movement that crosses the midline of the body. Imagine a line that runs from the top of your head, between the eyes, and downward. It forms a line of symmetry with the two halves of your body. This is the "midline." All movement requires a sense of balance, and this involves an awareness of one's midline. When the equilibrium is deficient, it can affect how we sit and may produce an increase in fidgeting and restlessness.

Poor midline skills can also cause the learner to have scattered attention. Movements that cross the midline are important for fine motor skills, directional skills (such as up, down, left, and right), and for interpreting symbols (such as letters or numbers). If a child has difficulty with handwriting and copying written work, often they may have challenges with midline moves as well. Can your child do jumping-jacks? (Jumping the legs from together to out, while clapping the hands above your head with straight arms.) Has your child failed to establish a preferred hand, righthanded or lefthanded? No dominant side will always cause a slight hesitancy in the child's movements. The child who has ambiguity of handedness has to decide with each movement which hand to use prior to action, which is automatic for others and slows cognition and causes confusion.

Eye movements are affected by the ATNR with the sign that when an object passes horizontally in front of a child, when it passes the nose or midline, there is a pause in eye movement. This affects reading fluency by the interruption in the visual process. As children grow from six months to a year old, their vision improves. Now, they can see farther than their arm and out into the distance. If the ATNR is unresolved, this distance vision development is inhibited and delayed and keeps their field of view of their arm's length longer. This prevents the next stage of development, which is tracking or the ability to visually pursue objects far away. This tracking skill affects reading because the process requires you to move eyes across words and track as you go. See more about this in the Vision Stress chapter. You can see why we should be screening children as standard protocol for resolved primal reflexes and training them accordingly in preschool before entering elementary school for their benefit. Do not get me started on my soapbox!

To look for an unresolved ATNR, begin assessing balance when your child moves their head from side to side. Are they able to maintain balance without an issue? A simple check is to ask them to walk on a two-by-four on the ground (safe if you fall only two inches but challenging nonetheless), and to walk slowly and, keeping pace, look right and then left. Can they balance? Does your child alternate their arms with their feet when walking, running, and skipping? Meaning, when the right leg takes a step, the left arm is swinging forward, and vice versa. Does your child switch hands for the same task as if to indicate they have not chosen a preference? Do not reward this behavior, as being ambidextrous is actually confusing to many brain functions. Parents should see which hand is used for eating most of the time and which hand chooses to write when the child is coloring or using a pencil most often. Then encourage their natural preference. Notice which hand the child uses most often when there is no prompting. Then encourage that hand each time.

The next reflex to discuss is the Rooting reflex. Sucking and swallowing are key to an infant's survival and this is why the rooting reflex is crucial. It develops about twenty-four weeks after conception and should be resolved by three or four months of age. If you lightly touch a baby's cheek or edge of their mouth, it will cause the baby to turn their head and open their mouth with an extended tongue in preparation for sucking. Nature's instinct to nurse, so to speak. The subsequent sucking and swallowing movements follow feeding. The rooting reflex is the strongest the first couple of hours after birth and is why new mothers are encouraged to nurse their newborn baby to allow this learning to occur. The gratification of the newborn is essential for this reflex to develop and sometimes premature babies are unable to eat, and this reflex is not fostered and then is difficult to develop later as they are able to eat.

When you see children have drooling issues or food dribbling problems when eating, this can be a sign in a school-age child that their Rooting reflex is unresolved. If the reflex is unresolved, the muscles in the front of the mouth do not develop properly to control saliva or eating food. Manual dexterity may also be affected as immature sucking and swallowing movements affect the hands, causing involuntary palming movements to occur in time with sucking, also called the Babkin response. Speech issues may also be present with the articulation of sounds being difficult in the front of the mouth. The muscles required in feeding or nursing to eating solid foods with proper control are the developmental grounds for speech. Often you will see the tongue too far forward in the mouth. This correlates with poor manual dexterity, which I would describe as the ability to use your hands in a skillful, coordinated way to grasp and manipulate objects and demonstrate small, precise movements.

The Spinal Galant reflex forms twenty weeks after gestation and should be resolved no later than nine months of age (but may be as early as three months). This reflex can be seen by lightly running your hand along the spine, and the baby will arch his back, extending the leg, flexing the hip joint. Stimulating the Spinal Galant can often lead to the ATNR being activated with the head turning. It is assumed that this is another reflex to aid the birth process as the spine is stimulated of the baby as it travels through the birth canal.

Interestingly there has been a link found between the Spinal Galant reflex and hearing. This is because the vibrations of sound, in a liquid environment, like that of a developing fetus in utero, are experienced through the spine. Fascinating, is it not? And there is a sound therapy for speech issues that also produce resolution of the Spinal Galant reflex as an unexpected result by Dr. Guy Berard called Auditory Integration Training. His work is important enough to take a few paragraphs now to understand. In Dr. Berard's own words:

"It is obvious that people who cannot hear well will experience difficulties in many aspects of life, and particularly that children who cannot hear clearly what the teacher is saying will be at a great disadvantage in school. In my practice as an otolaryngologist – an ear, nose, and throat specialist – I worked with many children whose hearing problems were affecting their schoolwork and came to see two important things.

"One was that there was a direct rather than an indirect connection between poor hearing and disruptive classroom behavior. That is, it is a common assumption that the child who cannot hear well becomes frustrated and bored, and because of this boredom and frustration 'acts up.' There is something to that, of course, but it became clear to me in the course of my work that hearing problems had a much more direct effect on behavior, and later work and tests confirmed this.

"The other major discovery concerned the nature of the hearing problems affecting behavior. Traditionally, hearing is regarded as ranging from 'good' to 'bad,' from being 'able to hear a pin drop' to being extremely 'hard of hearing,' and hearing function tests are performed from this point of view. However, it became evident that there were variations in hearing dysfunction, and that either abnormal sensitivity or abnormal insensitivity to certain

frequencies — rates of vibration — of sound waves, independently of overall hearing ability, were clearly associated with many behaviors and learning problems, including hyperactivity and dyslexia.

"I devised a technique of auditory training, in effect a 'reeducation' of the hearing mechanism, which in almost every case brought about the normalization of the response to the frequencies involved-and, almost always, the amelioration of the behavior or learning problem."

Dr. Berard developed a scientific method of retraining the ear's acoustical reflex muscle, known also as the stapedius muscle, so that the participant will be able to listen and to process sounds more normally without distortions and delays. AIT is also documented to improve the flow of blood to the brain. AIT is based on Dr. Berard's theory that the use of his specifications to electronically modulate and filter selected music retrains the ear and auditory system to work properly. Dr. Berard discovered that hypersensitivity, distortions, and delays in auditory signals contribute to inefficient learning. Read more in Auditory Integration Training (AIT) and the brain by Dr. Guy Berard. It is worth mentioning the checklist on my web page to see if hearing abilities are worth pursuing AIT therapies. But back to the Spinal Galant reflex.

The Spinal Galant reflex, if unresolved, can be activated anytime with slight pressure to the lumbar region. By lightly running your finger down the spine of a baby, you will see them lift one shoulder and slightly twist. If this reflex is present in a child, teen, or adult, you can easily tell by running a finger down the spine softly and seeing their relaxed and natural reaction. If they raise one shoulder, and slightly twist, then it is present. Those without will enjoy the stimulation with a relaxed response. This reflex is stimulated when sitting in a chair at school! Wiggles and the need to squirm can be involuntary when initiated by the Spinal Galant reflex. To complicate this further, this can activate the Pulgar Marx reflex, which will cause the infant to urinate, but also cause a student to want too many bathroom breaks. Poor bladder control is, therefore, sometimes associated with this reflex. Interestingly enough, adults with irritable bowel syndrome have a high percentage of those with unresolved Spinal Galant reflex.

The wiggly child in their chair who just cannot sit calmly and comfortably would be a reason to check this reflex. The child may dislike clothing around their waist. This affects concentration and short-term memory as this is a constant irritant and is always vying for the child's attention. So, to review the symptoms of an unresolved Spinal Galant reflex you might see fidgeting, bed-wetting, poor concentration issues, or poor short-term memory issues.

The Tonic Labyrinthine reflex (TLR) develops in utero and should be resolved by about four months of age. The Moro reflex and the TLR are closely related in the early months of life. Both involve the movement of the heads and alteration of position in space. TLR is the baby flexing forward when lying in your arms and arching their back when the head drops below the spine. This reflex is a response from coming from an aquatic environment to the air and experiencing the full effects of gravity. If this is unresolved when a child begins to walk, then the child will not experience gravitational security, or will often "trip" and stumble. The child will have difficulty judging space, depth, distance, and velocity. A sense of direction is based upon our knowledge of where we are in space. If our point of reference is unclear, then our ability to determine direction may not be reliable.

Balance is on the same circuit system as the eyes. Messages from the body pass to the brain stem, then to the eyes. Messages from the eyes pass to the brain stem and then to the body to do as instructed. The process is a superhighway of information zooming around at high speeds. Perception is formed by the timing of all of these messages. A present TLR will affect vision because of this relationship. If your child, as a baby, struggled with crawling, there is a correlation.

The Symmetrical Tonic Neck reflex (STNR) will remain "locked" if the TLR is present, preventing the coordination needed to crawl. These are classic cross-body movements that are a crucial part of brain development. Babies need to crawl, period. During this time, the child develops a sense of balance, space and depth are validated, and the collaboration between seeing and moving are synchronized for the first time in the brain's experience. The brain essentially learns how to perceive and move through the world.

Symptoms of an unresolved Tonic Labyrinthine reflex are poor posture, weak muscle tone in general, poor balance, propensity to get carsick, dislike of sporting activities, visual perception issues, poor sequencing skills, and a poor sense of time.

The Symmetrical Tonic Neck reflex (STNR) emerges at six to nine months of life and should be resolved and gone by eleven months of life. This reflex helps a child from the head down position on hands and feet (or knees) to lift his/her head, and causes the legs to flex and the arms to straighten. This allows the baby to go from head-down crawling to head-up and to be able to see where they have arrived to. Babies struggle at first. Then their muscles grow, and their eyes learn to perceive and decide what they think about the new location. Crawling and creeping are crucial to teaching the eyes to cross the midline. The eyes focus on one hand and then the other. This process is very important to strongly establish in the neuropathway, which is a superhighway of messages needed for future thinking. There is a high correlation between reading problems and children who omitted the stages of crawling. Bear walking on hands and feet is not considered crawling. Unsynchronized crawling is a concern. Also, children without the ability to spend time on the floor during the ages of three months to a year old – deprived of the opportunity to crawl –will also have present STNR and TLR. These cases have been successfully remediated with physical therapies. These details are for parents to realize that there are neurological developments that correlate with physical developments.

Noticing any sign of these primal reflexes in your child or teen indicates that you should work with a specialty physical therapist to resolve these traits or reflexes. It will open up the thinking and learning aspect impacted by their presence. This is a secret key holding learning back in many students in my experience, and resolving them has opened up higher levels of thinking and reasoning that would have been otherwise stifled.

All of this study and research by pioneers began with Rita Levi Montalcini, who in 1986 won the Nobel Prize for her work with nerve growth factors. Then came Jean-Pierre Changeuz who proved that when you paralyze a chicken's reflexes that help it break free of its shell, it grows to have brain abnormalities. The muscles develop the brain. What makes the muscles develop? The reflexes innate to the genetic codes in the brain begin the processes that lead to the essential neuropathways on the stepping-stones of the brain development pathway.

When I think of children, I am very aware that we all are a combination of our abilities, and as far as this chapter is concerned, the foundation I am looking for is resolved primal reflexes. And then there are behavioral patterns. These are habits. When I decide whether something is a missing skill or a behavior pattern, I am looking for any times or motivations where the child contradicts their actions. This shows the ability to override a behavior. When a child is so consistent in all situations and unable to vary how they are presenting to you, it tells me that there might be some underlying issue. The therapy I am speaking of is part of many academic transformations for which I have witnessed. Uncovering all of the influencing factors is key. Each reflex with recognizable descriptions helps you identify this need through your observations and interactions with your child. Listen to your intuition, and if you suspect anything, it is well worth the screening.

I recommend that you seek out a specialized physical therapist trained in resolving primal reflexes. They exist, and you may need to interview a few therapists to see which reflexes they test for and their experience in resolving them. Now you know the names and can ask for a thorough check of these reflexes. This is not something a parent can do on their own. The good news is that a good therapist will aid their therapies with some home exercises that support their sessions. You could expect a three-month to a twelve-month regime to reteach the body and resolve most cases. Further research this topic by reading Sally Goddard's books on the subject.

RECAP: PRIMAL REFLEXES

- Infants are born with primal reflexes to assist in the birth process and early survival skills.
- The reflexes should disappear within one year with typical physical and neurological development except for the Landau reflex.
- When a reflex remains, there are negative blocks or consequences in brain development.
- The physical and neurological brain links are directly related as seen by what thinking and focus challenges accompany unresolved primal reflexes.
- There are physical therapies to assist in unresolved primal reflexes which remain into adolescence or adulthood.
- A primal reflex screening is a great idea for a struggling student to learn if there are therapies available to remove barriers that may be present if there are unresolved primal reflexes.
- Teaching will not succeed when an unresolved primal reflex is inhibiting certain brain capabilities.
- This brings a whole new light to the importance of physical activities and the importance they play on brain development. The brain-body connection is complex and very related.

10

SOCIAL-EMOTIONAL FOUNDATION

Every child has emotional needs and how those get fulfilled has a big impact on their self-image. Let's talk about the essential emotional needs. A child needs a sense of belonging. This is true at school and also true at home. This is closely related to a child's need for self-worth and significance. One of the ways they feel that they belong is by feeling significant. Humans are social beings, and the brain responds to symbols of love, belonging, and being significant.

This was the exact reason I left public education. I felt that no matter how hard I tried, I could not make my students feel significant. I was assigned one hundred and fifty students each year. And my sons were made to feel they were not significant at school, despite talented, well-meaning teachers. There is a capacity to how many students a teacher can competently teach. I chose to have class sizes of ten in my school. And, over ten years, I felt that it was perfect. I began my public high school math teaching career in 1993, and in my career, I have found my best results working one-on-one. Academic challenges can be addressed and overcome with appropriate guidance and support. I left my public education career because it was too painful to not make each student significant and service them as I saw they needed with the workload.

The cynicism students have toward their teacher's sincerity in high school exists because they have felt betrayed in the relationships they needed in the formative years when they hit struggles. They learned that we say they can count on us, but we are not available when they need us. I tried to remedy that by greeting each student at my door as they entered each class. I made efforts to acknowledge each student through my everyday classroom practices and address all of their needs. I respected introverts and extroverts equally. I walked around to check practice papers personally, spent my lunch periods offering help, and allowed retakes to every test if students showed they understood the ones they missed. I made after-school hours available as well. Because I cared, even a few failing students, out of one hundred and fifty, hurt more than I could bear.

I gave much more than most high school teachers in terms of relationship to the students, and my success stories were many, but it was impossible to succeed with every student in that setting. My reason for leaving was two-fold, and the second reason was to find the solution for public education on the outside. I set off to open my school. Emotional safety was one of the key premises for my school and I think a large key to our amazing data of effectiveness, like the fact that all students, even those at risk, moved eighteen months in literacy skills each year.

To provide emotional safety, kids need you to help them to belong and feel significant and in order to accomplish these essential things, you must actively listen and clarify to prove you are trying to understand them. You need to appreciate and value their contributions by the tone of voice and eye contact and attention. Those mean more than verbal confirmation without matching tone and attention to children. Remember, children decide a lot by feelings. These are key ideas to create emotional safety.

Negative emotions are cumulative throughout the day. Just imagine if you are the child and your parents are disappointed in you for something in the morning and then you forgot something your teacher asked you to bring, and then you get a low quiz score. Finally, it is recess, and you lose a game and, on your way to sit down and rest, someone knocks you down and you hurt yourself. Feel the cumulative emotion just reading that. All while dealing with large amounts of people in your classroom, at recess, and in the halls. It can feel like too much. Children do not know that learning can feel another way. The day can feel less hostile while learning. They cope and they cope because it is expected of them. At some point, the exhaustion is why their stomach hurts and they do not want to go to school. It is not one thing, but a culmination of small failures to please. The demands are all day long. Be on time, follow the rules, turn in your work. To a student, even though students are not being mistreated in any way, and no one person is unkind, emotional safety is not there.

We create all this stress around learning. Being in large social groups can be stressful. Students have not established trust with everyone around them. The crowd mentality likes to notice anything that can entertain, and it is usually at someone's expense. It is impossible to monitor with a thirty-to-one ratio, or more. There are many more than that on the playground for elementary supervision and many more in high school halls and quads.

Does learning need to be associated with large crowds and include so many time constraints? These include timed lunches, timed classes, and timed assignments with due dates and points lost if the assignments are late at semester's end, whether assignments are ready or not. The rigidity of public school is strict and stressful, on a good day. Sometimes, one has to deal with a mean person or teacher in a bad moment. Managing the stress of a typical student is one thing but handling it when you are struggling to succeed in what is being asked of you and you have the shame of your peers knowing how badly you are doing (often) is a lot to ask someone who is under eighteen years old.

The emotional safety perception a student feels is what is important. You can get a range of emotional safety readings from a class of thirty students. Why is that? Students arrive with different vulnerabilities and needs. A struggling student is always attempting to save face in front of their peers about learning achievement. Teachers are not as confident about scores and grades as they could be, and the low-scoring student fears others finding out. That is not emotionally safe in a sea of emotional stress. Adults do not see their day the way kids do and can easily forget how they may feel.

Resilience is a skill. Some students have it early. Other students you see grow resilience sometimes before your eyes. Other students are far from building their resilience to where they need it. This includes resilience to stress, resilience to struggle and challenge, and resilience in maintaining their self-esteem.

As a person who has been in many schools, I have observed many teachers do their job. I have worked in three different high schools with over eighty teachers in each public school. I have observed student teachers in over forty schools in elementary, middle, and high schools. I have managed a staff of seventeen teachers in my school. I have visited my students and observed and met with their teachers in another large number of schools I cannot count. Then I have volunteered in my son's charter school and public elementary schools. It is a unique viewpoint that has been explained to me by many struggling students when they find out I will listen. It takes so much work for a child to deal with the emotions around the hurt that happens in an environment that makes them feel bad on top of being worried about not being "smart enough."

It has been rewarding to advocate for those who cannot advocate for themselves, for their emotional safety to learn. I feel like a student's bill of rights needs to be rewritten. I found the National Youth Rights Association has a student Bill of Rights you can read in The Action Plan. But nowhere in it does it say that students have the right to an appropriate curriculum for their learning needs. This is a source of stress and harm that is systemic and avoidable if we reinvent how we teach our children. I feel so strongly about this that after my many years of work, this may not apply to your child, but by reading this you can teach your child about empathy for others. Not being a part of a group mentality when someone is being ridiculed for a learning challenge would be a good topic. Being a good friend earns a good friend and a child needs to learn to be their own best friend. They should be helped to encourage themselves in their own self-talk and not put themselves down. Putting themselves down quickly erodes their sense of well-being with devastating results.

Here is a description of a common tactic of a struggling student. The component of a child's ego wanting to appear *with* their peers in a learning situation is an undeniable force. Your child may hide their confusion and go to great lengths to appear as if they are doing fine. Look and see if your child's ability matches how they behave with strategies to learn. Do they have learning strategies or do they just have hiding strategies? I often see students who have given up on believing they can learn, so they focus on hiding, which is the extreme case of a silent cry for help.

I write this chapter without filtering some of the emotions I feel while trying to help students who are coping with their learning struggles and not feeling emotionally safe in their learning environment. To feel their pain and stress in learning situations they often have no chance of succeeding in, is painful to be aware of. And there are many students where after a few meetings with school staff involved, we can help them feel valued, as though they belong, and significant. It can be done with a team approach in a public-school setting in schools with an administration that values neuroscience and the child's perspective. If a school is not led by a team with this value, it is much harder. You cannot change the culture for one student, unless there is an event that impacts everyone involved, without the admin team modeling this priority. Even then, a teacher who feels overwhelmed and burned out may not be able to support the intentions of the meeting as they manage their stress.

The bottom line is stress and learning do not go together. It is conclusive in all neuroscience research. Notice that I have not mentioned the increasing school violence issues our schools face, such as school fights and injuries caused through altercations on campus or on the way to or from school. We, as parents, protectors of our children, need to assess each child individually for how the setting is impacting their learning. Learning, not the setting, is most important. And social interaction is not a reason to stay when a child's learning is being significantly negatively impacted. American parents value social interaction so much that I watch parents debate the loss of it and making a change. I hear parents lament about the inconvenience of a change, and the impact on driving them to a school farther away, or the inability to take on a homeschool year.

Often, the easiest way of advancing a student who is far behind grade level is to temporarily remove them from a typical classroom and introduce a learning situation that is a better fit for them. Perhaps allow the student to work at home in a safe environment for a year, focusing on the weak area, to catch them up. Once the desired level is achieved – and yes, I have done this many, many times with great success – a student can return, hopeful and actually ready to succeed in a grade-level setting. After we transform confidence and prepare kids for the reintegration into the public classroom setting, they are different. They are wanting to show their new skills and be "like the other kids" who learn well. The student now approaches school proactively and not reactively. It is a different stance, a more prepared version of themselves, which kids transform with the hope that they can be successful. It is not so hard to understand. Public school design is archaic and insensitive to struggling learners that need a different curriculum than those able to succeed. But I will save my school reform thoughts and focus on the student.

Learn more about the SEL or Social-Emotional Learning movement that is addressing the hostilities I am highlighting in this chapter. SEL education is school-wide training for all members of the school community. Here is their definition of themselves:

"We are committed to highlighting the potential and urgency of leveraging SEL to promote educational equity and excellence. This is explored in a 2019 research article, Transformative SEL: Toward SEL in Service of Educational Equity and Excellence, and through our research-practice partnerships to advance ways that SEL supports equitable learning environments and optimal developmental outcomes for diverse children, adolescents, and adults."

A survey in October 2020 by the nonprofit RAND corporation titled "Support for SEL Learning in Schools" found that teachers believed that they could improve the SEL quality of their classrooms by implementing SEL training, but they found barriers. See the link to the study in the Action Plan. "However, teachers identified limits to what they could do in their classrooms. Many teachers expressed a belief that factors beyond their control had a greater influence on students' SEL than they did and that pressure to improve students' academic achievement made it difficult to focus on SEL."

Another finding from the survey found that about 90 percent of elementary and secondary teachers agreed that promoting SEL would improve students' academic achievement. Further explaining the stress I am referring to in schools across America, the survey uncovered some very real and alarming teacher feelings. Ninety percent agreed it would improve academic achievement!

The report goes on to say, "Teaching can be highly stressful work. Stress on the job can affect the teachers' sense of well-being, which, in turn, can detract from their ability to support their students' social and emotional development in addition to their academic performance. Teachers reported generally high levels of satisfaction with their work (e.g., a large majority of teachers reported that they looked forward to work each day) and high levels of well-being, including a sense of connectedness, frequent positive emotions, and feelings of creative engagement in their work. At the same time, however, roughly half of the teachers indicated that they felt burned out by their work. We found that teachers who reported higher levels of well-being reported engaging in SEL practices to a greater extent than those with lower reported well-being. We also observed differences in well-being as a function of the school poverty level, with teachers in lower-poverty schools reporting higher levels of well-being — including job satisfaction — than those in higher-poverty schools."

This is a shocking admission by the teachers surveyed that they many feel burned out (half!) and they felt improved results when using the SEL training. Teachers need help. My experience concurs with this impartial survey's findings given without biases. (That is the

AP Statistics teacher in me.) The secondary teachers surveyed felt a greater need for SEL training in general than the elementary teachers. This comes as no surprise. Teachers want more professional development.

Parents of struggling students, please address the needs of your child and promote the SEL inclusion in school design and redesigning how we handle students who are struggling. In the meantime, it is the very keen parental intuition I encourage you to rely on to promote your actions on this topic. Listen to your gut instincts, and if you are unsure, you can employ a psychologist or psychiatrist to assist you in the judgment of a student's social-emotional state of mind. In the associated workbook you will find some activities to try at home to support your child's SEL development.

RECAP: SOCIAL-EMOTIONAL FOUNDATION

- Children form their early social-emotional foundations from their feelings of significance and belonging both at home and at school.
- Children make a lot of decisions by their feelings and perceptions.
- By listening to children and teens, you are giving the most valuable and sought-out gift of time, which equals love and significance.
- Stress and learning do not go together. Eliminate the stress at all costs.
- Resilience is a skill to grow, but not reasonable when a student feels unsafe.
- Struggling students hide their confusions and questions to try to fit in, to their detriment.
- After surveying many teachers, they feel that their social-emotional safety is beyond their control, which is another reason the system needs revamping.
- It is a parent's responsibility to choose learning situations that meet the criterion of social-emotional safety to their child's needs.

11

DEVELOP YOUR CHILD'S EXECUTIVE BRAIN SKILLS

The next step in helping your child grow in school is to develop their executive brain skills. Executive skills are essential for school and efficiency in life. These skills include paying attention, organizing, planning, starting tasks, planning small steps to a bigger outcome, and staying focused on each step, managing emotions, and keeping track of what you are doing. These skills can impact students at home, at school, and in social situations.

The three areas of your brain involved in executive functioning skills are working memory, (see Chapter 21 for tips and strategies to grow and support working memory) cognitive flexibility, and inhibitory control. Working memory is the ability to keep information in mind and then use it in the short or long term, like reading something and then answering questions about that reading or holding a math fact or formula in mind while planning for its use. Cognitive flexibility is the ability to think about something in more than one way and consider the usefulness or applicability. When asked to find an equation of a line in algebra, you can do so in several ways. Knowing three ways to solve the equation is required. Testing requires cognitive flexibility. Literature discussions show the interpretations of the same text through different lenses of possibility, which also requires cognitive flexibility. Inhibitory control is the ability to ignore distractions and resist temptations to accomplish a goal. Some students struggle to control people-watching in school when it is time to work on an assigned task, which is an example of poor inhibitory control. Or, when a disappointment occurs in public, the child cannot prevent a public display of tears and disappointment.

Having strong executive function skills saves you time and makes the process less stressful for the clarity one feels knowing the systematic steps to the process for the outcome they desire. Helping your child grow their executive brain skills and capacities can be essential in their academic transformation to end their struggle in school. I believe parents mistakenly deny many opportunities for their child and do far too much of the thinking and planning themselves for the child in our American culture. I also see in my work with parents that they readily and willingly give away the responsibility of the task of their child's brain development solely to the educational setting to develop these skills along with teaching the curriculum. It is accepted in our culture to do this. I am asking parents to rethink this choice and take back monitoring this growth in their child. You can have a very large influence in assisting this essential skill. This is my goal for this chapter, to help you understand how to do that for your child's developing mind.

Every brain has executive capacities acting as the "CEO of the brain" orchestrating the brain functions, as I learned at Dr. George McClowsky's 2019 "Learning and the Brain" conference. This brain supervisory system includes executive capacities, emotions, thoughts, perceptions, and actions. It is not what happens that is important; it is what we decide about what happens that determines behavior. Children are good perceivers but very poor interpreters. Parents can help their children by influencing their interpretations with conversations that encourage, empower, and motivate their children. Remember, children are always making decisions based on their interpretations, and there is a belief behind every behavior. Parents are the ones who can influence a child's belief system and also help them reframe unhealthy belief systems. This is a daily task that involves communication. This communication grows the language center of their brain. Talking and influencing your child has these consequences for their thinking and brain development. The emotion your child feels for you is the frosting on the cake of why this is so important. These underlying emotions for you make your conversations more impactful and powerful in these goals because the brain judges importance by an emotional reaction. I want to empower parents to the best impact on their child's brain growth.

The executive capacities are made up of neural circuits in the frontal lobe of the brain, and these are the superhighways that connect all other parts of the brain. Remember, these neural circuits can be formed by you engaging in the interactive tasks shared here with your child. The brain is plastic or malleable, and you can intentionally grow these skills. Brain growth and repair can be seen physically with the technology we have today, so this is not a claim but a fact – the brain is plastic, or moldable, and we can grow skills with the intention that might not occur without prompting. This idea is a powerful one because you realize that we can very much shape our child's thinking and reasoning skills, and better prepare them to handle the rigorous thinking required to just operate our cell phones or computers, not to mention the ups and downs of twenty-first-century life. Life is very complex and requires savvy and strong thinking skills. The brain is a complex system that learns to be cued when and how it should use its parts to perceive, feel, think, and act.

First, successful students must learn "self-regulation," which is essentially a set of control skills that cue and direct the function of how a student perceives and regulates their emotions, their cognition, and their actions. You can grow your child's ability to self-regulate by allowing, encouraging, and expecting them to do so. Is your child aware of what triggers their emotions? Are they making choices to positively influence and regulate their emotions, or are they depending on you to do this? If this expectation is on the parent, it can be exhausting! Noticing how one feels in any given moment is called "metacognition" (thinking about your own thinking) and it is something worth talking about with your child. Does your child attend to asking questions that will clarify their understanding? This requires monitoring of themselves. For example, many students read right through vocabulary they do not know and do not stop to address, to learn the meaning. We need to model and encourage them to take the time to attend to *their* learning. It is a recognition of their responsibility to do so. Does the child think before they move, speak, or act, or do they move dangerously through the world? Self-regulation can be taught, kindly, and with patience. Learning happens in all the little conversations.

Students in elementary school often need to produce a monthly book report as part of their reading expectations. Sometimes, they choose from a project about their book, like a diorama out of a shoebox or maybe dress in costume as a character and present to the class. Other times, it is a written summary with character analysis or plot summary. Whatever the case, it is a great opportunity to grow executive functions by planning and deciding the steps that would help that process of completing the book report slowly over the month. Taking time to think and plan about this expectation is a process some students significantly struggle with and try to avoid. Is your child panicking and producing a last-minute book report? Are you doing too much of the planning and thinking around their project to *help* them? You are not helping their brain do this type of thinking with your suggestions. I commonly see parents engage too much with these types of homework tasks. These elementary assignments are to encourage reading and develop the executive function of your child, not *your* executive functioning. Helping your child too much is a common problem I see with parents. I have one client in mind who feels upset when I ask them to not help their child, and now that her daughter is in fifth grade, she relies on her mother's nightly homework support. Since the mother is a working mother, she has some guilt and caves in at each request because she enjoys being needed by her child who is nearing middle school and growing up. This is frustrating to me, as I can see the child entering middle school with the habit of allowing Mom's skills and brain to assist way too much on homework. The student's independence is not growing for this reason, and the parent tells me she wants that part of her daughter to grow, but yet, she cannot say no to the request, and the two of them are headed for rough waters. Some parents in my experience continue this throughout high school and contact the teachers for clarifications on assignments, which clearly should be conversations the high school students have with their teachers, not their parents. If you see yourself enabling your child too often with homework or planning of projects such as research papers, science projects, or book reports, take a big step back and allow these to be your child's responsibility. That was the teacher's intention, and your child's product needs to be their *own* work. You can give feedback, but changes should be made independently by your child. You can do it, and yes, it will feel hard to stop helping too much. Take a big step back, and allow your child's independence to grow, please, for their sake.

Second is "self-determination," which occurs when the child has the foresight and long-term planning skills to generate a goal or desired outcome. This requires the use of cognitive processes to construct visions of the future and plan for actions. For a kindergarten student, that may be something they plan for the next hour. For a second grader, they might plan their afternoon or a weekly project. For a fifth grader, they might form a routine to accomplish a patterned behavior or a several-days project, like collecting data and showing results in graphs learned in school. For a high school student, they might plan to study for the SAT or ACT for a certain period of weeks. These large cumulative tests required for many college applications expect and require preparation to succeed. This should be on every parent's radar: how is your child developing their self-determination skills? How are you helping them grow with the increasing duration of planning tasks? This can be done simply by involving your child in tasks that need to be done as a normal part of everyday life: Need to plant a garden? Let your child plan it. Need to plan a party? Let your child plan it and think of all the details, or better yet, collaborate with others in planning the party. Older kids can plan and execute one meal a week for the family, planning a list of groceries needed. Give your kids responsibilities and enough instruction for safety and boundaries and let them do the work. If you are always in charge, you are missing an opportunity to help your child's brain develop. And if this type of engagement is not expected at home, teachers will struggle to see your child succeed in group work at school.

Supporting your child with developing the goals and then challenging them to plan and implement them will help your child function as an adult who can plan and achieve high-level and complex goals. A recommended read here is *Age of Opportunity: Lessons from the New Science of Adolescence* by Laurence Steinberg, PhD, where this is discussed further.

The third skill is "self-realization," which is the realization of oneself and noticing and reacting to other's needs. This skill directs the cognitive processes that engage awareness in oneself and others and reflects with self-analysis. Then one can realize and cue cognitive processes to access information and apply it to specific situations. Does your child notice when good eating and sleeping habits are followed, there is a more stable mood and productivity? Do you see your child choosing to go to bed to feel well the next day, or is it a nightly fight? Do you see your kids learning food choices that promote well-being, or does your child eat too much? Do they consume too much sugar or candy despite feeling sick over and over? Look for decisions that have negative consequences and discuss these with your child and see if they can make better choices with the awareness. This is a skill and requires taking long-term consequences into consideration for their actions. This is an essential awareness to grow in your child, and this is part of executive function.

Conversations of cause and effect and helping them see the bigger picture is very helpful. When something has been left to the last moment, it is very stressful to complete. How could you have gotten more done ahead of time, so you would not be in this pickle? This is an example of asking them to rethink their actions and look forward to the next chance to avoid this situation.

By the time they attend high school, students should be able to make choices to support best-case outcomes for their goals. We often see this in sleep choices and eating habits. Is your child making reasonable cause-and-effect choices? Have they made that connection? Teaching and modeling informed decision-making along with mindfulness techniques to regulate mood, sleep, and healthy eating patterns are important life skills you can give your kids. Mindfulness techniques include using deep breathing to lower anxiety, fear, and blood pressure. Did you know that taking five deep relaxed inhales for five seconds, then slowly exhaling, can reclaim a person's control from an anxious reaction? What a small but powerful tool to teach and model.

Notice when fear, tension, and anxiety are a stumbling block, and teach the use of breath, positive affirmations, and reminding yourself of goals set, to keep on track with positivity and control. These are learned skills and all people need to learn them. Why not give this gift to your child? Teach these skills by taking a walk with them and listening to all sounds, and then share. Quiet time and reflection are not happening enough in our loud world of noises from so many sources.

Teach breathing techniques so they can experience for themselves the shift in their blood pressure. Learning experiences can be extremely effective and impactful. Make the experience age-appropriate: call it "Spiderman meditation" for those kids who are superhero fans. Ask kids to activate their "Spidey-senses" and focus their minds on smell, taste, and hearing in the present moment. Try this at times when sounds and smells are new to identify. This can be a fun mindful game for kids seven and under. Older kids can have a different name for the same task, such as the "Identify as many senses as you can" game. Have a contest to name as many things your senses experienced as you can. Competition motivates awareness in a fun way.

Asking your kids to notice other people's feelings and observe strangers from afar and suppose how they feel and what they are doing is a simple conversation with lasting impacts in developing self-realization. It's also an easy, fun, and engaging game with powerful effects when played at an airport or train station when traveling. What can your child observe accurately in the strangers around them? Discussing ambiguous observations can be eye-opening during this "game."

Lastly, "self-generation" is where the brain puts all the above skills into action. To develop this skill, you can pose speculative questions related to the meaning and purpose of life. These questions ask the child to find larger meaning than the task at hand and to put the task into the context of why and what goal we are aiming for.

Finding comfort in living consciously and with purpose, a focus on love and loving relationships, feeling loved and valued, and giving and receiving respect all form strong self-generation skills for life. There are three facets to self-generation: intention, discernment, and compassion. If you are a parent who is reading this, please don't panic! At any time, development can happen in any of the areas we are discussing. And you may find that you are already naturally having many of the discussions suggested here, and feel positive right now. If I am identifying areas for you to shore up, all the better. You cannot change what you do not identify.

My goal is to provide a new awareness with which to think about your child's development. Some of the most important skills involve being observant, curious, resourceful and having critical thinking and problem-solving skills. A sense of patience and willingness to make mistakes and learn from them along the way are important skills as well. You are the primary teacher of these skills, not schools. These attributes heavily influence attitude.

If you need your child's attitude to change, then the ideas here are the root of many attitude issues. Organizations like www.www.DeeperLearning4all.org are applying the science of learning to teaching and school expectations. If we all grow in our understanding of helping children's brains develop stronger skills, we influence their overall intelligence and ability to function in adult life.

We are in control of our own choices, and every behavior is a choice. This is called "internal control," but most of us behave via "external control," which is the belief that we are not responsible for our own choices and that things happen to us rather than being chosen by us and coming from within. This belief is foundational to helping your child on the journey of developing their executive function. Is your child living by internal or external control? I suggest this as a starting point. Make some notes as to what your child's weaknesses are and make the plan to strengthen these over time, as situations allow. Part of what clever parents do is to keep this list in mind and then integrate purposeful tasks and responsibilities utilizing their child's brain challenges. This creates the opportunity to revise and reconsider and discuss, which is where the teaching opportunities lie.

Executive function is required to be a skilled reader. This is a fact. Your brain can know the vocabulary and how to spell words. It can understand sentence structures and the rules of punctuation, but to use it all together, it requires executive function skills. So, yes, I am saying, you can do all the reading remediation needed and still not develop executive function growth. If this is the case, your child will never master being a skilled reader. This is the underlying skill of higher-level learning and thinking. It is essential to allow your child to take the planning and implementation role in their own life. This will help them refine and grow in this much-needed brain development by *doing*, not *watching* you.

I hope I have inspired you to add to your parenting toolbox growing your child's executive functioning skills. Help your child self-regulate, self-realize, and self-generate and this will help them to be a person who accomplishes deeper learning when exposed to instruction.

"Deeper Learning" occurs when students can exhibit these skills while participating in the curriculum of school: effective communication, collaboration, critical thinking, problem-solving, and self-directed learning. Together with these skills, an "academic" or "growth" mindset is required to progress through these skills confidently. Think of your student and when they earn a poor grade on something. Do they look to themselves to learn, improve, and grow? Or do they blame others and point fingers at what is essentially their responsibility? Do they condemn themselves to a pity party of disappointment, which is very unhealthy, or do they immediately turn to solutions? How your child handles these events is of paramount importance. We cannot shelter our children from all strife and struggle in this world, whether it is in academics or matters of the heart, but we can help them view these incidents as stepping-stones to learning. A "growth mindset" views failures as opportunities. Successful people do this, and it is a core skill that is often not discussed. This is opposed to a fixed mindset, which views failures as stopping blocks and promotes limiting beliefs. Being resilient is a product of having a growth mindset. Each failure reframed becomes a pathway to resilience.

According to Deeper Learning 4All, a non-profit organization focused on promoting more effective education, deeper learning is necessary because: "The fastest-growing job sectors are those that require problem-solving and critical thinking skills, while jobs that require routine manual skills are in decline. By 2020, two out of three jobs will require postsecondary education and training beyond high school. Consequently, high school graduates need to master challenging academic content and develop skills in communication, collaboration, critical thinking, and problem-solving that they can apply to complex and new situations. Yet too few of the nation's students, and even fewer traditionally underserved students, demonstrate the college- and career-readiness skills necessary to succeed in an increasingly complex economy."

This was written several years ago, and my opinion is that schools currently are not implementing the executive function research which clearly shows that we must teach with a higher expectation to meet the needs of our technologically developing society. Here we are in 2021, and while there are trades and success stories that are the exception, almost every occupation requires additional training beyond high school in some capacity. Academic training or training in the field or trade both require the skills of effective communication, collaboration, critical thinking, and problem-solving, and self-directed learning skills. Improving your child's executive function skills influences all of these tasks.

Remember, IQ is not fixed, and growing the executive function skills and capacities discussed here is a valuable part of preparing your child to become an insightful, goal-oriented, communicative, and productive adult. Refer to your workbook for an age correlation for the executive capacity demands to develop with regard to school. Help your child to form their own solutions by encouraging the growth of their executive function skills. By modeling reflection, and asking for your child to reflect, you are teaching. Reflection is a process that allows people to stop and think before they respond to something. This skill is key to solving problems. The more kids practice reflection, the better they get to the best response.

As students progress through school, the demands of executive function skills increase. In kindergarten through second grade, your child will be expected to be able to give their attention to and be engaged in learning activities. As students enter third grade, they are expected to optimize their tasks and time management to accomplish tasks. As students enter into fourth grade, they are additionally expected to show efficiency and memory abilities that extend over time. Once a student enters high school, then the added executive function skills of inquiry and solution are added, requiring critical thinking and decision making. Each step of the way in education requires executive function skills to be developing and growing in scope and skill. Do not let your child's education be hampered by any discrepancy in their executive function skills.

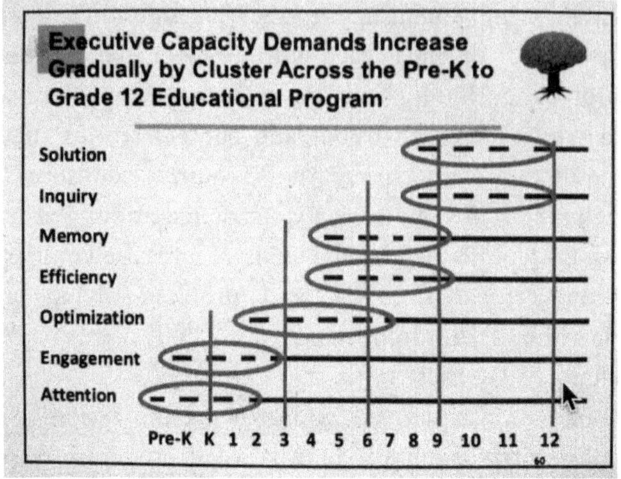

If you want to read a book about the American culture's tendency to over-nurture our children, I recommend *NurtureShock: New Thinking About Children* by Po Bronson and Ashley Merryman. Po Bronson also wrote the *New York Magazine* article "How Not to Talk to Your Kids," where she shares the outcome of research on praise. We learn that praise can cause the human psyche to avoid struggle and mistakes for fear of losing the praise they once received. This is not the intention when parents praise, so learning that "over-praising" can be very detrimental is a surprise to many. In *NutureShock*, the authors also discuss many topics parents in recent generations struggle with, including why kids lie, why siblings fight, the science of teen rebellion, and whether self-control is taught. It also outlines how parents can do too much for children, actually hampering their ability to grow the critical skills discussed here. It's a great parenting book for the twenty-first century, all based on neuroscience.

As a closing thought, I highly recommend you not dismiss this chapter. It is paramount for your child's brain development into young adulthood and independence. You can test your child by going to my web page and giving your child the "marshmallow test" to see how they are doing in the area of executive development. Ask them what they think they should do instead of thinking for them. Do not do it. Allow your child to have their own thoughts and realize their own consequences. This is a big deal, and well-meaning parents are actually hurting their children rather than helping them by doing too much for them.

RECAP: DEVELOP YOUR CHILD'S EXECUTIVE BRAIN SKILLS

- First, successful students must learn "self-regulation," which is essentially a set of control skills that cue and direct the function of how a student perceives and regulates their emotions, their cognition, and their actions.
- Second is "self-determination," which occurs when the child has the foresight and long-term planning skills to generate a goal or desired outcome.
- The third skill is "self-realization," which is the realization of oneself and noticing and reacting to other's needs.
- Executive function is essential for skilled reading to develop to put all the skills together.
- Executive function grows when students plan, execute, and orchestrate the desired outcome that requires steps over time.
- As a student grows, the complexity of tasks they should be able to independently accomplish should increase.
- School tasks naturally grow in complexity and students who are not keeping up with those expectations need to have attention in this area.
- Exploring the deeper learning definition helps to define how to grow executive function and further reading is recommended on this concept.
- If you are a parent doing too much for your child, thinking you are helping them, stop now.
- If stopping that coddling instinct in you causes stress, then please buy the book *NurtureShock: New Thinking About Children* and read it to understand further how you are actually hurting your child.
- Let your child live their life, and you live yours in terms of work output.

- Share experiences and accomplishments.
- Do not ever create work that your child calls their own. A rule of thumb for all parents.

FEARS, PHOBIAS, AND MATH ANXIETY

When your child's brain is in fear mode, learning is not possible. Their brains are programmed to survive above all else. When tests or projects are happening, and they do not see success in it for them, fear is a natural response. Primal instinct is behind our innate ability to react to new potentially dangerous situations in the interest of self-preservation and survival.

Remember Jaime Gardner, the mom, physician, and author of my foreword? A successful psychiatrist and human being, client and friend, she recently reached out to ask for my help with her middle son's math phobia and frustration last fall. She knew me from attending my private school with her two oldest children about eight years ago. Here is Jaime's version of how her son overcame his math phobia by working with me and transformed into a successful independent learner. I would say he was math phobic and anxious when we began last fall. He was upset and unwilling to do math in general.

JAIME GARDNER'S PARENT STORY

"My middle child now approaching seventh grade was a different problem than my older child who brought me to Lisa's school.

Different kid, different challenges, same story: frustration, refusal, and tears. Traditional schooling was too stifling and 'boring.' Nontraditional was too permissive and expectations were low. I had learned the hard way with my older son and wanted this one to be academically motivated. I could tell we were at a crossroads on what kind of learner he was going to be. Moving to another state in a metropolitan area did not afford me Lisa's school or any more tools. I again found myself at a loss of options and resources.

"One very frustrating evening, my son approached me with tears and said, 'Mom, I just cannot stand this school anymore.' It dawned on me . . . you actually do have a resource. So, I picked up the phone and called the one person who I trusted could help. Like coming home from a long, challenging journey, Lisa listened to all of my frustrations of our school experiences since the CLA. She jumped right in. Fortunately, we had all adjusted to remote interactions since COVID, and we could work together again even out of state. Just as suspected, after Lisa tested my son, we identified some major issues. As Lisa said, 'Jaime, this is not smoke, this is a fire!' He had huge missing math concepts and was totally confused. He had figured out just enough pattern recognition of math to appear like he knew what he was taught. As usual, he figured out a way to stay under the radar, chugging along in *good enough* land.

"Well, if Lisa thought my older son was a challenge, here was my feisty middle son. Lisa and I decided to put him in homeschool and divide and conquer. She would take on math and I would do the other subjects. This was not Lisa's first rodeo, and she prepared me for the upcoming challenge of getting him up to speed and his potential. It became very clear early on that the biggest challenge was reprogramming learned helplessness. We had to fortify him with the necessary ingredients to return to the living of being a learner.

"I was struggling with, 'How do I show Lisa's magic to the reader?' So, I'm going to let *her* show you. Below are a few sentences taken from Lisa's email exchanges to me that show her accurate read of her students, her ability to find missing pieces causing the issues, the progression of her effective interventions, and her awesome personality!"

The Beginning, Lisa Reports the Following to Me (Red Zone)

"He has this misconception that he needs to be *interested* from the outside, and not internally motivated. His internal motivation is hampered by the preference to avoid the recurring math failures which were occurring more often as math was getting more challenging.

"He needs support in facing challenges, striving through tasks with standards of achievement.

"His standards are too low for himself with regard to math. It is in the math anxiety zone, I am afraid to say.

"These are beginning signs of Learned Helplessness, avoidance, and excuses because he is actually avoiding the feeling of failure which he associates with math."

Interventions Applied, Lisa Reports My Son's Progress

"When he understands, he feels better. We talked about bringing a positive attitude and that I am trying to create a feeling of math = happiness. He agrees when he understands, he likes it better.

"He likes to say: 'What is the purpose?!' I told him that everything in math will be needed later, and he is not in a position to judge the purpose. He is the learner, and each lesson is for you to make sense of, not question . . . He will make a great lawyer!

"No, he is not wearing me down. I am still helping him have the right approach and attitude.

"His debates are about fear and avoidance.

"Today, he shared his apathetic attitude about paying attention to details ('I don't pay attention'). We got into a *big* talk about this. He wants to not care about the future and so the rationale of why you might need something is met with debate. This is his 'game.'

"So, he was trying to argue that *not thinking* of using his resources is OK. We need to *learn* to use them, I said. He tried to argue again, and I said, I expect you to say, 'OK, Lisa.' He did, and I said, 'Thank you.' (Tough love in math.)

"The problem is, he hits the wall as soon as it gets harder that way . . . not a long-term solution.

"Dax is testing the waters. Holding steady here. He mentioned that teachers in his past never cared and I said, well I do. (Wide eyes . . .).

"He has a visceral reaction to division. There is a *big* threat in the past with division. I am supporting it softly.

Making Progress, My Fiesty Middle Son Turns the Corner

"Just please cheerlead to him for these things from this week. (Do you have pom-poms?) Make a *big* deal about these things:

Great job for getting all your homework done this week! Proud of you!

Great job for focusing in class. Lisa's Friday report says that you were prepared and on time for class both Tuesday and Friday. Excellent job, Dax. (Hugs and kisses.)

Lisa said that you really are trying to show your work like an *Algebra student* and that there is a bit more to learn about that but that your homework on Friday was much, much, much neater than it was on Tuesday.

"I am firmly trying to motivate him. You do not need to discuss the challenges; it shames his ego for Mom to do that at this age.

"We discussed a *fixed mindset* toward math. I taught him about what that meant and how he is unteachable, and how to change that to a *growth mindset*.

"We talked about the process of learning from confusion to perfect understanding and how everyone has to deal with that feeling of being unsure along that path. We also talked about not feeling bad or putting yourself down in your self-talk.

"I have been deliberately teaching Dax with a lot of security and clarity for him to relax and gain some confidence. Dax was very insecure about his ability to do math when we met and would hide in his speed and lack of effort. I think it was too scary to really try."

Into the Green Zone, Lisa Reports Success

"He admitted his work was unreadable and I said that teachers in his future will not work hard to read his work; if it is unclear, it is wrong. His job is to make it clear. We discussed letters and numbers that need attention, and he was *so agreeable*! Super sweet and I can tell he feels safe with me and safe with math.

"Super happy about everything about Dax right now! We will pick up the pace on content when he feels successful and this attention to detail skills is so essential.

"I often asked him if that was fair, how I took points or gave partial credit. He agreed fairness along the way and also was very open and verbal about saying, 'Oh, I did not see that.' Or how he thought of something incorrectly. It was a great exchange, and he was so awesome at communicating!

"What a great day Dax and I had with his work shown! We were able to tell *why* a problem was wrong if it was.

"Dax has improved *so much*! This homework shows me that he can show work neatly . . . almost the whole time . . . and that he knows what to do . . . but when he gets tired . . . he needs to take a break!

"I have not been writing to you because everything is going so smoothly.

Dax is *easy breezy*, and having attention to detail. He calls me out on details now. Ha!

I love it!"

"As Lisa was moving through math, I was mirroring her efforts in the other subjects as I homeschooled him this year for the first time. I was applying the same tough love while raising the bar. All while being supportive and understanding along the way. As a mother, it has given me so much relief to have a co-leader to help navigate the best practices in educating my son."

ADDRESSING YOUR CHILD'S EMOTIONAL JOURNEY

This example Jaime has explained from a mother's point of view through her child shows academic growth and how it can evolve. Their absolute proclamations of being bad at math forever, or however certain or dramatic your child presents, are really cries for help, and not to be believed. Change is always possible, and so many times I see parents accept these childish perceptions as absolute. Nothing could be a bigger mistake. Be the adult, guide your child back to a reasonable perception, as shown with Jaime's son. It is possible. Jaime thought he was going to be a tough case, but actually, most students have that soft vulnerable place you can get to and nurture. We are all sensitive human beings, I believe.

Reassure the fear, and teach to the missing skills, strategies, and knowledge without judgment, all while holding high expectations. Kids know when you believe in them, and they must feel that from another person sincerely to begin to believe in themselves, in my opinion. We are all humans seeking positivity and acknowledgment.

Addressing fear is essential. Sometimes the focus we put on avoiding something is self-defeating because then all we are doing is thinking about not thinking about it. These fears are a form of thought distortion. Is there really a threat or a perceived threat in academics? The experience needs to be re-experienced so that the misconception of the fear is realized to be unnecessary and illogical. This takes work and patience, and a bit of success to prove the brain wrong. It helps to understand the biology of fear.

Fear is a response to a threat. If your student is fearing something at school (bullies, a certain subject, writing, speaking in front of people, changing in the locker room, pooping at school, or being called on in class, etc.), this impacts their ability to learn all day. These are common fears I hear about when I speak to struggling students. We can understand anxiety and worry and how they often go hand in hand with fear. Learning is impossible when the brain feels threatened.

Fear is an emotion which we are learning is not located in just one part of our brain, but rather a network in our brain involving the amygdala. Fear is an adaptive but transient state responding to a confrontation with a threat. Anxiety is more of a toxic state related to prediction and preparedness, whereas fear is passing and not a state. If we relate them in an analogy, fear is to anxiety as emotions are to moods.

We need to address fears to control anxiety. If your child is living in a state of anxiety, it is unhealthy, for one thing, and it is stressful. Their threshold for those times of extra stress may not be coped with well, and you can see why. If is enough to overwhelm them, then it is too much stress and it must be addressed. Reducing and managing the perception of fear is a form of executive function that relates to managing emotions. This skill is developing in children and teen brains. It requires and deserves nurturing conversations and emotional support in their growth, specifically in the ability to not react with a fear-based thought.

Children are careful observers and very poor interpreters. Fear may be a child's perception based on an experience or a friend's opinion and influence, perhaps even your influence. Help your child interpret their world in perspective. These are the conversations I want to encourage in this book. Parents are often so busy that they lose sight of what to discuss that can make the biggest impact on their child's growing needs of perception and fear management.

When fear is present, the brain responds in the amygdala and can cause you to stop and freeze or be ever vigilant. When fear is in the hypothalamus, the brain is motivated to find an escape. When the fear is yet another neural network, you have the flight or fight response. The flight is in any direction, but away as fast as possible – it is a panicked moment.

The thinking around fear is much about anticipated anxiety. Then anxiety occurs sort of as we planned. When you realize that life begins with a thought, then you understand that you must control the initial direction of your thoughts. They are your choice. We learn our phobias by repeated thoughts. We can desensitize ourselves if we experience contradictions to our predictions. Then the narrative in our mind changes.

Teach your children that they are in control of their thoughts. They may have a thought, but then they get to decide if it stays or goes. Who is in charge of our thoughts? We are! Your encouraging words in your child's ear are trustworthy and powerful.

Since the amygdala in the brain also has a well-known role in memory and attention, it is understandable that there is a learning-related role with fear. Fear makes learning not accessible to the brain. That is a good way to think of it. The brain decides if the fear source is "escapable" or "inescapable." That decision results in the response to the fear. When the "escape" is identified, then efforts toward that are a priority.

This moment makes me think of a boy who was a seemingly competent sixth grader who avoided his work with many creative strategies. He was a jokester and very adept at charming adults. I found that he had a convergence insufficiency vision issue, and his eyes could not read and think of comprehension. He was very fluent and a perfect reader. He had a strong sense of vocabulary, so his lack of comprehension skills was a mystery. He developed a fear of most all comprehension-demanding moments in school. This happens in all subjects and his master of avoidance techniques included cheating as a last resort. His fear was because he could not figure out a solution, so his mind went to escape. After teaching comprehension skills and after a vision doctor provided therapy to correct the convergence insufficiency, this handled the primary reasons for his inability to comprehend. Lastly, we had to remove the perceived threat and teach him to view comprehension without fear to access what he knew. It took practice and coaching to change the thoughts and internal negative self-talk. But dealing with it and challenging him repeatedly with graduated tasks grew his confidence and decreased his fears. Fear is something to overcome and succumb to. Another life lesson in academics. We cannot live by our fears. I am writing this book during the COVID pandemic. The world is learning this lesson right now. I am coaching you, so you can coach your child with these ideas. They are rooted in science and research and have served me well with many fearful students.

There is conscious and unconscious fear. I say this for the difficult cases out there that seem to have resilient fear. Fear can be an unconscious motivation for avoidance and attitude. If the student is accepting of the emotion, they may not be aware of the fear behind it. The brain often hides experiences in the unconscious to protect us but reacts the same. I say this because sometimes a student will deny the fear, but if every behavior points to fear then maybe it is something your student has not analyzed or acknowledged. For example, there was a high school teen whose math anxiety stemmed from her parents' arguments over money and numbers. The emotional anxiety of her very early childhood memories caused fear of numbers. She did not know this was her reason for her fear, but after hypnosis memory regression, she was able to learn math without the heightened emotion preventing her from thinking clearly.

Math anxiety. Test Anxiety. They are not the same, but they can coexist. The last example is math anxiety and a fear of numbers themselves. In recent research, over 90 percent of adult Americans have experience with some level of math anxiety. Wow! That is a big number. If you have shared this opinion with your child, you are a negative influence on their math success. So, asking for a good grade in math and sharing your math anxiety with them is a conflict for your child. Conflicts are stressful. Parents, please filter yourself from sharing any math anxiety. I leave you with this thought: numbers are one thing in life you can "count" on. I hope you are smiling now.

Test anxiety is common in math classes. As a high school math teacher, I have had students cry, pass out, get sick, and panic on a scheduled math test, which we reviewed for! This list provides examples of how test anxiety can manifest. Other students' symptoms may be invisible to observe but they may be experiencing an upset stomach, a headache, or heart palpitations.

Here are some effective tips and strategies I love to teach students to help them regain control of their anxiety. It is essential to control your breathing. Slow, deep breathing directly affects the lowering of your blood pressure and relaxes your heart. Breathing reminds your brain you are in charge, not the hormones excreted from the state of anxiety. Tell the student to count to five while slowly breathing in and then out to a slow relaxed one, two, three, four, and five. Ask them to repeat this five times. I call it "Five In, Five Out for Five." When you do it with them, they will admit to feeling better. What is stopping them from doing it anytime? It is empowering and a form of self-soothing. You can think of this as permitting them to self-soothe and feel worthy of self-soothing.

Change the self-talk by asking them to verbalize *everything* they are thinking while taking a mock pretend test. Write down the negative thoughts and positive thoughts. How many of each did they have? What was helpful or not helpful? Reframe how they could think the same thoughts more positively. "I am not good at this," can change to "What am I not seeing or missing?" Or "I give up," can be "What strategies or ideas do I have to try?" "It's good enough," to "Is it really my best work? Do I have any other ideas?" "This is too hard," can change to "This may take some time and effort." I like to say, be your own best friend silently in your head. Would you say those things to a friend? "You are not good at this or you should give up." No, I do not think so. Why say them to yourself? This journey changes and helps them monitor when despair takes over. The best self-talk to teach is empowering phrases for your subconscious. If we can choose our self-talk, and we can, why not say, "I will score well tomorrow on the test. I will remember everything I studied. I will feel happy at seeing each question which I prepared for. I will stay calm and breathe deeply as I enjoy knowing everything on the test." This, along with proper study efforts, will yield a good, if not excellent, score. Each test is a chance to refine the process and so begins the positive journey that was once fraught with fear and anxiety.

Math anxiety and test anxiety may share the fear of being wrong. Where was that learned? Being wrong offers the opportunity to learn something new. Grades are not what matters. *The learning matters most.* Make it a learning opportunity, pat yourself on the back, and move on. Teach your kids that mistakes are expected, respected, inspected, and corrected. That is positive, and it rhymes. And, gosh it sure feels better than the alternative.

Has math embarrassed you in the past? If you talk about that secret, it will have less power. A conversation is often just enough therapy. Timed math tests are a cause of some cases of both test and math anxiety. I am not a fan of "mad minutes" as a class activity. But I like students preparing for them and taking them when they decide they are ready. That is a completely different feeling. If you can minimize the threat, it helps students prepare for timed tests. Test-taking strategies help also and give a healthy focus.

There should be positive reinforcement, like a compliment for effort in math from teachers and parents. Again, we are intentionally associating a positive emotion. Motivate through positive reinforcement, not through threat or punishment if math is not complete.

Read stories and news about math purposely. If bedtime stories can include math and numbers, they become more comfortable and improve math learning potential. Calculate costs and use numbers in conversations. Talk about the total cost of everyone going to the movies. Talk about the cost of popcorn! Estimate a per-person cost with the different choices people made. Simple math ideas are important to have talked about with their parents before they hear them in math class. Simple interest problems begin in third grade. Banking ideas and positive and negative numbers in a checking account is something they need to be comfortable with at some point. There is no time like the present. Pretend with young children that they are a banker and you come in to make deposits and withdrawals. Counting money needs to happen at home and at school.

Math is not to be memorized. Math is to be understood. It is always important to know why each step happens. If your child does not know the *why* in each step of math calculations, teach your child to ask. Without knowing why, you are memorizing something that will look different next time.

Math is deductive reasoning where you need to follow steps logically to simplify things, like equations or expressions based on rules and logic. Using the order of operations (PEMDAS) is a deductive process, step by step, for example. And learning all the theorems in geometry and needing to decide which one to apply in this particular proof is an inductive-reasoning process. In math, you sometimes have to be creative and try different ideas to see if they make sense or help you progress. You can change your mind. That is why erasers were invented.

Calm, creative strategies, logical, with inductive or deductive reasoning, step by step: this is what math should feel like. Questions need to be asked for a teacher to help someone learn math. It is the student's job to think, *What confuses me?* Then they should form questions and ask them. Asking questions is very difficult for many students. They want to stay silent and appear to understand. Some questions can be in class, some can be in a private one-on-one moment with the teacher, and some questions can be asked when they work with classmates. Good students do all of these and ask a parent at home. Too many questions are a sign of a lack of courage to try an idea. Turn those questions into questions back at them to decide. Don't forget to praise and encourage.

Math ebbs and flows from stuck and unstuck moments. The key is to teach your child to manage their emotions and stay calm and think inductively when they feel stuck. "What do I know to try on this problem?"

I want to leave you with some motivational math thoughts to pass along to your children. There is a culture that seems to accept that math is hard and that it's OK not to like math. It is a silly thought. Math is not hard when you understand it. And math is nothing to fear; it is learnable and fun when you get the right answer. Math is like a game. Learn the rules to play, and you will enjoy playing. For sure, with your adult financial decisions, you cannot ignore numbers. Numbers are a necessary component in life, so make friends with numbers. You cannot talk about money without using math. Maybe your child's career will build things, as there is a lot of math in that. Maybe your child's career will be to design things, which employs a lot of math. Maybe your child's career will involve counting things or thinking about the probability of things. Math-related careers generally have a higher pay rate, and this is not changing.

Math is in nature and art. Look up the golden ratio. It occurs naturally in living things, like our bodies, plants, and nature. Artists in the renaissance, like Leonardo da Vinci, knew of this relationship and used it in art. Look up the golden ratio hidden in his paintings of the *Mona Lisa* and *The Last Supper*. It is fascinating and to be appreciated with wonder once this ancient secret is revealed. When I asked my geometry students to go out and search for the golden ratio in their life and bring it back, the class was always mesmerized by this ratio of 1:1.6 (approximately), which has fascinated mathematicians since Euclid. Remember him? He wrote *The Elements*, and this was the beginning of geometry as we know it. My students would measure their pets, and sure enough, a cat's tail to the whole-body length is golden! Their nose and ears are golden. A pinecone is golden, and if you measure a rose and where the first thorn grows, it is golden. Why? It is a long-pondered mystery about math in nature, and it explains why it is pleasing to our eyes. Artists incorporated this ratio to make art pleasing to our eye, too. There is a lot to love about math and the patterns within it. It is so fun to collect items or measure your pets or body to find the golden ratio all around us.

You can celebrate Pi Day on March 14th, and eat pie and read about the history of the circle. How many digits is Pi calculated to? People make a career around looking for a pattern in that decimal. It's mind-boggling. Make math cool. It is possible.

Help your child with the things they are afraid of head-on and you will be impacting them for the rest of their lives.

RECAP: FEARS, PHOBIAS, AND MATH ANXIETY

- When the brain is in fear mode, learning is not possible.
- Calming down the brain is a skill to learn and practice.
- Working through triggers of perceived fears in academics is necessary work.
- Addressing fears is essential for struggling students.
- Fears can be reframed with positive experiences and gentle re-exposures to redefine perceptions.
- Fear is a debilitating and painful feeling and should be reserved for true threats and not learning challenges.
- Math anxiety has roots in fears of being wrong.
- You can make being wrong viewed as a learning opportunity, which supports a growth mindset.
- Teach your child to view mistakes positively and not fear them.
- Prevent the self-criticism that might feed their thought distortions and create fears.

13

INTEGRITY WITH SELF

ntegrity is doing the right thing when no one is watching. It can also be about thinking the right thing inside your head. Are your child's solutions to avoid their fears at the cost of their integrity? Doing your own work is a big concept in academic integrity. Plagiarism is an offense that can get your child expelled from colleges or be a reason to fail a course at a minimum. It is a crime in the school environment.

The concept of academic integrity is expected and often ignored in the middle and high school arena by rebellious teenagers. They feel as if they are getting away with something when work is shared when it is intended to be done on their own. Often, this is dismissed as a common thing that everyone does. In America, the student-teacher ratio promotes the opportunity and is yet another reason for small class sizes. Collaboration is allowed often, and when it is not, it is considered cheating to not do your own thinking. This is a rampant problem, especially in grades six through twelve and among students who struggle as a coping mechanism for surviving a school product or curriculum above their ability. We encourage students to cheat by not offering school where they are functioning.

Most struggling students cheat. This is a tough one for many parents to deal with positively. Cheating, when caught, is punished and reported from elementary school through college. Cheating is often ignored and tolerated in reality because it shows some involvement and effort when doing nothing is often what a teacher is faced with, with too many students. When a teacher notices the same unique errors on homework and tests, they can group clues and surmise who collaborated on the work. Proof becomes a challenge and then with the busy day with being pulled in so many ways, as teachers are, the effort of the accusation is often what outweighs the consequences. Teachers have many battles and choosing to ignore some is a survival strategy. Students unfortunately learn that this is the culture. Cheating becomes a way to cope, please the teacher, and please your parents.

There is a confounding variable to the simple scenario of the previous paragraph. Students are tired of plowing through the material and answering questions about that material. The motivation for the lesson is often weak. And the amount of material that is crammed into a semester is enough pressure for kids to cheat to get through their work.

Yes, often work is designed to be collaborative. But that is a whole different conversation. Collaboration requires contributions. These contributions require social confidence, academic confidence in the topic, respectful culture in the class, and clearly designed roles in the collaboration. Often there is a missing component in the planning of cooperative groups. Often one student does more than their share and then all the group members get equal credits for a not very collaborative product but the effort of one or two group members when that was not the task. Sometimes this happens for a show of ability to manipulate someone into doing the work. Teachers with talent and classroom management skills can monitor this properly. But often I have seen group work left unattended and students in a dysfunctional group left unsupported.

Children know they should not cheat on tests, but a child's perspective is often situational. A teen's perspective is clouded in ego, due to their egocentric brain development stage. You will find that cheating is not a black and white concept to your student. They need help in understanding the concept of integrity.

Teaching that work is something to honor. Your child needs to understand that if they tried their very best and earned a D, that is *their* D. The next time they earn a grade in that class or subject, they have something to beat. They do not need to fear a D or an F, but they should plan on how they will conquer it next time.

Parents who focus on grades promote cheating. If the grade is the be-all and end-all measurement of success or failure, then a student rationalizes that it is "worth" it because it is such a big deal. You know how I feel about the subjectiveness of grades and their place in the role of a student, but it also has a role in parenting. Understanding the context and meaning of grades and how grades are earned makes each grade either valuable or not. Parents can do a lot to grow their student's integrity by focusing on rewarding their hard work, process, or effort involved. This will grow the skills of a successful adult. Not the grade earned by whatever means necessary. Did you ever think about it like that? Learning has been minimized to a game of minimal effort. It has become about checking the boxes and getting minimal feedback on their mistakes, only grades.

What is offered after a poor grade? Think about it. Most of the time, classroom life moves on. What does that teach? Yes, there are those exceptional teachers who offer retakes, who will help students prepare, and then go through the extra effort to make sure their students succeed. Bravo to them! When I taught public high school math, I always offered retakes. A few of my fellow math teachers were annoyed because they felt the pressure to do the same.

Kids engage more when they feel they can succeed, and a relationship of kindness and respect helps. Learning is a vulnerable process. You need to try to learn from someone else and work through your confusion until you reach a total understanding. Language often stops the middle step of working through confusion. If you cannot keep up comprehension, you cannot form questions. This is why all students need to be learning within their independent learning level. It can be done. Older students can be offered age-appropriate topics and material at many grade levels. If this is done, they will grow their literacy by participating in class. If not, they will remain lost and look for survival mechanisms like cheating.

If we are driving kids to cheat, think of what consequences that will have on them as they grow into adults. Education needs to meet the needs of the student, or we are creating the next generation of criminals and drug addicts with negative self-esteem from lack of success. Social humiliation is enough to wound a person for life and forms a sort of PTSD reaction to learning on demand. This is pretty debilitating on the job front and then economic disaster follows. Maybe I am overdramatizing, but if 66 percent of students are entering high school below grade level, it will be a bumpy ride.

Many of my clients ask me what I think the solution is. I want to answer that here to end a chapter that delves into the dark psyche of survival for adolescents with my hope and solution. I think America needs to focus on building literacy, math, and critical thinking skills in our kindergarten through the eighth-grade population. This should be done using social studies and science learning as content, not leaving it out but making literacy growth a priority and reading leveled appropriately. This way we can revolutionize the high school experience with prepared minds. It is possible, but parents must demand it. And can our over-politicized system realize the main work has been done, and let go of the control? Will it allow science to guide our strategic planning for learning? It exists. We just need to implement it. I can see it clearly. I hope this book helps you see your child more clearly and also imagine my dream for education really addressing these issues and preparing kids much more uniquely for our transforming world. There is room for us all, and we do not need any child on a path of shame to adulthood. There should not have to be a chapter on integrity with self with the discussion of cheating and surviving when we discuss educating young children.

Often, students who are pushed to succeed when they do not feel that they can do so will cheat to save face. But what they really traded was their integrity for a moment of acceptance. Learning is a vulnerable process to the ego. Students go to great lengths and sometimes sacrifice their morality to survive the threat of school timelines, tests, and pressures. Once that trade for moral integrity happens, it is a value, whether conscious or subconscious. Losing sight of honesty and integrity is not what we are intending when we send our children to school. I am not defending it but rather trying to explain why a student's ego would rather save face with cheating than be "found out," if they care about their grades.

It is even worse when students start failing assignments and tests because they aren't even motivated to try or cheat. This is a big red flag. This makes me refer you to the "Drastic Times Call for Drastic Measures" chapter.

The measure of someone's character is integrity, and this chapter is asking you to see the desperation in cheating. Yes, it can be laziness or a bad habit too. But usually, there is a catalyst, something like, "I will earn a better grade if I cheat." The reason why a student cheats is more important than the actual cheating itself. I have seen very creative cheating from students who cannot do the work based purely on their literacy skills. They will copy sentences instead of writing their own. Many students cheat as a way to get through the day in a curriculum that does not fit their skills, and we pass them along. Learning is vulnerable. Putting a student in a classroom is an unspoken expectation that if they can do it, then they are good enough and if they cannot then they are not. I would like to also refer you to Lawrence Kohlberg's *Philosophy of Moral Development* as a guide to growing this skill. This is the bible of understanding and moti-vating each state of your child's moral development. Many adults never get beyond the first stage of moral development, which is behavior that is "good" only for fear of punishment. One would hope that as one progresses through life, an adult would see their place in society as a commitment for behaving in a way that is "good" for soci-ety, not just to avoid consequences. There are universal principles of ethics that define right and wrong, and the perspective of every party is considered to determine what is acceptable as positive for society. Acting in a selfless way and realizing that your actions have effects and consequences to others is the ultimate moral development a person can attain. Think of our actions as parents and realize we are setting moral examples for our children which heavily influence them.

The second stage "aiming at a reward" is seen in preschool-age children who fashion and choose their behaviors for a reward. As kids grow into elementary school-age children, they choose behaviors to secure approval and maintain friendly relations with others. Preteen children focus on rules and begin to understand that morality is about maintaining social order. They should start to realize what is good or bad for society. Teens begin to understand mutual benefit and reciprocity in relationships. Moral rights and legal rights are not always the same. Then in adulthood, we ideally achieve morality based on principles that benefit society.

Only when our brains reach the teenage years and beyond can we think theoretically and hypothetically, and consider reasons for and against a moral decision. Parents can influence their children by being fair and honest with their children. Taking responsibility for themselves in conversations serves as a model for what is expected from your child. A great conversation for parents to have is asking their preteen or teens about kindness in different situations. Practice taking the perspective of others after expressing about their perspective. Empathy often needs to be grown and modeled for children to make the consideration of others a part of their decision-making process. Is your child considering others, or making decisions from a selfish point of view? Maybe this is what you have allowed or maybe you have not modeled this enough for your child to emulate you in this positive attribute. All food for thought.

Empathy is rooted in attachment and when your child has strong attachments to their parents and family members, the seed of empathy grows. A parent interacting and smiling with baby begins the love connection and fosters the attachment necessary. A child must feel love to give the loving thought of empathy to others. Love and empathy are a loop, and one supports the other. While it is true that empathy grounds morality, be careful not to assume that it secures and guarantees it. Morality goes beyond empathy. If you are upset on behalf of others and you get upset for them, that in and of itself is not helpful to them. You might be considered self-indulgent, in a martyring way, if you only cry for others. To act and ease the suffering of others is beyond empathy. Here is a quote from William Damon, author of *The Moral Child: Nurturing Children's Natural Moral Growth:* "Neither the most empathetic emotional response, the sharpest awareness, nor the best of intentions can do very much for the social good if one lacks the strength of character necessary to take responsibility for one's actions." This book is a great read if interested in this topic further.

The biggest thing I see eroding children's development is when a parent models situational morality. Let's say that a child is taught not to steal by their parents. But one day, while shopping with your child, the items on the bottom of the shopping cart are not charged when checking out of the grocery store. If you realize this and follow through on the belief you taught your child, that stealing is wrong, you will then go back and pay for those items to rectify the situation. If you do not do this, your non-action will then erode all lessons you have taught and will teach. Situational morality is modeled and can be a rationalization for that child to not hold to any values. I see this all too often – rationalizations for immoral behavior that are self-centered and situational. Character is determined by the ability to live by a set of standards. Are you raising a child of high moral character, or promoting (by modeling) a self-benefiting situational morality? These moments are hard for children to contextualize, especially if they are younger than thirteen years old. This can cause a lot of confusion that often carries into adulthood.

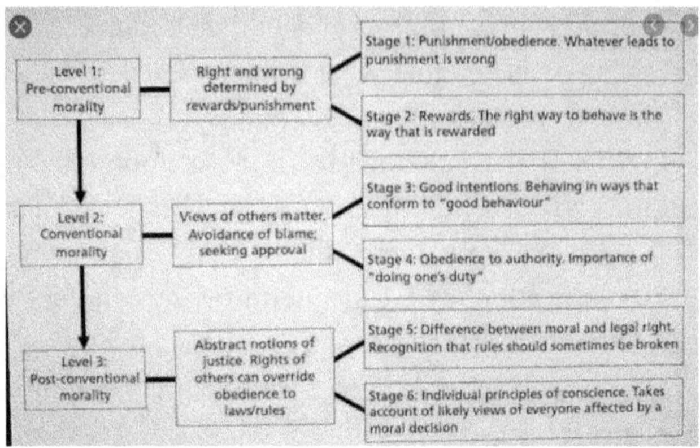

Every day we can support our children moving up the morality scale and form the lens of how they judge their life's actions. Can you think of a more noble reason for the conversations that also impact your child's language skills and relationship with you? I remember one Thanksgiving my mom and I went shopping for the big holiday meal. I think I was in fifth grade at the time. She had the turkey on the bottom of the shopping cart. The checker did not see this big turkey and did not charge my mom for it when we checked out. As we walked to the car, she was inspecting her receipt because it was less than she expected (that was my mom's number sense kicking in, a great thing to have). She noticed that the turkey was not charged in the total. We did not unload it into the car but marched back in to point out the error. I remember saying to my mom, "We could have had that turkey for free!" She said immediately to me, "There is no way I could eat that turkey if I had not paid for it." I was so confused because I felt she had a stroke of luck, but she insisted that there are needy people and if the store may want to give turkeys away, that was their choice. We could afford the turkey and had no reason to deny the store their profit. She said she would feel wrong about it. It would ruin her holiday. I learned a big lesson that day, about integrity and conscience. Do not let your conscience be bought for the mere price of a turkey. You are better than that.

Integrity matters, at least in the character traits of those I admire. Look at the failed marriages, the lies, and cheating on one's spouse so rampant in our country. Half the families are divorced in America, and many divorces end up losing trust. Trust requires integrity, and this is taught from a very young age. How is your child's sense of integrity? Teachers need parents to teach this concept at home, and school requires that learning be done with personal integrity.

If your child is pushed to cheat in school, it is a cry for help. Integrity is a concept lost in an education system not working for two-thirds of those who attend. Is it no wonder American prisons are at capacity, and crime is rampant? Integrity in school spills out into life, you can be sure of this. Situational integrity is what I often observe and that does not move a person into higher moral development as an adult. It seems there is an acceptable concept of trading integrity for a momentary reward, but I assert that you trade your soul to the devil, so to speak. You lose the pride of earning your grades if you cheat. Where is the pride in cheating? There is only shame. Make the connection with a positive self-concept with having integrity; it will serve as a character-building block that future moments of integrity will stand upon. Talk to your child about the value of integrity and know that you tried your best. Maybe the grade is bad, but you learned. Learning is the most important thing, not the grade, remember?

Moral development will be a foundation which guides your child in school in those moments where cheating feels like an option or an escape. If your family culture views failures with a healthy attitude, there will be less pressure to cheat. You will also be supporting your child's moral development by helping them make decisions based on what is right and wrong, and feeling good about earning their poor grade, rather than knowing a good grade was obtained through immoral behavior.

Make poor grades something the parent takes action about on behalf of the student showing there is a need for intervention. Show your child you believe they can do better and then help them along the way with integrity. This is a positive response to a failing grade. Anger for a failing grade from a parent, and maybe associated "punishments," can push a moral child into immoral behavior and should be carefully reconsidered. Poor grades are a sign the child needs help, not punishment. Promote your child not cheating by being the parent they can tell that they have failed, and show them how to learn and plan accordingly after a failure.

As a final note, an observant parent can surmise, or at least get an intuition about if their child can possibly succeed at the subject or task which he or she has failed or attempted cheating. If there is no way that your child's skills can succeed because they are ill-equipped for whatever reason, then remove your child from this daunting task. If they can succeed, maybe succeed is aiming for a C or D in a very challenging situation. That is fine. Redefine success, and make it attainable. I view cheating as a behavior cry for help, and it should be carefully analyzed as to the reason the child feels compelled to cheat. Often, struggling students who are unwilling to try any further and have a pattern of failures fall into "Drastic Times Call for Drastic Measures," Chapter 25.

RECAP: INTEGRITY WITH SELF

- Integrity is doing the right thing when no one is watching.
- Some schools have an underlying culture of cheating.
- When students see it happening around them, they join in because others are "getting away" with it.
- Often, academic survival is the cause of cheating; the student sees no other way.
- Cheating is a form of hiding.
- Cheating is a way to please those around you when you cannot do it on your own, via grades.
- Modeling situational morality is damaging to their resistance when it is convenient to cheat in school.
- Morality is learned and something to support your children in developing.
- Refer to Kohlberg's Six Stages of Development for reference.
- Reconsider how failures are discussed and viewed in your family culture to bring about the best learning for the future.
- Failures should promote a positive action plan that includes studying and using more resources like meeting with the teacher first.
- Analyze how your child is studying and consider new approaches for a better outcome.
- If a child is failing, and you can see their skills do not allow a chance of success, then remove them from that expectation, as it is too damaging and not serving the child.
- Redefine success to be reasonable for the child to attain.

CORE SKILLS

14

SPELLING

If your child's spelling knowledge is lacking, then the rest of the literacy skills will be held back. It is paramount that spelling is addressed to promote maximum growth of literacy skills. Many parents discount the impact of spelling, with computer spell check and texting changing casual communication. Is this a reason to compromise reading comprehension? Since missing spelling knowledge holds back reading comprehension and writing skills, that would be a very, very big mistake. No, spelling is not something to discount.

Literacy is like many strands of skills braided together, each strand with its own purpose. The braid of literacy begins with oral language. We speak to our children and show them the meaning of our words, and your child learned to understand oral language. Great, your child can learn, you have proven it to yourself. Stories that you read and tell your children teach them more about language. Every conversation enhances your child's brain. Literally. Children who have many stories read to them very young are listening to language and making meaning from the ideas that flow in a story. That strengthens the language center of the brain, grows vocabulary, and associates love with reading – all excellent associations that are subliminal reading influence and promote brain development. Never too much reading to and with your child. There is evidence that reading to your child in utero is helpful to brain development. Wow, right?

ORTHOGRAPHY

The next component of the braid of literacy is the student's growing knowledge of spelling. Literacy specialists prefer the word "orthography" over "spelling" because it refers to the letter patterns more specifically in words that represent sounds. When used as a noun, orthography means the study of correct spelling according to established usage, whereas spelling means the act, practice, ability, or subject of forming words with letters, or of reading the letters of words. They sound similar and synonymous, but they have a definite difference. Orthography comes from the Greek and means "correct way of writing." It includes punctuation and *spelling*. Rather than a mere activity, it's the part of grammar that studies, and is related to, the correct way of writing, whether it is about single words, punctuation, etc. Spelling is *"the process or activity of writing or naming the letters of a word."* All aspects of orthography are a strand in the literacy braid.

The reason I am teaching you the word orthography is that I have been taught (and I have validated over my career) that if you teach orthography, which includes spelling, it is better than isolated spelling teaching.

When you see a misspelled word in your child's writing, come up with *all* the words in that spelling pattern to learn and group in your child's mind. For example, if they spell "hach" instead of "hatch." There are words that rhyme with hatch, snatch, match, and catch, etc. They are all with the silent "t" and a short vowel. Learn them all as a group and simplify the complexity.

If you want to read more on how to teach spelling, then you should purchase *Words Their Way* by Donald Bear, Shane Templeton, Marcia Invernizzi, and Francine Johnston. These are also the authors of the Houghton Mifflin language arts curriculum, which has amazing data of effectiveness and is in over thirty-five languages worldwide! Maybe there would be homeschool mothers or fathers motivated to know how best to fix their child's spelling issues. You will also learn how to purchase the supplemental spelling books, each of which teaches all the spelling lessons in each successive reading stage.

Just like math, orthography has stages of learning that are sequential. There are assessments and you can just teach them what they do not know and fill in what is missing from their past.

Orthography is the "leading literacy indicator." This means that spelling or orthographic knowledge will hold your student's comprehension, fluency, and writing skills back if there is missing background information. It is a strand missing in the braid of literacy, and it can appear that a reader is unable to progress. Orthography is the hidden variable causing the rest of the literacy skills to appear "stuck." Many other supports can be put into place, but until the missing orthography is learned, literacy will continue to stumble, be out of concordance, and will have limited potential.

I cannot teach you all the aspects of *Words Their Way*, but I can tell you that it is an essential tool. It is a program that required literacy specialists to practice for about a semester to feel competent to deliver to students in its intended way by the brilliant professors who created it. And delivery is 90 percent of the proper learning and discovery of this program, teaching the brain to notice and attend to patterns.

You can use a strategy that is generally helpful every time you notice a misspelled word. You can make a word study notebook where students jot down words that they misspell as they write and cannot spell, even after a second try. These become a road map to what they have not noticed. Some learners ignore word structure when they learn a new word. They hear how to say it and learn what it means but they ignore the letters, and hence do not notice patterns.

You need to help your student, at any age, notice patterns. I would like to give you an elementary and a secondary example. Let's say that your child spells make as "mak" or "mack." You see that they are not solid on the "silent e" pattern with the "long a." You can gather lots of "long a" words, and even generate them by sound with your child. Then sort all the long a words into the spelling patterns: "silent e," "ai" words, and "-ay" words. Maybe you have a neighbor as one of the words, and yes, ei is also another vowel team that can sound like long a.

Ask your child to sort the words by how they are spelled and explain that when you say any of these you can try the long a sound! When you are trying to spell long a, you can try each of these, and one should look familiar. Say the spelling and write the spelling. Younger students can write it in the air or in the sand or with anything fun and colorful. Older students can keep a word study notebook. Here, blocks of similar words become tools they can revisit and have multiple exposures to help them remember. This is a method to capture and study spelling words you need to learn.

A secondary example might be if they misspell bicycle. The word root cycle has a prefix in front of it: "bi" which means two. Hence two wheels, right? We can learn the word cycle and also learn unicycle, tricycle, pop cycle, and cyclical. Looking up the meaning of this word root, you learn it is Greek.

The "cycle" root comes from Greek, where it has the meaning "cycle; circle." This meaning is found in such words as: bicycle, cycle, cyclo, cyclone, cyclotron, recycle, and tricycle. Looking further into that word or doing "word study" you can find lots of chemical and medical words using the word root "cycl." These would include:

- doxycycline
- cyclohexane
- macrocyclic
- cycloserine
- cyclization
- encyclopedia
- anticyclone
- carbocyclic

This is a very mature learning exercise for an older student or an adult. Make a word-study notebook and begin to decode words and roots as you need to. It is an engaging activity that is sure to surprise and sometimes delight you.

Any parent can keep a word-study notebook for their child if they are unwilling. You can discuss and play with words as I have modeled and quiz them when they feel they know the word. Expose your child until they can spell words like it and that word itself on their own. Small spelling moments regularly along these lines will begin new habits of noticing patterns in spelling.

An older student may feel empowered to have a method to repair spelling. The word study notebook is nearby whenever they edit. Collect the words for later investigation.

Imagine all the strands of literacy now braided together: reading comprehension, vocabulary, writing skills, sentence structure skills, literature and genre knowledge, spelling, figurative language methods, and fluency. The thing that makes a skilled reader is now dependent upon your child's executive function abilities to use them all in conjunction as they read, think, and write. It is all of these skills working together that is the goal. All of these skills working together and in concordance (or at a similar level) are needed for your child to grow and follow the grade level increments required in reading and writing each year of their kindergarten through twelfth grade academic journey. So, this may make you reread Chapter 11: "Develop Your Child's Executive Brain Skills." You may decide to hire a literacy specialist to grow your child's orthographic knowledge. And then hire a psychologist to help you create a family culture that encourages your child's executive function skills if they have been enabled loving and mistakenly by one or both parents. Maybe you buy a book on helping your child and retrain you in this area. There are many good books on the market. Now you know two essential priorities in improving literacy skills.

RECAP: SPELLING

- If your child's spelling knowledge is lacking, then the rest of the literacy skills will be held back.
- If you teach orthography, which includes spelling, it is better than isolated spelling teaching.
- Spelling leads all literacy skills: reading, comprehension, and writing, and can equally hold all literacy skills back.
- Just like math, orthography has stages of learning that are sequential.
- New learning must stick to something already learned, and in this idea, spelling needs to be carefully taught and built upon previous understandings.
- Short vowels first, then long vowel patterns, then r-influenced vowels, then diphthongs and other ambiguous vowels, then beginning and ending complex consonants, to begin the sequence of learning.
- Spelling is worth paying a professional to teach, as long as they subscribe to the stages and beginning at the first weak area and moving forward.
- Recall www.TalkingFingers.com as a spelling program online with two parts that bring learners through the long vowel patterns.

15

READING AND COMPREHENSION

Reading and Comprehension is fundamental to learning. In this chapter, I will share with you relevant and up-to-date information from prominent researchers in the field to help your struggling child. These researchers include:

- Joanna A. Christodoulou from MGH Institute of Health Professionals at Harvard University
- Dr. Jeannine Herron, neuropsychologist and founder of www.TalkingFingers.com
- John Gabrieli from the Department of Brain and Cognitive Sciences and Martinos Imaging Center at the McGovern Institute for Brain Research, MIT

When we send our children to school, one of the most important skills we want the school to teach is reading. Reading can be thought of as many strands woven together to create a skilled reader. The first strand you need to build is word recognition, and that involves phonological awareness which is knowledge about the phonemes (sounds that letters or groups of letters make), syllables in words, and the way sounds blend together in a word, as well as the ability to add or delete a sound and understand rhyming words (words that end with the same sound). Word recognition also involves decoding, which is a spelling sound pattern. Then you need to form sight recognition of familiar words. This is what teachers call "sight words." You can reference which words your child should know at about one hundred per grade level. I am a fan of Fry's Sight Word lists, which should be studied in order as they are listed in order of frequency of occurrence. That is the math geek in me to have an ordered list of frequently used words to learn to begin to allow fluency. No need to sound them out; the goal is to know them by the sight of the whole word, instantly.

The second strand of learning to read is language comprehension. In this, you need five skills. The first is background knowledge, concepts, and awareness enough about what you are reading that your mind can reference something to attach new learning to. A secret of a good educator is to know that all new learning needs to be attached to something we already know. In doing this, we are creating an association or retrieval process and a memory location for the information. You also need the vocabulary to know the breadth and precise meaning of words used. Then you need to understand language structure such as syntax, or form of sentences, and semantics, or the meaning of phrases or different ways to express detail. Language comprehension also requires verbal reasoning such as inference, where the reader needs to draw conclusions beyond the written word and assume things implied, like figurative language such as metaphors and idioms. Favorite metaphors are "raining cats and dogs" or "heart of gold" or "life is a roller coaster." Idioms are often misunderstood by children when reading if they are not exposed, like "speak of the devil" or "that was the last straw," which are not referring to straws or devils. Literal mistakes when reading of idioms are common unless children are exposed to them, and this can upset comprehension. The last skill required for language comprehension is literacy knowledge like genres and types of print for context.

All the skills required in word recognition (phonological awareness, decoding, and sight recognition) need to blend in the brain with the skills required in language comprehension (background knowledge, vocabulary knowledge, language structure, verbal reasoning, and literacy knowledge) to form skilled reading. Skilled reading can be thought of as a fluent execution of coordination of the word recognition and text comprehension. As a reading specialist, I am looking for these skills and finding a level where I can create concordance, or all the skills in the same level together. Then it is like an orchestra with all the players, and the brain takes over and reading happens.

In kindergarten, students are learning the twenty-six letters of the alphabet. Then in first grade, students are beginning to learn the phonemes. These are sounds for letters and groups of letters, of which there are forty-four phonemes. For example, "igh" is a phoneme for the long "i" sound and is one of the longer phonemes with three letters. Likewise, the letter "g" can have a g-sound like in the word "go" or a j-sound like in the word "giant." Students need to learn the phonemes and when and where they occur in words.

In kindergarten the brain is engaged in pre-reading activities which include phonemes and phonological awareness. Then in first grade, the brain is learning to read by putting phonemes together to build words and simple sentences. In second grade, the brain is learning to read accurately. The phonemes are not all mastered yet and the brain is learning to use them in different combinations. In third grade, the brain is learning how to read to learn, learning to comprehend, and think about reading in new and deeper ways.

Reading problems are labeled as learning disabilities or LD, which is a way of saying the brain is struggling in this area or not keeping up as we expect. In the past, educators were ill-equipped and underinformed as to what to do. To get clinical, educators began to label problems and form assumptions that these problems are fixed. These learning challenges are just that. I have learned to view them as things to explore. What I find is that some are easy to solve and were just missed at the time or not encoded properly at the time. Other times, I can see the struggle the student has to learn something that is not usually so difficult. Then, my challenge is to find a way that students can learn what they are missing and grow skills in areas they are missing. The skills I am referring to are the language comprehension and word recognition skills I described above, the eight skills that are used to create skilled reading. I cannot teach a parent my master's degree as a literacy specialist in this chapter, but I can give you a global overview of what I have found works in repairing reading skills.

Students learn uniquely, which I see when I am trying to teach through a "learning disability," which is a phrase that rubs me as having inaccurate implications. For example, there are signs labeled as "dyslexia," which can present in many different forms and combinations of things. I also do not subscribe to using that word. It has lost its meaning due to how broad it has become. I like how I have heard some neuroscientists refer to it as processing reading in inefficient parts of the brain. That explains it accurately and you can understand that if the brain is randomly assigning reading tasks to various areas of the brain, that some choices would not be as efficient as other choices. Neuron pathways need to connect ideas and put together the parts for reading to occur, and so I think of it as teaching a new skill and creating and strengthening the new pathways to function where they did not exist before. This serves me and has helped me visualize my reading remediation process. I am thinking about the eight skills working in conjunction and shoring up the ones missing.

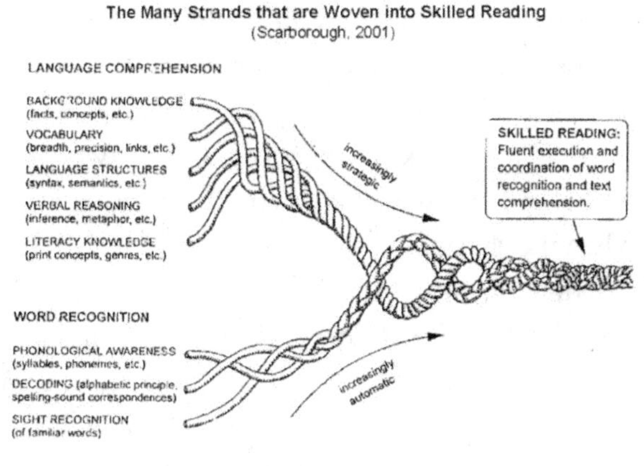

But then, I learned about Dr. Jeannine Herron at a conference in the early 2000s. She is a neuropsychologist who I had the pleasure of listening to at a brain conference and her session was about dyslexia. I had a particular student in mind who was a very challenging case, so I was hoping for some insight to help that boy. Tears swelled in my eyes as I could not believe what I was hearing. This soft-spoken articulate lady, whose humility touched me, shared her research. She showed brain scans of struggling readers and what parts of their brain were active while reading. She showed strong readers and their brain scans and what parts of the brain were active. Well, poor readers are not processing reading near the language center of the brain and therefore the brain has much longer neural pathways to accomplish the task of reading. Seemed so logical. She went on to explain that her work focused on whether the poor readers could move where reading was processed in the brain. The short answer was *yes!*

I remember my eyes were filled with tears at this amazing research and the best part was she created a spelling program that utilized her findings. You can read all about her work, and more importantly you can have your struggling reader use her two ten-lesson programs that review and reteach the first phonemes and spelling ideas typically taught in first through third grade. These are the key foundations that are predictors of reading struggle in later years. Her programs feel like a game to children and even older kids. And you will not believe it, but it also teaches typing skills to the beginner. If your child cannot spell the long vowel patterns and shows any dyslexic tendencies, this program will change their reading future. It is a no-risk and everything-to-gain tool: www.talkingfingers.com. The two programs can be monitored behind the scenes by a teacher, and parents may not realize this when purchasing.

Dyslexia is first diagnosable in second and third grade and the most effective time for intervention is kindergarten and first grade, so there is research happening at MIT to try to diagnose earlier. The early predictors of reading difficulty are phonological awareness skills, rapid naming (ability to recall letters and their sounds quickly), and letter knowledge. When these skills are slow, you cannot build other skills upon them. Older kids then have large gaps in knowledge that hold back the brain's ability to read. My findings are that I can find these gaps, and work on them and their reading improves. Rhyming is something where children who are not read to with whimsical children's rhymes like those found in Dr. Seuss and nursery rhymes suffer in their phonological awareness. This is a good thing to tell parents and this can be made up of listening to poetry and having older students find the rhymes and become better at listening for them. Skills once learned stay learned.

The students with permanent retention problems are fetal alcohol syndrome (FAS) babies and some babies born addicted to drugs. There is damage to the memory systems of these innocent victims. These are the cases that lowering standards apply to. This is a small amount of the total reading problems, and so the hope and progress I am explaining is possible for all but this group. They are truly learning challenged in my experience. The retention rate is so low that the sheer amount of time it takes to is not feasible. The other group of students I have more than a typical reading specialist's experience with is our children with multiple concussions. Offering an adaptable but rigorous educational alternative for ski athletes was one of the things that my school specialized in and this group of students regularly experienced concussions. Ski racers, big mountain skiers, and aerialists all often took large spills at high speeds and this can be dangerous. Even with helmets, students were injured sometimes. Without their ski helmet, damage might have been unimaginable. For this reason, I asked my boys to please keep their skies on the ground. There is an edge of control and my recommendation is to have fun and keep hold of control, and I say this as a skier myself.

There is such glamorization of dangerous mountain adventures year round. I caution parents to allow their daredevil children some thrill often in safe environments, so they are not taking risks to get their adrenaline rush. This is becoming more and more of an issue to manage, thrill seeking! Parenting in the twenty-first century. Just put the risks to learning in perspective. Remember, *learning* is most important.

Seven out of eight students with reading problems in first grade continue to struggle with reading in ninth grade. They get better but never catch up. I feel this is because in our education system we do not try, and we could if we handled things differently. My work has proven to me that if you try, you can markedly improve most all regular education students except those with FAS or traumatic brain injuries like concussions. Improving listening skills is often the easiest route to improving reading skills. Since both use the same part of the brain, it is incredible to challenge your student to listen. How about listening to the scavenger hunt? Listen to a poem for tone and predict the author's mood. Our world is so noisy one wonders if the over-stimulation of a loud world is a factor. Just take commercials on TV for an example of learning how *not* to listen.

We have talked about the eight areas of reading skills that need to be blended into skilled reading. Well, that blending of skills requires executive function skills. Yes, everything I wrote about in Chapter 11! Yet another reason executive functioning is essential for learning and should be developed at home. Parents need to make yet another preperation so the teacher has a teachable brain, which is to develop and grow their child's executive function.

Reading comprehension is a process of improving the five language comprehension skills over time. These skills are taught and refined each year of school through twelfth grade. The knowledge is refined and expanded and increases over time in all five areas. Then the word recognition skills also grow over time and one's sight words continue to grow. I look up words all the time. I am a lifelong learner and modeling that attitude is what it takes to continue to develop the three word recognition skills. Older students for example learn the concept of word roots and prefixes and suffixes that add meaning to the root. This expands our decoding skills yet again in one of the last stages of reading which happens in sixth through ninth graders.

In 2012, there was a survey of public perceptions of LD, and one third of people attributed LD to causes that were inaccurate. Of those surveyed, 22 percent thought LD was caused by too much time watching TV, 31 percent thought that LD was caused by a poor diet, and 24 percent thought that LD is caused by childhood vaccinations. None of those ideas have any validity. Another one third of people surveyed thought that a lack of early childhood parent-teacher involvement can cause LD. None of these ideas are proven to cause LD. Fifty-one percent of people thought that LD was the result of laziness. Not true. Fifty-five percent of people think that LD is a product of the home environment. So, if you have any of these ideas, please let them go.

Thirty three percent of classroom teachers and other educators believe sometimes what people call a learning or attention issue is really just laziness. How shocking is that? Do you think a child can feel that hostility and judgment? I think teachers are very hard-working people and can be "worn down" over time to get these opinions because it is hard to know the invisible workings of a child's processing capabilities.

Forty-three percent of parents say that they would not want others to know if their child has a learning disability. Yes, there is shame to the label even to the parents. This label is real and it is what we do with it that matters to me. Push the boundaries of the child's capabilities and you will find what skills can grow with pointed attention and what skills are less able to grow and might need other strategies to compensate. This is what goes on in my head. I see the areas of deficiency and I then systematically try to grow each area and note the retention of these new learned abilities. I find that often, the brain needs assistance to grow, but most always can. I rarely find a child unable to progress. I am looking for potential and I do so with hope and optimism.

Doctors who recommend having a child evaluated for learning and attention issues say parents follow their recommendations only 54 percent of the time. There is a natural avoidance to learning where your child's weak areas are. I understand this when no one is addressing them with hope, but rather limiting beliefs. I say, dig in and understand what a weak processing area is and then exercise that area. Do something proactive about that developmental area not keeping pace. You can approach this whole area with positivity with the knowledge that the brain is incredibly plastic. There are so many sound strategies to apply, and growth can be measured. That is the math geek in me. I love to use data for student progress, not labeling and stifling.

Let's clarify the labels attributed to reading problems. Dyslexia is a term used in research and clinical education settings. It is a specific word that implies a high level of difficulty in reading. Dyslexia is used when there are extreme letter reversals, visual problems, problems planning and organizing and executing, slow speed of processing, and seeing backward. It is often associated with motor coordination issues and trouble linking letters and sounds. It can be one or more or any combination of these things that cause the term "dyslexic" to be used. Dyslexia is best thought of as reading being processed in inefficient parts of the brain.

Educational terms for a reading problem are Specific Learning Disability (SLD) and we use these terms as legally defined terms in education. Dyslexia is a term used as a type of SLD. The label does not typically change how the system teaches the student from the student's point of view, and they are not served by being labeled. Teachers are asked to "understand" and "accommodate" but rarely does the student get specialized instruction, as I recommend.

Medical terms for reading problems are called Specific Learning

Disorder (SLD) and they are clinically based and not specific to any reading issue. Medical terms consider dyslexia as a type of SLD.

Neuroscientists know that dyslexia is neurobiological in origin and it centers around difficulty with the sounds of language, the phonology. Reading comprehension challenges are the result. Other things that contribute to reading problems are the exclusion of culture, education, stimulating environment, or other disabilities. Reading problems and dyslexia cannot be diagnosed from a brain scan. These are performance diagnoses.

About 13 to 14 percent of students have dyslexia. If your child does not have the reading problems described here (letter reversals, visual problems, problems planning and organizing and executing, slow speed of processing, seeing backward, motor coordination issues, and trouble linking letters and sounds), then your child has a reading problem and not dyslexia. I need to emphasize that letter reversals are not a defining feature of dyslexia as this is a common condition up until third-grade brain maturity.

About half of the nation's population who have qualified for special education services have a learning disability of some kind. And about 85 percent of those with LD have a disability in reading and language processing. Now, this group of students is the easiest for a reading specialist to repair. And it is a majority of the group of struggling students. They are missing building blocks of knowledge that their brain did not catch when taught. But now their brains are older, more mature, and are more adept at learning than the last time they attempted to learn ideas they need, and it is surprising how ready they are and excited I might add, to learn what they have missed. It is like handing out epiphanies to children, and they are so happy to figure out things they never understood.

The best instruction for students with reading problems derived from dyslexia or LD is multisensory instruction which uses all the senses. Another best instruction is explicit, instead of a discovery approach. Additionally, structured and sequential instruction is a successful strategy and provides many opportunities for review and practice.

We want to create cognitive resilience and focus when we work with a struggling reader. We can do this by strengthening and nurturing oral language skills. Early problems in oral language such as articulation or sentence repetition should be identified as early as possible and given intervention to build up that skill. Students should be encouraged to practice using their vocabulary knowledge to grow their vocabulary with intention. Students with reading difficulties will need guidance setting goals and self-monitoring their behavior and progress. Strategies to build executive function skills should be taught, supervised, and practiced.

To address the social-emotional resilience necessary for children with reading difficulties, here are some protective factors that contribute to success and intervention. Students benefit from a sense of coherence, self-determination, and an internal locus of control. Students with an "internal locus of control" generally believe that their success or failure is a result of the effort and hard work they invest in their education.

Students also benefit from family cohesion. Divorce is a cause of reading problems for one to two years and delays in reading development following divorce are well documented. I recommend intervention when the emotions have settled down and the student can regroup. Often during a divorce, the student's world is too tumultuous to be teachable. Strong parental attachment and parenting support and understanding of their child's reading disability and struggle was paramount.

Parents need to promote hopeful thinking, focus, and work ethic as positive traits that a person practices and grows. This is also called a growth mindset. Peer relationships are important to the child's sense of self-worth. Having teacher support and small class sizes is also ideal. Students with dyslexia need to feel they have a sense of control of their lives, especially their academics. They should be given resources, strategies, and choices to bolster this sense of control. Parents can increase a child's sense of worth by seeking to understand each child's patterns of learning strengths and weaknesses as related to dyslexia.

Here are some excellent resources for different versions of print materials available to assist you and your child's teachers or reading specialists:

- National Instructional Materials Access Center (NIMAC)
- Bookshare
- Learning Ally
- American Printing House for the Blind
- Best Evidence Encyclopedia
- National Center on Intensive Intervention
- International Dyslexia Association (IDA)
- What Works Clearinghouse
- Usable Knowledge, Harvard Graduate School of Education

The biggest barrier to comprehension is a lack of fluency. Less than 15 percent of learning-challenged students would have comprehension problems if they read accurately and read faster than seventy to eighty words a minute. It is like teaching a child how to steer a bike before they learn how to pedal. We want to build the skill of fluency by reading things they can be accurate with and slowly increasing the difficulty of text while maintaining fluency.

Reading too slowly makes it hard for the brain to remember the beginning and end of the sentence to make comprehension meaningful. Reading too fast is not allowing adequate time to process the meaning of words. There is a sweet spot with reading speed. I have a boy right now whose main reading problem is speed. He has decided early on in school that getting things done means free time, and getting things done faster is better, equaling more free time. That is the reinforcement he received in school in the beginning. Now as a fifth grader, he has skipped paying attention to the structure of words. You need to teach your child to learn new words in three ways, notice their structure (spelling), learn how to articulate the word, and lastly, learn the meaning of the word . . . and often multiple meanings. This boy is so driven to be fast, and to slow him down causes tears and struggle. He is struggling with spelling severely, and grammar and comprehension are challenging too. Having attention to detail is something he is learning to attend to, and he is a high-performing student and a charming young man.

We have overviewed all my magic fairy dust to repair reading problems. Reading independently promotes more reading because it is able to flow and be enjoyable. This requires that your student is reading at their independent ability, as a top priority. The more your child reads, the better they will be at reading. Fluency increases as you continue to read. The more your child reads, the more their brain will be able to sustain the mental effort required for meaningful comprehension. The more your child reads, the more they will learn about the world in their reading. The more your child reads, the broader their perspective will be during their life. A motivated parent can dissect these ideas and make progress using resources and suggestions here. You got this, and I know if you are still reading, you have what it takes to help your child.

RECAP: READING AND COMPREHENSION

- Reading can be thought of as many strands woven together to create a skilled reader.
- The first strand you need to build is word recognition, and that involves phonological awareness which is knowledge about the phonemes (sounds that letters or groups of letters make).
- Then, in first grade, the brain is learning to read by putting phonemes together to build words and simple sentences.
- Sentences grow in complexity from simple to compound to complex from second grade through fifth grade. The brain is also learning more spelling as words grow in complexity.
- The second strand of learning to read is language comprehension.
- For Language comprehension you need five skills.
- The first is background knowledge, concepts, and awareness enough about what you are reading that your mind can reference something to attach new learning to.
- Next, word recognition skills also grow over time and one's sight words continue to grow.
- Model learning new words as part of a natural curiosity and look them up with your child.
- Older students, for example, learn the concept of word roots and prefixes and suffixes that add meaning to the root. This skill moves reading comprehension ability.
- Reading comprehension cannot grow without executive function braiding all literacy skills together. See chapter on Executive Function.
- The biggest barrier to comprehension is a lack of fluency.
- Fluency requires some resilience to processing reading at a rate that the brain can see and interpret words while articulating accurate sentences with voice inflections that make sense.

- Fluency must be practiced to grow.
- Students who avoid reading do not improve their fluency.
- Dyslexia is best thought of as reading being processed in inefficient parts of the brain.
- See www.TalkingFingers.com to promote reading to be moved to efficient parts of the brain through spelling intervention.

16

WRITING

Reading and writing skills are related. A good reader can have writing challenges, but the writing process is more complex than reading. As literacy grows, let me restate, spelling is what leads the knowledge growth in literacy skills. Vocabulary grows while reading and the correlation to verbal language is made when it is seen in print. Learning by reading about words and their uses together by different authors allows writing skills to grow. Writing is the last literacy skill to follow spelling, reading, and vocabulary growth, and then writing brings up the rear. Do not be concerned about this; it is the nature of literacy progression. This chapter will explore and inform you on how to influence your child's writing skills positively. It would be worth reading, even if your child's writing is not concerning you.

Skilled and insightful writing is different than being able to write. Writing receives less than deserved time on tasks typically, and adding writing to your child's education, especially authentic writing, would exercise their writing muscles and result in improved skills. Letters or emails to relatives is writing. Social justice and letters for community concerns or a new skate park, for example, are excellent examples of authentic writing, the very best type of writing for your child to engage positively with writing.

The beginning writing is learning how to print. Forming letters, holding a pencil, and taking the proper body stance, which is more important than I can say. This means sitting with feet on the floor, shoulders leaning slightly forward and the paper at a slight angle to parallel your writing hand forearm, and the other hand holding the paper that you are writing on. Create this posture so the body can learn the advantage of the posture, which promotes comfort in writing and a relaxed approach.

Does your child have awkward body positions when sitting? Do they squirm around in their chair? Writing posture and becoming comfortable while writing is an important habit to develop or reinforce. There is a positive feeling when one is comfortable and relaxed with good body positioning. Children do not know that and some really struggle in this area. Teens are classic for saying this does not matter and preferring strange positions on the floor or curled up on a couch. Children and teens often do not know how to value comfort and posture. Help them learn this while writing and are you promoting a positive writing experience right off the bat.

Reminding your child is expected for a period of time and is often needed. Creating a "code" word or signal for this posture can be a fun reminder and more positive way to remind a younger student. Buying your teen an ergonomic office chair and then allowing them to set up a personalized workspace reflecting their personality and interests encourages writing at a desk properly. Computer use encourages using a desk for comfort and refers to an ergonomic seat. Students cannot write for long when they are curled up and not sitting in an ergonomically correct position. See the chapter "Primal Reflexes" if sitting in this position is something that needs to be reset frequently. A wiggly child or teen often may need some physical movements to think. Most of us can for at least ten minutes at a time at a minimum sustain writing. You can write a lot in a ten-minute increment.

All letters should be formed from the top down, with attention to the height of and proportion of the letters, attempting to write in a level straight line. I am a huge fan of Handwriting Without Tears program. They have different books for each stage of printing or cursive practice. I am ok with personal preference on the cursive debate because it is a smooth convenience that may be helpful to some students with particular reasons, or preference. The priority is to print neatly and properly, with attention to proportion, clarity, and proper letter formation.

My second priority is to teach typing. Finger dexterity is a kinesthetic language and can be easy and fun to learn. It builds upon the proper sitting stance you have taught and moves to a keyboard. The new iPad covers that also function as keyboards are great for small fingers. They are vinyl, easy to clean, and do not have any extra keys on the keyboard. The keyboard feedback is light, making it easier for small hands. There are several online programs that deliver age-appropriate typing lessons for both kids and adults. You can check out a few online typing platforms on my blog. Typing can become a daily online "game" time. Watching your words per minute score is something I would have students at my K-grade twelve school graph and share with parents. Graphing your score is a motivator for kids. This also models a growth mindset about learning a new skill with diligence and practice. They will earn the pride of accomplishing something that is not easy. Learn to view a challenge as possible and something to plan for.

We need to teach tolerance for the writing process. In the first draft, you write down your preliminary ideas. After that, the student can continue to polish, edit, and fix errors. A first grader allowed to skip over writing errors will encounter difficulties in their writing development. You cannot better your writing skills by ignoring mistakes. Punctuation, capitalization, sentence structure, spelling, word choice, and the organization of ideas into paragraphs and a simple or complex logical flow or sequence, are all part of the writing process.

First graders learn to write simple sentences. Second graders can combine multiple simple sentences and maybe begin to use conjunctions (acronym FANBOYS: for, and, nor, but, or, yet, and so). It is a warning sign if your student cannot use conjunctions properly. For example, when using "but," the first sentence is usually something positive and the second sentence is a negative aspect of that first idea: It is sunny today, but it might rain later tonight.

Just because someone does not notice something like the purpose of a conjunction, that's all there is to it. They did not notice that. Teach the concept. They will use it properly moving forward. It is not a conclusion of ability or intelligence if they do not notice this. It is a sign of a language processing propensity that needs support to grow. So many of my students that needed that lesson grew into competent readers and writers. These details shouldn't stop progress. Writing instruction is not detailed enough for the learner. As parents you can add the detail. We can all do it, especially if you have a college degree yourself. If not, I have helped parents who are on the learning journey alongside their kids. Your love and interest convey that writing is important. Your children want your love and strive to make you proud. Make it easy for them to do that with their effort and incremental improvements.

Here is how one objective of the writing standards is expressed in the Common Core Curriculum for a second grader:

"Write narratives in which they recount a well-elaborated event or short sequence of events, include details to describe actions, thoughts, and feelings, use temporal words to signal event order, and provide a sense of closure."

That is a pretty big expectation for a second grader. Writing expectations lag reading expectations by three to six months prior to third grade, or in later grades the lag of skill is typically about a year. Their writing skills should match the complexity of what they are able to read. This will not happen unless the student is actively writing. This is why writing should accompany everything they read in a productive literacy experience. The most important part is feedback on their writing. Peer editing is powerful and considered more fun than receiving it from a teacher. I like talking to students about their writing without marking it up in red. That is so stereotypical, and the red is negative and a harsh color. Remember, the brain associates the feeling of everything with the experience. The goal is to make writing feel collaborative, with trust and a respectful relationship. Too often, editing feels threatening or punitive. Avoid that at all costs. I like to write in pencil, underlining and talking about the changes. Then I see if they can revisit and improve the error with their own skills and not my telling them what it should have been. Every mistake is a learning opportunity.

Responding and rethinking about what you read, analyzing the plot, and learning how to think globally about a lesson learned or the main idea are skills to be learned. Every bedtime story is an opportunity to discuss these things, but you don't have to make it academic. Teens are fascinated by the dangers of the world, the wonders of nature, and often thrilling daredevils and unbelievable adventures. No matter the age of your child, you can find compelling short stories, read together, and discuss afterward. Comprehension questions help students learn how to reflect on what they read.

Use their interests and curiosity to keep them writing about things they enjoy. Biographies can be inspirational for students of all ages. Find a role model along the way. Below are all the aspects of writing standards for a fourth-grade student. Write opinion pieces on topics or texts, supporting a point of view with reasons and information.

Here are the essential key elements of writing skills that apply to all grade levels for a general understanding of the progression of writing curriculum. A general goal of writing is to clearly introduce a topic, state an opinion, and have an organized structure. By structure, we are looking for your child to be able to write a simple sentence by the end of kindergarten. By the end of first grade, your child should be able to write a more developed simple sentence. By the end of second grade, your child should be able to write sentences using descriptive details, with some figurative language.

Recall that figurative language is writing elements that describe using techniques such as similes, metaphors, idioms, hyperboles, and alliteration, to name a few. Figurative language skills can be simple or very savvy and cleverly written by the best of writers, so this skill is expected to grow through twelfth grade and most likely to be considered "developing" even by the best of writers. I recommend reading children's books that are rich in figurative language to children and encouraging exposure to novels which are rich in this area to enrich your student's ability to apply it with confidence.

Continuing with the structure of writing expected by grade level, by the end of third grade your child should be able to write a cohesive paragraph with a concluding sentence using simple and compound sentences. By the end of fourth grade, your child should be able to write in distinct paragraphs and be able to edit for spelling, punctuation, and capitalization accurately fusing simple, compound, and beginning complex sentences. By the end of fifth grade, your child should be able to construct a cohesive three paragraph essay, with an introduction, thesis statement, and conclusion. Throughout middle school writing is practiced and polished, and increased grammatical skills are taught and expected. In middle school the ideas of tone and voice are introduced. Middle school is the time when vocabulary demands become increased in the content of the core subjects, and new vocabulary is expected to be incorporated into writing. By high school, the analytical expectation of what is being written steadily increases over ninth through twelfth grade. Writing is expected to "cite textual evidence" and have increased purposeful structure and succinctness throughout high school. As an example, the essay prompt on the SAT is a task in analyzing the persuasive elements used in a reading passage of a famous speech or writing excerpt. Students have to refrain from their personal reaction to listening to tone and changes in tone, listening for the use of statistics or data to persuade, or the use of word choice to persuade, or the types of appeal used to persuade, like logic or emotional appeal, etc. Explaining the rhetoric used in a given speech or writing, and citing examples used in an organized five paragraph essay is the SAT writing task in a fifty-minute time period.

To accomplish the SAT writing task and other high school writing requirements, writing needs to flow. This cognitive process grows with practice. High school students need to write in a variety of tasks, such as research papers, persuasive essays, informative essays, summative essays, analytical essays, creative stories, personal narratives, news articles, mathematical explanations, retelling and analysis of historical events, character analysis from novels, historical events and biographies and memoirs, scientific justifications with data analysis, and science lab papers using the scientific method.

If your child is a struggling reader, then use the grade level general expectations I have outlined here to guide what you expect them to write competently. For example, if your child is in seventh grade, but their reading comprehension is in fourth grade, then expect them to write just a paragraph or two. That is where their literacy skills are and doing that much well is reasonable to teach and expect. That makes sense that if their reading skills are low, the writing skills will also be delayed respectively or just a bit more, since writing is the last literacy skill in the progression of skills to develop.

Writing is in the four core classes and not just in English class. Then there is writing an outline and deciding what is most important. The skill of writing with transitions eloquently is developed during high school and continues into college. The ability to develop a topic using concrete details, quotations, and other information including examples is developed during high school. Lastly, using precise language is an art that comes with being a skilled writer.

The ability to be descriptive and detailed while being succinct is rarely seen in high school but can be achieved by a student willing to engage in a detailed editing process. Editing is a skill that requires revisiting and time management to accomplish. Editing is very challenging for some students and the trick of coming back at a later time is only afforded if your child can plan ahead and allow that time and effort to do so. This requires executive function skills which are so important in so many academic areas, hence a whole chapter dedicated to the topic in this book.

Writing is the progression of understanding how to form a simple sentence, then how to link sentences together to convey an idea. The complexity of sentences grows through reading and reinforcement of how a sentence sounds. Sentence structure understanding should originate from speaking and how a proper sentence sounds. The sound of subject verb agreement develops from those speaking to the child properly. The sound of a complete sentence is also learned from listening to complete sentences. Speaking properly is a component of writing properly.

Editing is a process. The more you edit, the more polished your first draft becomes. This is true! When a student is forming the ideas they want to write, it is normal for their knowledge of conventions to not show up. But in reexamining their thoughts on paper, the attention can turn to conventions of writing. Those conventions are capitalization rules, punctuation, sentence structure, paragraph format, best vocabulary for the situation reconsidered, sequencing ideas, and lastly, thinking if any good ideas are left.

All students from kindergarteners through twelfth graders should be involved in a writing project in one subject at all times. Daily reading is something we all accept as important. Thank you early elementary teachers for making reading every day a priority! But writing should be a weekly project. In my perfect school, I would have a coordinated effort for teachers to follow rotating when writing is to be assigned. When language arts ignores writing, then it opens the door for social studies, science, or math to assign a writing project. Math can involve a writing project! I wrote a guide to writing the mathematics classroom as a part of my graduate work. I could write a chapter just on that topic. Below are a few types of writing that we need to expose our students to beginning in third grade and developing throughout twelfth grade:

- Narrative writing
- Expository writing
- Descriptive writing
- Research paper
- Persuasive writing
- Poem
- Creative writing
- Formal letter

If you are the homeschool mom, then you can orchestrate this idea pretty readily! If you are sending your child to a school, then you are delegating this to them. You can convey to your child that to supplement school is prudent.

I know parents whose children have a wonderful life. They enjoy a lot of fun, family, and activities and they routinely have academic practice. For my family, I asked my kids to devote Sundays from about 4:00 - 7:00 p.m. to academics. If they had nothing pressing to work on, we used the time to engage in something of their choice in the area of writing. It was a time we all had. It did not interfere with sports, sleepovers, or skiing. It worked for us. A client whose oldest daughter came to me in the first grade with a reading comprehension problem is now at an Ivy League college on the east coast – yet another example of an "average student" that rose to excellence with perseverance and hard work because of practice, family culture, an involved mother, a clever use of competition, and positive encouragement. Intelligence is secondary to that. Her mother made binders of weak areas and test prep practice for the International Baccalaureate schools which they attended. She gave them a rigorous and excellent education and then also supplemented their confidence with practice in a supportive non-graded safe way.

It is amazing to create habits that have such an impact on one's future. I am a passionate mother and educator. Math and literacy skills are essential. Parents are every child's first and most important teacher.

To further give you a better understanding about writing, let's look at ninth-grade and twelfth-grade writing standards side by side to know where the American education process is taking your child.

Writing is therapeutic. Giving a child a journal for private writing is often a comfort to growing children. Their privacy should be respected. I encourage you to take what your child is writing seriously. If they are writing dark thoughts, they must feel that way, as it is not typical. If they are writing violent thoughts, it is a big warning sign to share with a professional psychologist. If they are conveying desperation, or any other concerning tone, it is like a cry for help to process these emotions. Honor the writing and remember it is personal to people. Compliment first and then softly ask questions and seek to further understand their intentions.

My hope is that you are motivated to grow writing in your child's student tool kit. Do not lament about where they are at this time but begin the process. I recommend you save each piece in a special binder, in plastic sheet protectors. You are saving evidence of the growth and documenting the learning. Showing it to a good teacher, can help them help your child much faster. It is like saving a bit of their innocent youth to peek at later and feel happy, and very nostalgic.

Just as valuable as their art, is your child's writing. Cherish the writing in all the phases. If your child is in middle school or high school allow them to keep their writing in a special binder to save their work and be able to enjoy looking back and feeling proud. Teens are in an egocentric brain stage and to ask them to write about themselves is often a hook to get them involved, which is motivated by their brain development stage.

Students who have abandonment issues or who have been punished by writing need sensitivity often to express themselves in writing. Students who feel only criticized when their writing is graded may be negatively impacted by a teacher with good intentions.

I recommend looking into a writer's workshop approach if you are a homeschool parent or someone who is taking the writing remediation task on for their child. This involves peer edits and a supportive collaborative approach to writing. The approach encourages editing skills and provides social interaction over the writing process which is often socially rewarding attention that teens enjoy. You can find many online resources on this topic.

Bottom line is that writing is an indicator in life as to your education, intelligence, and ability to communicate effectively. Writing is not to be overlooked. It is important, and undeniably valuable, so model being a functional writer to your child and ask them to read your writing. What a great conversation to create to get to know your child better and deepen your relationship, over writing. If you are a busy working parent, consider a communication journal. Write to your child thoughts or questions, and they can answer you. This is a great tool for your relationship, and for developing writing skills in an authentic way. Ask them where they would like to vacation next, or how they are feeling about something or someone. Ask them about their friendships or music preferences and see if you can use writing in a communication journal to solve disagreements or anything too emotional to comfortably discuss.

Writing on the computer has many tools to help you write well. You can use spell check and look at the recommended edits. Encourage computer writing by teaching typing. Look into a typing program to teach typing with an online log in. There are many to choose from. And if spelling is also an issue, remember I recommended www.TalkingFingers.com in the spelling chapter as a typing program that also teaches spelling from first-grade skills through third-grade skills that can be used as a jumpstart in both areas with students even as old as middle school. No, it is never too late to improve your student's writing skills.

RECAP: WRITING

- Writing is the last literacy skill to develop. This is normal.
- Students who struggle to read will also struggle to write.
- Have your writing expectations match the grade level described in this chapter where they can read independently as a guide of where to begin.
- Teaching typing promotes writing and offers support for writing development.
- Do not underestimate the expectations of various types of writing.
- Your child's writing always has room to improve.
- Authentic writing is the most engaging for your child to learn to enjoy writing.
- Writing can be therapeutic.
- Writing skills progress each year in school and it would be a big mistake to ignore them.
- Writing is a life skill, not just a school skill.

17

MATH SKILLS VERSUS NUMBER SENSE

When a student is weak in math, and math confidence, I recommend repairing their number sense. This can be described as their understanding of the size and relationship of numbers and generally what size of the number is expected after addition, subtraction, multiplication, or division of numbers. A broader understanding of number sense is a group of skills for students to work with numbers, grasping concepts like "more and less" and "larger and smaller" which sounds simple. Do not assume this when you consider which is larger, ¼ or ⅓? This is often confused.

One skill is understanding symbols that represent quantities (5 means the same thing as five) and ideas like equal, less than, and more than. Another skill is understanding the order of numbers in a list: 1st, 2nd, 3rd, etc., and the naming protocol of place value. Students with number sense have an understanding of the size difference in decimals such as 0.1 and 0.01. Struggling with number sense can lead to challenges in school and everyday life.

When a student struggles with number sense they are always unsure of the solution, a sign of eroding confidence. Without a basis to quantify and expect a certain result, errors often show this lack of realization. Number sense can be integrated into your child's or teen's life. A great place to start is to find examples of units of measure beginning as young as second grade. Unit conversions are first explored deeply in pre-algebra. Pre-algebra is typically taught in seventh grade. If you cook with your child, they will have an advantage if they know what a cup of something looks like, or what a teaspoon is as opposed to a tablespoon, or how many ounces are in a cup. Give your kids a night a week to cook for the family beginning as young as fourth grade! Kids can practice doubling or cutting a recipe in half. What a great way to experience authentic math.

If your child engages in measuring activities, they will have an advantage in several ways. First, number sense and familiarity with units of measure are both valuable and depend on exposure and experience. Look at tools that measure, and draw, walk, and drive these distances and practice estimating all of them. Do the same with units of volume: teaspoons, tablespoons, cups, pints, quarts, and gallons, and then liters and milliliters. Measure them and estimate them and compare them to each other. Cooking is great for employing these skills. Units of weight need the same attention: ton, point, ounce, grams, and kilograms. This prepares them for converting units and having a sense of what numbers to expect. Experience and exposure are what it takes to develop this very essential skill for high school math, science, and everyday life. The number of exposures depends on the individual, but you want to be able to discuss these units and hear their command of the ideas of each amount. Understanding the convenience of metric units and the common prefixes that all mean the same power of ten is also essential information. This is taught in the math curriculum beginning in fourth grade but more deeply explored in math yearly through high school. It is not going anywhere, so to master it in your child's elementary years is ideal, but never too late before they grow into an adult.

Developing a number sense with very large numbers and very small numbers alike is important. Does your student understand the size of a million relative to a billion? I love the book *How Much is a Million* by David Schwartz. I would read it to my high school algebra class. They listened with riveted eyes, enjoying the entertaining story. The graphics appeal to all ages. The book does an amazing job of showing students the relative size of a million versus a billion and is eye-opening to those who think they have a good handle on it.

Can your child multiply by ten or a hundred easily? Skip counting by different values such as twos, threes, fives, and so on is another way to understand numerical relationships. Knowing the prime factorization of numbers is a worthwhile thought for students over the fourth grade. Prime numbers are those that only have factors of "one" and "itself." Two is the only even prime, quite notable. Then there is three, five, and seven. These are all numbers that cannot be divided evenly by any number other than one and "itself." The next is eleven. But it is rarely needed when prime factoring any number. So, with the few primes, you can know most numbers and how they break down with multiplication. (See diagram.)

If you give your child this number sense, they will easily simplify fractions or square or cube roots in high school. They will understand factoring polynomials so much better than those without this number sense. Playing with numbers and understanding them and their relationships to other numbers is what grows number sense. Stop your younger students from adding and subtracting on their fingers by teaching them to think around the nearest ten. Help them to recognize all the pairs of numbers that add up to ten and then to use surplus numbers to understand the "ones" place. For example, 8 plus 6 can be thought of as 8 plus 2 is 10. There are 4 left over, so the answer is 14. No fingers, bravo. This is often referred to as chunking to ten. For younger children, familiarity with the *hundreds chart* can make some essential patterns visible. Adding ten on the hundred chart is merely going down one row, which increases the 10s digit.

Students need to be curious. My favorite Albert Einstein quote is, "I have no special talent. I am only passionately curious." In order to motivate this curiosity, pose a question, a challenge, or a competition. Cleverness makes the experience fun. Try to estimate the weights of items that can be weighed on a household scale and kitchen scale. Try to pose three quantities where two of which weigh the same and the third does not. Find the one that does not. Let them guess, and weigh to confirm the amounts. Walk a mile and understand how far one hundred yards is on a football field. Estimate and measure. You can make a scavenger hunt describing clues in units that you are learning. To get to the end, they will have thought through many number questions, and all be excited to be doing it to the next clue.

There are computational expectations involved in the number sense. No counting on your fingers, because when you realize the ten tens that make one hundred, you can "chunk" to tens when you add or subtract or multiply. For example, you can add 17 plus 6 by thinking of it like it takes 17 plus 3 makes 20, and there are 3 left, so 23 is the total. This would be mastered by second graders without fingers ideally. All third graders need to skip count quickly by 2s, 3s, 4s, and 5s to begin to be proficient at multiplication. Then the multiplication facts are not just memorized but experienced in knowing each set of numbers. When a student does this, they notice the commonalities in the skip counting patterns and realize they say 24 when they skip count by 2s, 3s, 4s, and 6s. In later experiences, they add 12s when they are thinking in larger numbers. No fingers and skip counting ease, are essential skills.

Next, you can move on to more complex computational strategies. This includes being aware of totals. If you add two numbers less than one hundred each, the total must be less than how much? The response should be two hundred. Younger students can use a one-hundred grid to use their finger to physically point out how addition and chunking with larger numbers works. For example, 47 plus 24. Start at 47 and add the twenty by jumping down two rows. Now, you are 67. Then add the 4 1s as 3 to get to you 70, so 71. To estimate this, 50 and 25 is 75 and so it should be less than those overestimates. Doing one to five of these is much better than counting fingers through many more. The mental math exercise is progress and foundational to number sense.

Thinking of money requires counting skills of 5s, 10s, and 25s. Counting money and "paying" for things are excellent exercises. You can give your child the task of purchasing several items with a limited amount of money. They need to estimate a total and tax. Overestimating 10 percent for tax is easy to do and effective. I love to teach high school students a convenient way to tip is to double the tax, since the tax is just under 8 percent and a minimum tip in America is about double the tax or 15 percent. Number sense is fun to teach in "sale thinking." Interaction with money and numbers under the guise of budgeting money is also an excellent exercise. Do not shield your children from money transactions. It is "consumer number sense" to understand how much things cost and how much is typically earned. The reality of costs and understanding the idea of inflation are minimal number sense skills to give your child.

Time increments and the passing of time are essential number sense skills. Many children struggle with learning to read a clock. Most students learn this at home and school reinforces clock reading. If school is the only exposure and discussion, the result is much different from the outcome parents see when they discuss clock reading with their children each day, during different time cues. Your child needs a working understanding of the five minutes between each of the numbers on a clock, yielding the sixty minutes in an hour.

After reading a clock is accomplished, elapsed time questions are the next idea to master. The movie begins at 1:45 p.m. and runs for two hours and forty minutes. What time will the movie be over? This type of thinking is required in planning successive estimates of appointments. It is important to discuss elapsed weeks, months, and years.

As students grow, the discussions of number sense turn to more complex ideas than those involved in the formula of distance equals rate times time. You can use them quite effectively with regard to teens who drive. How far can you go on a tank of gas if you get fifteen miles per gallon and your car holds twenty-five gallons? Thinking of this relationship and having the units make sense utilizes the discussion of the units earlier and then applies it and adds multiplying estimation skills and a formula relationship. These skills begin in fifth grade and continue through high school and are a focus on college entrance exams. Studying assumes number sense as a child is curiously interacting with their world. Parents who do interact with numbers for their children in an effort to care for them and serve them are actually hurting them by denying their exposure to these thoughts.

Manipulatives increase the growth of number sense. This is beneficial for younger students or those older ones who struggle with mental addition. A system of "ten" blocks and unit blocks that represent numbers often helps students grow into their number sense skills. When you are adding and have too many unit blocks, they can trade ten of them in for a "ten" block which is how addition works. The abacus was a classic visual addition tool and is quite handy. Toddler areas often sell them still.

CONVERSION FACTORS

When students begin to learn positive and negative numbers in pre-algebra or middle school math, they learn to have a sense of whether to expect a positive or negative number as an answer. My recommendation when learning to add or subtract positive and negative numbers is to visualize a number line. For example: -6 + 10. If you begin on the first number, in this case, -6, then use the operation to determine the direction. Addition goes to the right where numbers get bigger, and subtraction goes to the left, where numbers get smaller. So, we begin at -6 and then go to the right ten units, which clearly leaves us at +4. This solid number sense leaves no doubt what the answer is. Some middle school teachers teach rules like, "When the signs are different, subtract the numbers and make the sign of the larger." This is what I call "monkey see, monkey do," math. There is no understanding of what is happening.

Unfortunately, it is all too common for high school teachers to get students with little number sense and memorization of silly "rules" that fail under stress because they are not backed by any number sense! Kindergarten through eighth grade teachers are mainly reading specialists, and some obtain an algebra endorsement, but most are not overly math confident themselves. I might offend some in this statement and there are exceptions certainly. My recommendation for details and a champion of teaching number sense is Marilyn Burns. She has many books out on this topic and many examples and lessons to work through tied to grade-level standards. Check her out on her blog: http://www.marilynburnsmathblog.com/. Her work has improved mathematics education.

My first math department chairman, while I was teaching public school math, was a master at teaching patterns and explanations for high school level math reasoning. I learned how to teach students to think and have math number sense within the high school math curriculum from geometry to the unit circle in precalculus.

In geometry, students learn shapes. They also learn to calculate area and perimeters. The measurements of the shapes should promote an estimation of those measures. Students should understand one-, two-, and three-dimensional measurements and their corresponding units to the first, second, and third degrees correspondingly. They should realize that distance is a one-dimensional measurement. It takes one measurement and that is one dimensional. The area is two-dimensional and to measure the basic rectangle is the simplest example of that and the units are feet squared, for example. You measure the length and width of a rectangle and that is the two dimensions required to calculate the area which is A=LxW. Volume is a three-dimensional measurement. And when you think of a cube, you need the length, width, and depth to calculate the three-dimensional measurement of the space within it. The units would be inches cubed (or to the third power) for a three-dimensional measurement, for example. The geometric shapes and general formulas should be familiar by seventh grade.

Some families commonly discuss all of these math and number topics as a part of their interactions and conversations. Then there are families that would never include these discussions in their interactions. But the difficulty is obvious to your child's teacher. What is not taught at home is expected to be taught in school. This exposure directly affects students in school, and I recommend that there is no age limit to conversations about numbers.

To help you know how to meet your child where they are in your newly motivated

mathematical conversations let's talk about the stages of mathematical reasoning children move through. These are sequential and always progress in the order I am about to overview. You can investigate your child's or teen's reasoning ability by starting at the beginning and seeing how far you can verify as being a skill they possess.

Many questions were answered by French psychologist Jean Piaget in 1952 when he published his groundbreaking theory on cognitive development in children. There are four cognitive stages of childhood development as identified by Jean Piaget which can be described as follows, and the ages noted are typical of each stage:

Sensorimotor Stage: birth through about two years. During this stage, children learn about the world through their senses and the manipulation of objects. An additional characteristic of children at this stage is their ability to link numbers to objects, according to Piaget's 1977 work. Another activity that could enhance the mathematical development of children at this stage connects mathematics and literature. There is a long list of children's books that embed mathematical content and provide a delightful math experience bringing number sense as a bonus. Because children at this stage can link numbers to objects, your child can benefit from seeing pictures of objects and their respective numbers simultaneously. Along with the mathematical benefits, children's books can contribute to the development of their reading skills and comprehension. A resource will be shared with you for a long list of these books, located on my web page. (See my Thank You page following the conclusion of this book for details on how to access this list.) For an older student who has not been exposed to math in this entertaining, storytelling way, a favorite trick of mine is to ask an older student to read these to a younger child. This gives them a purpose for experiencing what they missed while entertaining a child. This is a win-win experience for both the older and younger child.

Preoperational Stage: ages two through seven. During this stage, children develop memory and imagination. They are also able to understand the concept of the past and future as well as think symbolically. There is a lack of logic associated with this stage of development. Rational thought is not typical. Your child will relate unrelated events, and he or she will see objects as possessing life, which we view as adorable as parents. Typically, your child does not understand the idea of point of view beyond their own. Your child's perceptions in this stage of development are generally restricted to one aspect or dimension of an object at the expense of the other aspects. For example, Piaget tested the concept of conservation by pouring the same amount of liquid into two similar containers. When the liquid from one container is poured into a third, wider container, the level is lower, and the child thinks there is less liquid in the third container. Thus, your child is using one dimension, height, as the basis for his judgment of another dimension, volume. Teaching your child in this stage of development should focus on questioning about characterizing objects. For example, when students investigate geometric shapes, you could ask your child to group the shapes according to similar characteristics. Here is an example of what question you could ask: "How did you decide where each object belonged? Are there other ways to group these together?" Engaging in discussion or interactions with your child will help him or her think about the numbers in new ways.

Concrete Operational Stage: ages seven through eleven. During this stage, your child will become more aware of external events, as well as the feelings of others, outside of their own feelings. They become less egocentric and begin to understand that not everyone shares their thoughts, beliefs, or feelings. The stage is remarkable cognitive growth when your child's development of language and acquisition of basic skills accelerate dramatically. Children at this stage use their senses in order to know; they can now consider two or three dimensions simultaneously instead of successively. For example, in the liquids experiment, if the child notices the lowered level of the liquid, he also notices the dish is wider, seeing both dimensions at the same time. Additionally, seriation and classification are the two logical operations that develop during this stage, according to Piaget, and both are essential for understanding number concepts. Seriation is the ability to order objects according to increasing or decreasing length, weight, or volume. On the other hand, classification involves grouping objects on the basis of a common characteristic. Hands-on experiences and multiple ways of representing a mathematical solution can be ways of fostering the development of this cognitive stage. The importance of hands-on activities cannot be overemphasized at this stage. These activities provide your child a pathway to make abstract ideas concrete. Because concrete experiences are needed, you might use manipulatives to explore concepts such as place value and addition and subtraction. The abacus is still sold as a toddler toy but is a powerful manipulative for playing with numbers and understanding the base ten number system. Here are a few ideas you can find online or at a teacher store in your area: pattern blocks, Cuisenaire rods, algebra tiles, algebra cubes, geoboards, tangrams, counters, dice, and spinners. Tangrams feel like a fun puzzle and kids love to match a given pattern which is very helpful for special awareness skills. But you are not limited to these teaching materials. You can also use household items in activities such as paper folding and cutting or coins or cotton balls. These experiences help lay the foundation for more advanced mathematical thinking. You can build their mathematical confidence by giving them a way to test and confirm their reasoning. They learn to predict and confirm ideas, using these items. "How many is half of these objects? How can you find out for sure?" For example, it may be difficult for children to conceptualize how a four-by-six-inch rectangle built with wooden tiles relates to four multiplied by six, or four groups of six. You could help your child make connections by showing how the rectangles can be separated into four rows of six tiles each and by demonstrating how the rectangle is another representation of four groups of six. Providing various mathematical representations provides multiple paths for making ideas meaningful. Allowing your child to present mathematical solutions in multiple ways such as by using symbols, graphs, tables, and words is very powerful at this stage for building understanding.

Formal Operational Stage: ages eleven and older. During this stage, your child wants to use logic to solve problems, view the world around them, and plan for the future. Your child at this stage is capable of forming a hypothesis and deducing possible consequences, allowing him or her to construct his or her own mathematics. Your child will typically begin to develop abstract thought patterns where reasoning is executed using pure symbols as seen in algebraic concepts. For example, the formal operational learner can solve $x + 2x = 9$ without having to refer to a concrete situation presented by the teacher, such as, "Jamel ate a certain number of candies. His sister ate twice as many. Together they ate nine. How many did Jamel eat?" Reasoning skills within this stage refer to the mental process involved in the generalizing and evaluating of logical arguments and include clarification, inference, evaluation, and application. Clarification requires students to identify and analyze elements of a problem, allowing them to decipher the information needed in solving a problem. By encouraging students to extract relevant information from a problem statement, parents can help their children to enhance their mathematical understanding. Children at this stage are developmentally ready to make inductive and deductive inferences in mathematics. Deductive inferences involve reasoning from general concepts to specific instances. On the other hand, inductive inferences would include choosing which geometry theorem applies to a certain proof from all the theorems learned. The process of thinking is important beyond knowing how Euclid deduced geometry so long ago. Evaluation involves using criteria to judge the adequacy of a problem solution. Evaluation leads to formulating hypotheses about future events, assuming one's problem solving is correct thus far. Application involves students connecting mathematical concepts to real-life situations. For example, the student could apply his knowledge of rational equations to the following situation: "You can plant your spring garden in five hours. Your sister can plant the spring garden in eight hours. How long will it take you to plant the garden working together?"

Number sense is the foundation of math confidence. I have devoted a whole chapter to this idea for making this point. Whenever you are doing math, you need to have a sense of the expected result so if you are way off, you realize it by common sense. You now know generally how to approach your child's growth of number sense and mathematical learning at whatever stage they may be in developmentally.

RECAP: MATH SKILLS VERSUS NUMBER SENSE

- Your child's brain develops to relate to numbers in stages.
- Check where your child is or may be stuck by beginning to test concepts from the first stage until you reach their maximum thinking ability.
- Then you will know how to impact them to grow in their thinking skills exactly.
- Hands-on experiences in measuring distances, volumes, liquids, and weight are essential. Such exposure will help your student to understand unit conversions in math and science.
- Having math stories read to your child with picture books illustrating math concepts is a very valuable and positive math experience you can provide to your child at almost any age.
- Have your older child read these illustrated math stories to a younger child to provide the missing exposure in a nonthreatening way for teens.
- Number sense is the backbone of strong math students and is very worthwhile to develop and grow.

18

20/20 IS NOT THE WHOLE STORY

As a reading specialist, I have worked with students of different ages with various reasons for their reading problems. Vision is one of the leading issues I find. There also is a genetic propensity. Can they see the letters accurately? I look for the ability to smoothly run the eyes across a line of text, and track to the next line. I notice if the eyes are aligned with each other when reading. Does the reader stumble on a word? After I help them, do they continue to stumble on that same word? Is there poor visual memory? Is the child rubbing their eyes or yawning while reading? The point is, I watch them read.

I watch the students move through their space and how they visually find the chair to sit in it, or visually grab a pencil with a reach. Their eyes are working, and I am looking for how well they can perform the job of gross and fine motor skills. I also listen for any complaints the reader may have, such as headaches, a feeling of eyestrain, or if words are moving around on the page. Can you imagine how difficult it would be to read then? Does the student complain of double vision?

These are the surface-level things I begin noticing when I meet with a client and continue to note over time. I look for patterns, consistencies over time, consistent errors over time, and the circumstances that they occur in. I will check each part of the issue separately like how a mechanic goes through an engine. Yes, it is receiving gas. And yes, it is combusting properly. My job is to figure out why they have a reading problem and decide what needs to be done to resolve each issue. It always involves missing content they need to learn. But I continue to be fascinated by the unique combinations of issues I find.

Remember, a person's view is limited by their perception of the world. I have had students who have sharp peripheral vision but struggle to see "in the middle" where reading occurs. I have had students that cannot discriminate the details of the printed word longer than about five letters at a twelve-point size. He would guess the endings of words because he could not work to see each letter until the end of longer words. This student learned to cope by looking at the overall shapes of words to get by and recognize them until I noticed his issue. If a student is seeing words above and below the line they are reading move around, how difficult would that be to focus on reading?

When a child has outbursts, usually emotional or anger outbursts, when the reading task gets difficult, there is a clue. The brain can feel so overstimulated or overwhelmed that it is an unsolvable problem, and an outburst is all that is left. Refusal to read or do homework is another thing to note. Think about it. The text is very large in kindergarten and first grade with only a few words on each page. Then by first grade, there are several lines on the page under the pictures and by third grade there might be paragraphs and fewer pictures on pages. So, the text gets smaller and smaller each year, as the sentence structure increases in length as well as the words. Also, the punctuation becomes more involved, and that is more to notice for the eyes. By fourth grade, the text is very small, and there are pages and pages of reading. Generally, this is called vision stress, but the forms are as unique as people. There are combinations of skills that present in varying degrees in each of my diagnosed clients over several decades. The issues that can be helped with vision therapy sometimes can be very difficult to observe but the symptoms add up.

Who should be considered for a functional eye exam by a specialist in neuro and developmental optometry? A person who regularly exhibits anything I mentioned regularly. Vision therapy can be a component of the issue with dyslexia, lazy eye, strabismus, autistic spectrum, ADD or ADHD, and athletes.

The treatment is therapy or training designed to strengthen visual performance. It can benefit people of all ages and can develop at different stages of life. Vision therapy crosses over with occupational therapy. But the factor that differentiates vision therapy is that it exclusively uses lenses, prisms, flippers, and anaglyphic (3-D) filters. Other tools would be patches, electronic targets, timing mechanisms, specialized card games, building activities, and more. I have witnessed powerful changes in visual perception and spatial awareness with clients who receive vision therapy while I am coaching them.

There are binocular vision problems which include these particular dysfunctions. Convergence insufficiency is a reduced tendency to converge eyes when looking at things nearby. Convergence excess is an excessive tendency to converge eyes when looking at things that are nearby. Then there is accommodative insufficiency where there is a reduced tendency to focus eyes when looking nearby. There is accommodative excess where there is an excessive tendency to focus eyes when looking nearby. The strabismus, which I mentioned earlier, is a binocular vision issue. In this matter, the visual posture of the two eyes is far enough out of alignment that visual fusion does not take place.

Fusion is the brain's ability to gather information received from each eye separately and form a single, unified image. Double vision is the result if this is unable to occur. The brain subconsciously suppresses or inhibits the vision in one eye to avoid confusion. Lastly, the "lazy eye" is often a case where the favored eye compensates for the amblyopic eye so the child or adult may be unaware of the problem. Poor depth perception is also a common association with amblyopia. The obvious lazy eye is not required to be present with amblyopia. Treatment is often delayed because the child appears to be fine. This condition is easiest to treat in the earlier stages.

There are also functional vision problems. The student may not be able to multitask and keep all aspects of their vision working simultaneously. The speed, endurance, accuracy, or agility of vision may be impeded. There could be visual attention problems.

Go over the following checklist and see if any of the following applies to your child:

- Blur when looking up close
- Headaches when looking up close
- Falls asleep when reading
- Writes uphill or downhill
- Poor reading comprehension
- Holds reading material very close
- Clumsy/knocks things over
- Homework takes "forever"
- Low IQ "processing speed"
- Reverses b/ d and p/ q
- Smart in everything but school
- Double vision when reading
- Words run together when reading
- Skips/ repeats lines when reading
- Tilts head/ closes one eye when reading
- Omits small words when reading
- Avoids sports or games
- Labeled "lazy," "slow," "ADD," or "dyslexic"
- Reverses was/ saw, on/ no, or 12/ 21
- Poor handwriting
- Struggles with reading/writing, better at math/science
- Low IQ "perceptual reasoning"

If your child is experiencing more than one of these problems, your child should have a Functional Performance Vision assessment from a certified optometrist in the area of neuro and developmental optometry. The occurrence of some vision issue in the general population is that one in every fourth person is affected in some way. That is 25 percent of the people in this world have this negatively influencing their ability to visually interpret their world in some way. The occurrence in prison in America is nine out of ten, or 90 percent of incarcerated people have this visual deficit causing them to feel stupid or incapable in the current education setting. This is a shocking statistic and the National PTA in 1999 passed a resolution calling upon all public schools to screen for the kinds of "visual skill deficiencies" which behavior optometrists treat. Keep your heart focused on the love and fairness to the learner. Is it OK to have the learner so disabled when it is fixable? For any learner to not be able to visually see while learning it is so neurologically overwhelming, the push to a life of crime is understandable pain to me.

I want to tell you a story of my first awareness of this very hidden issue. As a reading specialist, I had a very extensive curriculum at a school well known for their literacy program with world-renowned authors and researchers. Never was I taught about vision-related issues to watch out for when working with a struggling reader. That seems ludicrous to me now.

I was working with a very shy introverted boy who was a second grader for a year, and the progress was not being retained as expected. He avoided working on reading, it would seem, and sometimes got upset when it came time to put the effort a typical second grader should be able to put forth. He was unable and unwilling to do so. He was sad often too, overwhelmed with the simple task of making words from the phonemes he struggled to remember. After a day when he complained about a headache, I recommended the client get the eyes examined. This client took their child to a developmental ophthalmologist and they found conversance insufficiency along with some divergence issues also. This child was not able to sustain reading without considerable strain and stress. The student participated in vision stress therapy with committed parent follow-up and attendance to the sessions. The commitment takes perseverance and follow-through and interruption to the working day of one parent or caregiver to get him to the sessions. There are also support exercises to do between appointments at home, which aid the process. It is not about completing a certain number of sessions; it is about the rate at which you can strengthen and teach the necessary skills to the visual system. This boy's reading ability, fluency, and spelling improved like a jump once he completed the therapy. He was able to utilize and make brain space for using what he was taught. The brain was not strained or overwhelmed, and it could see, think, decide, and read promptly. It was an amazing case that opened my eyes.

That boy graduated from high school in 2020. He has never struggled in school and was accepted into a four-year university. His ability to participate in reading was changed by his vision therapy. This science became available in the 1970s. I found out from my mother that the school district where we lived in the San Francisco Bay Area offered to test and found that my brother also had a similar diagnosis to my nephew. He was given therapy in school and also overcame a reading problem with intervention. He now flies airplanes as a captain for a major airline. He has trained pilots overseas and is a talented aviator.

I know a girl whose grandmother is her after-school caregiver. The grandmother, a retired English middle school teacher, is an active, vivacious, passionate woman. She is well-known, well loved, and widely respected in her town. Her grandmother read *to* her and *with* her throughout her whole life, patiently reteaching school lessons. But even with all this effort, this girl was a poor speller and had comprehension struggles. A complete literacy assessment revealed that her spelling was the main gap in this bright student's results. Her aptitude was at first-grade level when she was in the fourth grade. She also had trouble tracking and would easily lose her place. She consistently made errors at the end of words. This is another sign that the eyes cannot finish the visual discriminating task of the letters. There was a mild vision issue alongside a language processing issue regarding most all structural rules taught in school. With a combination of vision therapy by a developmental optometrist and spelling instruction by a literacy specialist, this student is now excelling in school.

Parents cannot condemn themselves for "missing" something when a loving educator with daily contact with a degree in teaching English could not find the key to her own grandchild! This is a guilt-free zone for parents. I also value the resilience that inevitably occurs in a struggle. But a lifelong struggle is unnecessary. Answers are available to so many of our struggling learners. This vision issue is too important to not be included in this book.

RECAP: 20/ 20 IS NOT THE WHOLE STORY

- Vision is a complex process from the eyes through the visual cortex to the brain.
- Vision stress is often a hidden problem that appears to be laziness or avoidance.
- Vision stress often causes emotional outbursts. The child is unaware that their brain is overwhelmed with the task of seeing, often presenting while reading.
- The size of the text decreases as the grade levels increase. This explains why early readers are OK until the size of the text is fourteen or less.
- Do not assume your child's perception is the same as yours. Perception is truly in the eye of the beholder.
- Vision stress is treatable with therapy and does not have to be a lifelong condition.

STRATEGIES TO TEACH

19

STRATEGIES FOR BOREDOM

The key is to understand the claim of "boredom" or the bored behavior of a struggling student. The claim of boredom by students is a cry for help or attention or both. It is a loaded word that implies being let down by what is happening. There is something that I refer to as a gifted underachiever. This bright person is not being challenged to feel like they are succeeding at anything they value and over time it robs them of self-worth. Doing this work with so little challenge becomes something they rebel against and find very little value in doing. It is sad to say that if a gifted student is unable to have their needs met for a challenge, the student can have quite a negative reaction to education.

I have seen many gifted students enter the trades for autonomy after being forced to learn cooperatively much slower than preferred. Often this situation is not in the awareness of the gifted student themselves. They feel unsuccessful in school for their lack of interest or tolerance for the work expected of them. Could any of this apply to your struggling student?

Giftedness comes in many forms, and it is so hidden sometimes, even to the child. Frustration becomes the dominating experience, and what is underneath is lost in that label or behavior.

Everyone gets one childhood, so it is important to get it right. Scars from childhood influence one's life and being a failure in school is not a happy memory. Tackling your fears and challenges and making progress is something to be proud of, embracing your individualism and living what makes you happy and fulfilled is life's goal. With gifted kids, it may be hidden in a one-size-fits-all restrictive system. Consider your children not through the lens of your childhood or what you think of them but for who they are becoming. Being open to who they are and loving them with what you find is a gift every child dreams of, especially a frustrated gifted student who is in so much pain they are underachieving to cope. Maybe this chapter will help you help another parent see their child. That is my hope – that this helps someone. Ask and see what you get when you think they feel safe enough to share their truth.

"If you are bored, I get there is an unsatisfied talent or interest you are not exercising as much as you wish, or you are annoyed at the learning speed of those around you in class. What is it for you? Explain how you feel to me. I promise to listen and care."

This might be how you could start the conversation. I envision sitting by a mountain stream, but that is in my perfect world. I just love the peace of nature. It seems to bring out the truth and basics in us all. But I think the moment you try to have this conversation with your child, no matter the age, should be well chosen, and a time of connectedness would be a great choice.

You can have a gifted student who is working so hard with inefficient strategies and they are not achieving success. They do not realize that if they approach school differently, they may have a vastly different outcome. This student gets discouraged easily and cannot see a way to change. They need a learning coach who can help them be efficient in their approach.

Giftedness is the need to be challenged. The problem of boredom is one that no one seems too concerned about. If your child is bored, they are one of the greatest at risk. I say that because you are not seeing the best version of your child when they are feeling this way. Boredom is extremely frustrating and is as damaging or more than when you are unable to do the work because of being too low skilled. Boredom due to high skills and nothing challenging you is very anger-causing and isolating. There are so many students at risk by being low that very often the gifted student gets forgotten about or minimized.

In this book, I am talking about just the right amount of challenge when I say, "At their independent level." If you can do it on your own, and the challenge is perceived as manageable, then a student will feel motivated to participate. When is it too hard or too easy? When a student learns quickly and has to stay for the rest of the class to catch up to where they are, over and over. Can you see how that might feel?

If you have a student seeking more challenge, that is not a request to be taken lightly. That might be how they are expressing frustration or exasperation. How long will that feeling be present? Maybe your student is "gifted" and underserved. What is the learning capacity or desire for learning within your child? Some parents really need to ask that question and not assume that "the product" of their child's grade is a fit for them. I am sure that some parents reading this book have a gifted child who may seem to be a struggling student because of lack of engagement. If the challenge seems mundane and "stupid," a bright student may stop participating in complaining about the lack of value. Does this sound familiar? Are their foundational skills above grade level (reading for sure and maybe math too) or above the seventy-fifth percentile on standardized tests? Maybe they do not really take the test? I have seen that too.

The fluency exercise recommended earlier using the textbook would yield a very strong result. The comprehension questions might have allowed you to hear some insightful thoughts, proving they are more than keeping up with the text. So, you may already have an inkling that boredom might be a part of the problem.

Another characteristic of gifted students is that they were early readers and seem to learn quickly, a bit ahead of their peers. They remember what has been learned. Another way to say that is they have a higher-than-normal retention rate. Average retention rates are about 80 percent (if learning was in optimal conditions), but gifted kids can have higher rates than that! They often have passionate interests in one or several topics they would prefer to learn about other than school-directed learning. They surprise you with the ability to understand complex concepts.

Does your student ace tests without doing any homework? They do what is convenient often but not much else, and then the tests are very strong anyway. Teachers usually allow these kids to fly under the radar because they are showing competence. The power struggle over doing the assigned work may be about how this is not challenging and therefore not worth their time in their value system. This is often misunderstood as obstinate, or "being a difficult child or teen." Let's play detective here.

If they used to ace tests and not do homework, but now they are failing all tests and not doing homework, I would heed the advice in the chapter titled "Drastic Times Call for Drastic Measures." Time for a change.

Gifted students can often be very precocious in some areas and maybe average in other ways as compared to their peers. They tend to resist cooperative learning because they see the task clearer and faster than their peers. They might be emotional and get upset easily, because of the sustained frustration. Often, they have an advanced morality or sense of fairness. Gifted students have an advanced sense of humor and often daydream as a coping strategy. They are keen observers and usually do not miss a thing. A self-taught reader is a definite sign, as this is not typical.

A gifted student is sensitive. They are typically empathetic and caring. They appreciate and recognize beauty in common and uncommon places. The gifted student might be musical. They might have some skills they have developed that are not typical for their age, more like adult skills acquired through their interests.

Gifted students may be perfectionists. Their teachers often expect high performance all the time and hesitate to reward anything but excellence from a high-performing student. A perfectionist believes that what they can do is more important than who they are as a core belief. They get too much praise for being smart, and they fear they will lose that if they do not perform perfectly. Psychologists say some perfectionists who are self-critical to a fault have an "imposter syndrome" where the student does not believe they deserve their accolades and each challenge that may not feel easy, like most things, becomes very scary. Avoid the phrase, "Always do your very best," because it feeds the problem. Instead say, "Put forth your best effort." Reward the effort and not the result.

To help a perfectionist and very bright student, it is important to help them learn that it is OK to struggle with some things. They do not need to feel bad. It is rare for them, and they fear not being the smart person everyone thinks they are. Maybe you also teach them that when something is not easy, they have strategies to try. Do not panic or feel bad, but use creative problem-solving ideas. This brainstorming technique is a replacement for the panic when a perfectionist thinks they cannot be perfect. It replaces the pressure for the right answer with a step in the right direction, which is great and should be rewarded as much or more than the easy things for them.

TYPES OF GIFTED CHILDREN

There are types of giftedness and to try to name all types would be impossible. I can talk about the types I have met. First, there is a creative child, who needs to express new ideas often. This child rebels against routine and seeks independence and time to be creative. This need they have is passionate and will seek a balance with their creative energy. The creative thinker encourages them to explore their environment from many perspectives. Look for the creative outlets that fuel their daydreams between the times they can create. Allow and honor their daydreaming when they have free time. It is precious to them. Provide open-ended challenges of their choosing where there is no one right answer or outcome to explore. Allow them to participate in decision-making where possible in the family. Explore the fine arts and music. Creatives feel blocked when they perceive they much succeed at everything they do. It is also blocking when they cannot work alone. When their creativity is perceived as wasting time or viewed with disdain by adults, it is hurtful. The worst strategy is to be authoritarian and tell them to do as they are told, and this is also hampering how they operate.

Some gifted students are unique in so many ways and it may not be something noticed, yet. Be open to the source of your child's desires and intellectual needs. I don't like the word "gifted" because it implies others are not, which is against my philosophy. But the positive part about the word is that it implies something is special about them and needs to be nurtured.

There are kinesthetically gifted children, who dance around and move with joy. This is a type of "giftedness." Let them develop this after school. Let them shine in a way that confirms they are special. Good grades and maybe a change in schooling strategy can promote their dancing, ballet, or downhill ski racing, whatever it is. Let them live their gift while their body is young and asking them to try. I have experience with this passionate athlete who plays on the edge of what is possible and is so talented that it justifies the support around them. I would say that you need to operate within their talent level. Are they good enough for a private competitive situation or performance-based program? Are they Olympic material, based on professional coaching advice? Are they a talented fencer? I used to start and stop school for my athletes based on their competition challenges. Not having the pressure of school interfering with races gave them an edge. These athletes were children, but I saw how they pushed themselves. Their parents often encouraged less intensity, but the kids were winning and at the top of their sport. It is something to see. Some sponsored kids are able to afford education alternatives, but there is always a financial demand for this lifestyle. Creative solutions, I say. Do the best you can do, please, parents.

Negotiate school engagement, and best efforts and grades will be rewarded by more of the desired thinking time. You might consider changing to an online school platform. Your student may master the lessons and enjoy the self-paced opportunity with more time and freedom to pursue their passions. This is something to consider when you identify a need for more time in their desired passion. I can recommend kindergarten through twelfth-grade-online, charter schools that are available in most states. I have used it for gifted students to differentiate and eliminate frustration.

I have witnessed gifted students allowed to pursue a self-paced learning environment (in one or more subjects) accomplish up to three years of learning in one year with excited abandon. We filled their schedule with AP classes they otherwise would not have had time for, and they graduated with their peers. Since I was the school administrator, I did not have to jump through any hoops. It was awesome to give kids what they needed when I had a school. That was the best part.

You can have a gifted in one area child and a learning-disabled aspect of their performance. That is possible. Humans are complex beings, and I am often surprised at what needs attention to heal a student's struggles. I feel like the motto "never say never" is applicable.

I want to say here that generally, schools, districts, and states identify "gifted" students differently. The lack of consistency in this identification process is very much the case. Also, the narrow group of students that a district chooses to offer many services for is not necessarily all who need them.

If you aim to take a stance to work with their school to adjust the curriculum flow, you can ask to allow them the opportunity to "pass" out of the curriculum with pre-testing. Your student can choose an alternative course of study that broadens the curriculum and possibly benefits the class. This has helped give the gifted student some control where they had none. If that is not enough, consider an alternative learning situation, like putting an education specialist in charge of a more customized curriculum.

RECAP: STRATEGIES FOR BOREDOM

- Some gifted students are so frustrated that they choose to be underachievers.
- Not being challenged over time erodes the gifted learner's self-worth.
- The child's gifts may be hidden. Both the parent and the child may be unaware this is the problem.
- Finding just the right amount of challenge for a gifted student is the goal.
- Check their reading ability by moving from grade level up to where they cannot be fluent and understand concepts presented.
- Self-paced learning is often a huge relief to someone feeling held back in the classroom setting.
- Gifted students do not understand why others do not get concepts that are obvious to them. They often feel added frustration at the expectation for them to explain things to other students.
- The gifted student who is under-challenged has as much or more frustration than a struggling student.

2 0

STRATEGIES FOR REMEMBERING

I love talking about memory and memory retrieval to students and empowering them to learn how to use their unique, wondrous, and individual brain. Academics is about Deep Learning. It is the tool we need to be thinkers. Understanding big ideas, making connections, and being communicators demands education. How we can learn something that is useful to us because we understand it fully and can use that information when our life calls upon the need for it – that is the idea of ideal learning. Everything new we learn is best remembered when it is attached to something we already know. Making connections is our brain's main strategy, and it is how we retrieve information best.

Deep Learning also entails working independently on an idea, making progress, and understanding it. It requires working collaboratively with ideas and thoughts and moving them forward. By listening to others and talking in conversational turns, knowledge expands. To be involved in Deep Learning, students must collect the information they know and gather opinions they have formed about the things they "know." This higher level of learning engagement requires confidence in the ability to assess what you know.

In this chapter, we will explore how learning becomes memorable, how to study and how to learn where your individual strengths and weaknesses are regarding the use of your memory. When I work with students, this is the one thing that benefits all levels of learners, whether you are a struggling learner needing to be retaught critical content to raise your basic math or literacy skills, or a gifted frustrated learner that is seeking enrichment. All students must learn how to confidently study and remember or recall information when they need to; in both practice and testing settings which include higher stakes and more stress.

Our brain decides to remember something in the first few seconds of exposure to the information. There are four steps to using one's memory: encoding, storing, retrieving, and forgetting. This is the cycle of our conscious experience.

The subconscious experience is completely different. The subconscious brain is the one that makes sure our heart is beating, makes sure we are breathing, and is "on" 24/ 7. It is recording every aspect of our life experience. It is not happening like a tape recorder, but rather like the information we experience hits a blender once we perceive it inside our brain. Yes, we know from brain imaging research that when anything new happens and we take in information from all of our senses, the sight, smell, touch, and sound of the experience, our brain is active in many areas putting pieces into places where it relates to other past experiences. New information is the trickiest. You need to relate it to something you already know to help it have a place in long-term memory storage. When we are asked to recall anything, all those areas of the brain work in unison to help us recall all aspects of the experience or learning.

That concept of one memory stored in many places and then the many places must connect to remember the memory is symbolic of how complex the human brain is. To think of the human brain as using the billions or more of microscopic neuron connections like a superhighway at the speed of light, like electricity flowing to and from cells to create thoughts, is a very accurate image of what is actually happening. In everyone's subconscious brain, all information is stored. If you have ever experienced hypnosis or seen someone under hypnosis recall details that are not readily available to the conscious person, it is quite fascinating and proof of what I am sharing. Maybe some of you know this but may I remind you of this very human truth: we all are recording everything all the time. So, why then is it hard to recall what we need when we need it? Yes, I will answer that, but first, I think my story will explain why I have spent thirty-six years studying and reading about neuroscience and learning.

When I was twenty-one, I was at university. I was ready to student-teach as a high school math teacher. I had a slight stuttering problem with my friends, and many did not know I was managing a dysfluent stuttering issue. For anyone who has never had a speech impediment, it takes effort to think, talk, and try to be fluent. It can be exhausting and embarrassing when the listener finds your stuttering funny, which is usually the reaction. Sometimes I would slip and stutter socially, which was always met by snickers and giggles. But I was nervous about student teaching and I noticed my stutter was worse. I feared the students would laugh at me while I taught.

Since the age of twelve, I had stuttered, not before that, curiously to my parents, and myself too. It filled me with fears and anxieties, which I struggled to control when I spoke. I had had enough of the fear that was about to ruin my student teaching experience. I took myself to the speech pathology department at my university. I was motivated to face my speech impediment and work on it, despite being emotional at the thought. It was embarrassing, which you pretend not to feel bad about, but it hurts being the joke all the time. I was so inconsistent in my speech errors that the speech pathology people told me that I needed to go to the psychology department on their referral as it was "emotionally based." Well, I felt confused as to what that meant. Am I a mental patient? What? But I took the advice and tried to be brave about what they could offer me as I walked to the psychology department to make the appointment. Well, they offered me memory regression hypnosis to uncover the "emotional trauma" that caused this speech issue. I did not recall any "traumas" and felt I had a pretty awesome childhood: two loving parents who have strict and high expectations, but fun and family-centered too.

The professor seemed super nice, and he offered this big recliner for the sessions in a sun-drenched office. I agreed to try it. After attending once a week for maybe two months, I was enjoying the relaxing meditations, and he would ask me about my childhood going back a little farther each time. He was kind and soft-spoken, and I certainly did feel safe. I did not feel "hypnotized," yet he said I was "highly suggestable," which was hard for me to understand since my only perspective was my own. I felt relaxed and awake, so this was confusing at the time.

Living in the dorms at the time, I cannot tell you the appeal of his big recliner, as my world had only an academic setting, which looking back now I think it is funny how I just enjoyed the chair. Anyway, I felt embarrassed at this one session because it felt as though I fell asleep. Oh, my gosh. How long did I sleep? I felt my face get red and urgently wanted to apologize. I woke up quickly and a bit surprised. I felt so bad for slipping into sleep. He said I was not sleeping, but deep in hypnosis and he found the source of my stuttering! He said my mind was protecting me from the memory and that it was going to be OK. He said, go have a great week, and he would explain more next week.

I was excited to hear what he had found the next week and he told me to prepare myself for a recording of myself speaking at younger ages. He said he had two things to share: in one, I was twelve years old and the other I was just a toddler. He first played when I was eighteen months of age. The backstory is that I was a precocious, smart, sneaky little toddler into everything, my mom had told me. One day, I got into danger and ate all of her iron pills, which was way over the lethal dose for my size. The recording that the doctor played for me was myself talking like toddlers do, unable to pronounce my consonants, explaining the nurse was poking me with her fingernails and pins (because I was passing out with toxicity) and their white hats and dresses. Then I started gagging and explaining that they are hurting my throat, more gagging and crying. I was reliving the doctors pumping my stomach while I was fully conscious in a panic.

I recalled the stressed voices shouting orders and the bright lights.

As I heard this strange version of myself crying, I had a surge of recollections. I knew that I had taken all of my mother's iron pills while she was resting with an upset stomach when I was very young. I knew I almost died and that it was very traumatic for my eight-month pregnant mother who was only twenty-one at the time herself. I never realized that. I remembered that incident at the age my mother was. When I was listening to myself speak so authentically *toddlerish*, it was shocking. All of a sudden, I remembered the large floral pattern on the couch in the Navy base housing my parents lived in. I recalled the floor plan of their two-bedroom bungalow in an instant with a host of sensory memories, including the view out the window. I remember looking at the TV with my mom's purse on top and then peeking at her to see her not looking at me. I went through her purse on the floor with enjoyment. I found the pills which I opened easily (before childproof tops) and with excitement, found sugarcoated "candy." I knew I was doing something wrong by taking them and eating them and I remember peeking at her to see if she was still resting. I ate all of them. When I did get up, I said, "Uh-oh, Mommy," with a guilty conscience. I remembered it all for the first time, in an instant. It was as if it was injected into awareness. The tape was me remembering the doctors and nurses putting a tube down my throat to pump my stomach, fully conscious.

In the retelling of the story, in my toddler's voice, there was screaming and crying. "Stop it!" I yelled, and he stopped the tape. I began to cry. I just had emotional pain for the torture of that baby, and that baby was me. I had no recollection of this event in my conscious mind, but I knew it happened all my life. Knowing about it and having the memory were completely two different things! In the tape I also said, "My mommy is crying, and I cannot move." The doctor said I was in a coma and aware of my mother visiting me. I remembered when I was in a coma! Wow, that is unbelievable, but I was listening to myself recount it. In my life, my mom said it was a miracle that I survived. No one did anything to me, and my parents did the best they could. Learning that my trauma was an accident relieved me. The professor then said he had a tape from another session. In this session, he asked me about age twelve. I did not recall this session sleeping, and I had no idea of what he was about to play. He played me the next tape. It was my tearful account of the shocking death of my twenty-nine-year-old uncle in a helicopter crash the summer I turned twelve. It crushed my dad. And his pain made mine that much worse. Our family was devastated.

The loss was a terrible shock of a very loved and charismatic Vietnam War veteran who we all loved and worshipped. This event was so traumatic to me, he explained, and the only reference for this much trauma and pain in my brain was the terrifying poking, pinching, and then the choking incident, where I was frightened and felt out of control.

My brain related the two traumatic incidents and probably stored them in the same place together as life-threatening. I felt out of control with the loss of my uncle, my first experience with death, and the fragility of life. I did get very depressed at the time. I remember feeling so tired and was not able to function as a normal kid. It was hard to feel happy for a long while. This shattered my perception of my idyllic, loving childhood and what I thought life was. The brain related these two traumas, and the stuttering began. Tightening of my throat was my brain's way to react to stress and fear, and it was a subconscious connection at the choking trauma. The revelation was amazing and even though it was hard to hear, I felt empowered. I understood myself in a way I never had.

My journey with death, which I am speaking about here and I also spoke about in Chapter 9: "Primal Reflexes," is one that everyone must face at one point. Let's take a moment to realize this. How rare is it that one ends one's life, never to have lost someone they love? Only the young lay claim to this benefit, to be spared the feeling of losing a loved one, in their tragic loss of life itself. We must prepare our children for life's realities. Shielding a child from the pain in death is a parenting strategy I cannot condone. My parents did not discuss feelings. We all closed up. We should have talked about our own coping and supported each other. But a twelve-year-old cannot strategize their way out of that sort of shock. Their executive function is not that savvy. We need to remember our adult perceptions are nothing like those of our children, preteens, or teens. Death and pain are unavoidable parts of life. Being aware of this fact helps you live better. Bond through processing death together with your child, and it is never too late. Healing happens when you let it out and feel supported.

I went back to the psychologist's office for a few more sessions to break that psychological connection and this involved raising the scary incident to be perceived by my older brain differently. Those who choked me also saved my life. And I taught my brain to relax my throat during fear and stress. It took a lot of practice in the following years to not stutter after that, but eventually, it was gone completely. I knew what to do. I understood myself. This was the pathway to healing for me.

The power of the subconscious is almost unfathomable, and it remembers everything. Everyone's brain remembers what happens when you are awake, asleep, or in a coma. Pretty fascinating. Then why is learning, and recalling what we learn, so difficult? There is a simple answer. It is because children and many adults do not understand the way the subconscious brain relates to the conscious brain. I am going to give you strategies of thinking that are all based on neuroscience research.

When you learn something, you need to relate it to something you already know or have experienced. If it just reminds you of something in some way, that is enough. But it is important to think and explore what you already know about something new that you are learning. This is one way that gives your brain a pathway back to recollection. It is simply a set of neural pathways between ideas you are creating as you consider what you already know.

Use your imagination to visualize the new information. Make a movie in your head, give it fantastical ideas that amuse you, anger you, or cause any emotion you choose to relate to the new information. If you involve your emotions, you will automatically raise your interest and your ability to recall it. Get involved with your learning. Be amazed, explore more, and ask why. The answers will be a fascinating journey into our planet, human capabilities, and the wonder of the universe. Life is fascinating and those who act as if life is boring and predictable have not been introduced to life itself. That is my belief. I have not met a student who cannot be tricked into learning this.

Involve all of your child's senses when learning. When you involve the five senses, it gives the brain more ways to remember it. Recall the blender idea I shared earlier, explaining how the brain stores information. It also puts more tidbits into more places which are more triggers to recall. The visual input trumps all other inputs generally. Seeing is a very complex brain process as I discuss in Chapter 18. The visual process is not like a camera, actually quite the opposite. Seeing is not a reliable form of information, yet we all perceive it to be accurate and reliable. No, it is not. Your eyes notice lines, colors, shapes, and shadows. They interpret distance by clues. This is all taken in through the optic nerve which then floods the thalamus, which is an egg-shaped thing in our brain that serves as a distribution center for most of our five senses. It is like a big superhighway with thousands of speeding cars at the speed of light traveling into our minds, each carrying information we need to interpret. Then the information travels from the thalamus into the occipital lobe (in the lower back of our head) called the visual cortex. The thousands of cars carrying visual information now need to be sorted for things such as motion, color, and shadow interpretation. They are grouped together as needed. The brain must do this all quickly to calculate visual interpretations as we move.

I think of downhill skiing, which my husband and I enjoyed raising our family doing as a yearly tradition. Taking off downhill, turning and turning to control your speed, interpreting the snow before you, and making distance judgments all while zooming downhill makes you realize how fast your eyes can interpret your world. Visual misinterpretations could be devastating. There are those people whose brain speed of visual interpretations causes them the inability to do such activities as downhill skiing or other fast movements. I read about a case in the book *Brain Rules* by John Medina about a person who had a brain injury to the visual cortex and lost only the ability to interpret motion. They could visually interpret all other things, but not whether something was moving or not. We know that the brain is organizing visual information by type and then interpreting. The brain is not like a camera.

Back to using all the senses, Vanderbilt University is doing amazing work that is well funded on senses. Vanderbilt has more than fifty faculty members, across schools and departments, contributing to vision research alone. According to David Calkins, PhD, Professor of Ophthalmology and Visual Sciences, "If you ask people what they fear most about getting older, the No. 1 response is losing their mind. The No. 2 response is losing their sight."

According to "The Science of Our Senses" by Matthew Batcheldor, "Calkins is excited about current research on several tracks that he believes will restore vision to patients who have lost sight due to chronic disease or injury. One of the means being studied is identifying new treatments to encourage the body's own cells to regenerate the retina and optic nerve." The science of understanding our ability to maintain and interpret visual information is fascinating and exciting. Often it is also the reason we are not remembering. Are we noticing all that we can? Are we going too fast? Slowing down to experience learning is a big thing I look to see if students can do, at any age. Yes, it can be taught.

Think of the smell of baked bread and cinnamon rolls. That smell takes me back to my grandmother who would make the dough the day before and get up and knead it all night. Then before sunrise, she would get loaves of bread and caramel-coated cinnamon rolls. Oh, my gosh, it smelled amazing and actually woke me up. Or I think I told my mind to wake me when I smelled it. I was waiting for it. And the smell today takes me back to the love my grandmother gave me, and I do not have to eat it to feel every memory of her when that smell triggers me. You can trigger learning with smells. I love to teach my students to study with a favorite essential oil. Then use that oil for a quiz or test and the information is much more accessible if you have learned to relax and believe it is.

That comes to my next tip: you need to study something and think, "I will remember that." It sounds way too simple. But it is a very, very effective and powerful strategy. Your subconscious is paying attention all the time, now we know this. But what people generally do not realize is that your unconscious is literally listening and trying to comply. It does not understand humor, sarcasm, or know when you are "kidding." When you think negative thoughts, your brain is making sure it complies. Have you ever had this sarcastic thought while learning something big or tricky: *I am never going to remember all this!* "OK," your subconscious thinks, "I won't let you." Your student may have trouble remembering under stress but do fine when reviewing with you or their class. This is common to have test anxiety that causes trouble in recalling information. You can adjust the self-talk to address this to be *I will recall this information anytime I choose.*

Your memory lives in your subconscious. You need to work with it and not against it. It does what you tell it to do. That is why the people who think *I cannot do that*, usually don't. It has been called "The Secret" or many other things, but it is really the power we all have with regard to belief. We can use this believing something to "manifest our future" some believe, but that is another book. I actually do feel that when you are living your life's purpose and you are serving others, you get into a "flow of the universe." I have dedicated my life to advocating for and helping children and adults who struggle academically. It has served me in so many ways, and I feel truly blessed to be making a difference. I have to be open to each new student and learn what their strategies for learning are, and how they study. More importantly, what does your child (or yourself for that matter) say to themselves inside their head about their (or your) ability to utilize information and recall it when needed? Learn to listen to yourself talking inside your head and take control of that powerful thinking that determines what your subconscious allows. Listen, and if you can influence that conversation, you may influence their life. Oh, my goodness, while I wrote that sentence a rainbow appeared out my window. I must be saying something perfect for you, my reader, to hear. That is my wish.

I do not have magic fairy dust to offer, as many parents wish, but I have been called the Mary Poppins of Education, which I love, the biggest compliment! I wish I could sing, but sadly, that is not a skill of mine. She was magic. Now, the trick to use after you study with a belief you can access this again when you desire is to realize that you need to make sure the pathway to recall is there. There are strategies to help you get back to that information to put into practice. A strong student will get a sense of when they will be able to recall it and when they need a strategy, but that is advanced. Learning these strategies is the first step.

Seven is the magic number for the number of things you can hold in short-term memory. Anything more than that needs a strategy for short-term memory or long-term memory. The first long-term strategy is a mnemonic device. That means using the first letter to spell something to remind you of something else. Since I am also a math teacher, a common math mnemonic is PEMDAS: "Please excuse my dear Aunt Sally." It stands for, P-parenthesis, E-exponents are a priority, then M-multiplication and D-division are next priority. A-addition and S-subtraction are last priority when computing a numerical expression, as you read from left to right within each priority. These are memorable and easy to call upon as a pathway back to the information. Mnemonics can come in other forms too. You can have a musical mnemonic. An example would be, even though I cannot sing, I would teach my Algebra 1 classes to sing the quadratic formula to the tune of "Chattanooga Choo Choo," an old show tune. My students could always count on accurately writing the formula to begin the problem. Rhyming is a mnemonic device. Grammar tries to capitalize on this by the rule: "I before E, except after C or when sounding as 'A' as in neighbor and weigh." Pretty helpful when you are trying to spell receive (not I before E, because it is after C!) or Santa's Sleigh because it rhymes with "weigh"! Using slightly inappropriate rhymes might make them more memorable, but I would not say this to a student until ninth grade. The ninth grader will laugh because half of their thoughts are about their awakening sexuality. Let this help them in school. There are complicated mnemonics that are fun to study if you get into this technique. Look up phonetic peg mnemonics if you want to learn something complex and high level in this area. To teach a struggling student, start with something basic.

Another strategy is repetition. Yes, this is obvious, and this is the reason for the popularity of flashcards. They provide repetition and recall opportunities. The pathway does strengthen when called upon multiple times. Learn how many times you need to recall something to remember it. I recommend four times at a minimum for strong results.

Write it down and say it out loud are two strategies you can use together sometimes. Writing uses a kinesthetic movement and the language center simultaneously while thinking about the new thought which makes it more memorable. Speaking the new information uses your vocal cords, kinesthetics, and your sense of hearing which is another way to strengthen the memory. If you use these while connecting them to ideas and things you already know, it is very effective for most.

The method of loci is a technique whose research is very strong and competitive with other mentioned methods. In this method, you imagine a room or a place in detail in your mind. As you study, imagine "putting" each hunk of information in one place, then walk on an imagined "path" to the next place where you study and learn. And imagine "putting" it in this place. You keep doing that, forming a journey of learning so to speak. It could be a journey through a real or imaginary place. But a real and familiar place is recommended. Your brain is wired to remember how to return to the cave or how to retrace your steps. When you need to recall this information, do not stress out, just retrace your steps on the journey and each location should have triggers and associations to the information. This is a fun and secret way to study that can amuse and entertain you as you learn and when you recall. This method has research to support all types of learners, and the results in people with mild cognitive impairment is very promising.

Remembering what you read is a big part of comprehension. If you want to remember what you read, you need to have a place to *focus* on reading without disruption or distraction. You need to understand the vocabulary and sentence structure of the words you are reading. Lastly, you must *recognize* what you are reading, which is also called semantic encoding. Then you can apply a memory device that is required for information as you go. Take notes if it is an academic purpose. Or with visual imagery, see a "movie" in your head. Or imagine reading and creating the loci technique. Take a dry topic and make it memorable, like learning science facts as you walk along the beach or explore a cave. Associate each new scene and see it in the location as you go. We are the makers of our thoughts, and active engagement when reading is the key to remembering what you read.

Students who have struggled to succeed in testing commonly have negative self-talk about remembering. If your student does this, talk about it and see if you can encourage them to try another approach. Stimulate them to find something they will approach with excitement (emotions) and use all the senses (either real or imagined) while learning. The success will then introduce them to the possibility of discovering that it is within their power. It presents a creative solution to help with the task of remembering. Strengthen the pathways back to the information with a variety of strategies. Stay calm and confident as we try to recall is a behavioral pattern that gets easier and easier the more you do it. These are the secrets of dazzling students. They are just strategic and positive. Anyone can learn this mindset.

RECAP: STRATEGIES FOR REMEMBERING

- Study efficiently and positively.
- Academics is about Deep Learning. Deep Learning is the tool to be thinkers. It is how we come to understand big ideas and make connections. It enables us to be communicators about the concepts we are learning.
- There are four steps to using one's memory: encoding, storing, retrieving, and forgetting.
- The power of the subconscious is almost unfathomable, and it remembers everything.
- Involve the five senses to help make learning memorable.
- Practice recalling to strengthen your ability to remember.
- Repetition is effective at increasing memory ability.
- Positive self-talk commands the very literal aspect of your brain to recall since it does what it is told.
- Saying to yourself, *That is hard. I will never remember this*, is a sure way to not remember.
- Replace negativity with positive thinking. *I will remember this*, is a powerful suggestion to teach your child to say to themselves.
- Music is a powerful memory pathway.
- Associations, silly or novel, can be a powerful memory tool.
- All learning needs to attach to something we already know.

WORKING MEMORY

Does your child leave their things everywhere? Do they misplace things they care about and will need to find later? Do they have trouble completing multiple verbal directions? As parents, we are tasked with keeping our children's items together and somehow sending them out each day with what they need. Teens can be exasperated looking for items that are buried on the floor of their room, but not visible on top. Working memory issues are related to ADD, ADHD, and autism. Working memory issues are considered a "learning disability." This sounds like a permanent condition, right? Well, remember how plastic the brain is? I keep this in mind when I am teaching. In this chapter, you will learn how helping your child improve their working memory will in turn benefit them at school.

Is something a permanent condition or is it learnable, something that will develop, and something that I can strengthen? I find that with pointed effort, working memory can improve with specific efforts. My findings are ahead of research. As of 2020, there is great debate whether working memory can grow. Many apps have been developed claiming this is the case, but the research has not proven it. I find that human relationships and interaction trumps everything gained from human interaction with a screen. There is a value to the interaction and communication between two humans that does not exist with a computer interaction. The brain seems to recognize this as well.

A study, completed at Massachusetts General Hospital, Harvard Medical School, and the Massachusetts Institute of Technology, reported that daily mindfulness practice increased recall and allowed participants to tune out distractions by regulating sensory input. Mindfulness practices have many benefits including calming, relaxing, clearing, and resting your brain. Now, we can also include increased recall.

I teach my students to shift their thinking from seeing learning tasks as difficult, like "hard" vocabulary or spelling demands, or facts to recall in science or math, whatever the content, and to work to make sense first. Once a strong understanding is achieved, say to yourself: "I will remember that." It sounds strange at first, but the idea here is to tell your very literal subconscious, where memories are stored, to allow the memory to be recalled upon demand. When I work with a struggling student, they either say or tell me that they think, "I will never remember this!" This becomes a negative outcome prophecy, and they struggle to recall when needed. We can use mindfulness to imagine recalling and succeeding on a test, where you are very prepared. This can be an exhilarating experience.

Working memory, in my opinion, is influenced by self-talk at the moment, along with the student's perception of their skill on that task. Once you break a view of the difficulty and create success, you increase effort, motivation, and recall in the hope of success. That is an oversimplified process outline that can take time to create. Finding the nonthreatening starting point can lead to the next lessons they need to learn.

The problem is the "product" of their grade is often something they are not prepared to do. Whose fault is it that the student is ill-prepared? Is it the fault of the system, the parent, or the student? The truth is, all three. The parents, the system, and the student can all do better. My personal belief is that working memory is influenced by attitude, practice, and belief. The system, working with the parents and the student, can impact your child's scholastic outcome.

As we learned in the comprehension chapter, the brain needs to remember details along the way while reading information to put ideas together. When part of the information is lost and unable to be considered, the understanding is weaker. When you are listening to language, you need to retain information about the beginning of the sentence until you can make sense of it. If you hear Susan would like to visit the third animal enclosure in the room on the left, you need to recall that the person in the sentence is Susan. Then you need to retain the verb until you know what it is she would like to visit. And you need to retain the adjective (third) until you know "third what?" All of the pieces must be put together in the right order. Without sufficient working memory, the information would be lost before you could combine it into a coherent, complete thought. Often a mixed-up version of the details might be recalled. This is how it might feel to be challenged with low working memory.

Another example of how working memory is needed is when thinking about simple arithmetic in your head without paper and pencil. If you want to add 28 and 14 you may need to find that 4 plus 8 = 12. Retain the "2" and carry the "1" over to the "10s" column to make "2" plus "1" plus "1" = "4," in the 10s column. Then you integrate numbers with the "1s" columns, to arrive at the answer "42."

If you are searching for your car in a parking lot, you have to remember near where you think you parked while recalling the layout of the cars in the region you just searched so that you can avoid wasting time searching the same region again. Likewise, in the forest, a predator that turns its vision away from a scene and revisits it moments later may use working memory to detect that something in the scene has shifted; this change detection may indicate the presence of prey.

Working memory can range from spoken words and printed digits to cars and future meals. It can even encompass abstract ideas. For example, you can ask a person to bring a side dish to your house, but probably not to take a side dish to your house (unless you are not there), and not to send a salad to your house (unless they are not coming with you). These conditions can tax working memory. The concept of "bringing something" seems to require several conditions. The student's initial concept transferred from working memory to long-term memory may be incomplete or jumbled. Another exposure allows the student to amend their memory when falsehoods are discovered and or further learning occurs.

Working memory is one of the most widely used terms in psychology and education. It has often been connected or related to intelligence, information processing, executive function, comprehension, problem-solving, and learning. Let's talk about how it affects comprehension.

Working memory is the small amount of information that can be held in the mind and used in the execution of cognitive tasks. This is in contrast with long-term memory, the vast amount of information saved in one's life. Everything we have ever experienced is stored in our brains. Our conscious brain can only recall some of it, but under hypnosis, you can access much more of your memory. Students love to hear about how everything you experience is in your brain; the trick is to learn how to access it.

Working memory and long-term memory both play a primary role in learning and school bureaucracy. I use that word because students need to do specific tasks, such as turn in things in certain ways at certain times in certain formats to function in a classroom setting. A student's struggles with these tasks are sometimes the best indicators of a working memory problem. All too often this is mistaken to be an intentional avoidance or "laziness" when turning work in is involved. That is unfair to the student who is operating with low working memory ability.

I have attended many conferences about a struggling student where test results are shared with teachers and administrators. When working memory has been low as compared to norms for their age, it is accepted to be a permanent deficit. Working memory is expressed as a reason for the student's low achievement. It becomes a rationale for lower expectations and more "accommodations." It has been assumed to be a diagnosis.

An area that I can positively impact student performance in and find ways to improve with a student is in helping them lower stress and anxiety and increase comfortable exposures to the content. Then you can add strategies for learning and functioning that cause less reliance on working memory to improve overall performance. Making ideas visual as you go by outlining, making flashcards you can manipulate and organize, and highlighting are some of my favorite ways to help working memory. You gather important ideas, then return to them for conclusions. Do not try to gather and conclude using only working memory – add some tools. These ideas used in conjunction have positive effects in raising academic confidence. My experience, over many student transformations, has found that there is a secret key for every student to improve. I have never met a student performing at their potential, without some area that can grow. The human potential is amazing, and students fascinate me with the strides that can be made.

Attention and memory go hand in hand. More attention, and you increase memory. More exposures, and you increase memory.

In his article, "The Development of Working Memory," John P. Spencer reports the following: "Working memory plays an important role in child development, and many theories of cognitive development take increases in working memory capacity as a starting point for cognitive change (Case, 1985). For instance, increases in working memory capacity are thought to underlie improvements in speed of processing as well as improvements in children's reasoning ability (Kail, 1991). More generally, individual differences in working memory abilities correlate with measures of children's academic performance and general intelligence (Conway, Kane, & Engle, 2003). Given these findings, it is not surprising that deficits in working memory are thought to play a central role in neurodevelopmental disorders such as attention-deficit/hyperactivity disorder (Willcutt, Doyle, Nigg, Faraone, & Pennington, 2005).

"Recent studies suggest that working memory is open to intervention (Diamond, Barnett, Thomas, & Munro, 2007). This raises exciting potential to overcome the limited working memory abilities of at-risk children (Vicari, Caravale, Carlesimo, Casadei, & Allemand, 2004). Nevertheless, questions have been raised about whether working memory training extends outside the laboratory to affect how children deploy working memory in real-world settings (Diamond & Lee, 2011). One possible way to boost the effectiveness of interventions is to intervene early in development. This would capitalize on the massive brain plasticity evident in the first few years of life."

Working memory is a central cognitive brain system that changes dramatically over development with far-reaching consequences. We cannot gauge the rate of a child's physical development or verbal development, nor can we gauge a child's working memory development over their growth into adulthood. Then why would we presume to label them at any given time in their development? This is my stance, based on research. I recommend it to you. This supports my hope and view of all students I work with to achieve successful working memory skills.

If there were an app on your phone or computer that could improve your child's memory, would you try it? Who wouldn't want better memory? After all, our recollections are fragile and can be impaired by many things, such as diseases, brain injuries, mental health conditions, and for all of us, aging. There is a multibillion-dollar industry for brain training. Commerce is capitalizing on this perceived need by providing an abundance of apps for phones and tablets that provide mental challenges that are easily accessible and relatively inexpensive. I want to caution you about using online brain training. Some researchers have expressed deep reservations about both its reliability and its validity. There was even a consensus statement issued calling brain training into question, which, in turn, resulted in a counter-response from researchers who defended it.

I can personally endorse www.BrainHQ.com. It is a collaboration of some big names in neuroscience, several who have shared research at conferences I have attended and whose work I am familiar with. I have used this with an ADHD client with increased attention scores with a practice that has translated into the classroom. Some of the thinking is behavior-based. I also like the data report available after each session. Data-driven results as you practice with BrainHQ is a very motivating aspect of the program.

The second one is the only FDA-approved treatment thus far. In 2013, Gazzaley published a paper in *Nature* reporting that six weeks of training with a video game called *Neuroracer,* in which the player seeks to discern relevant cues from distracting one's during a car race simulation, improved attention in aging adults. The results were striking, given that attention markedly declines with age and the data was conclusive. With the new FDA approval, children can now be treated with a kids' version of the technology called EndeavorRX. Gazzaley is a co-founder of Akili Interactive, which produces EndeavorRx, and which conducted pivotal clinical trials of the game as an ADHD treatment with researchers at Duke University and elsewhere. Here is an excerpt from the FDA's press release:

"The prescription-only game-based device, called EndeavorRx, is indicated for pediatric patients ages eight to twelve years old with primarily inattentive or combined-type ADHD who have demonstrated an attention issue. EndeavorRx is indicated to improve attention function as measured by computer-based testing and is the first digital therapeutic intended to improve symptoms associated with ADHD, as well as the first game-based therapeutic granted marketing authorization by the FDA for any type of condition. The device is intended for use as part of a therapeutic program that may include clinician-directed therapy, medication, and/ or educational programs, which further address symptoms of the disorder.

"The EndeavorRx device offers a non-drug option for improving symptoms associated with ADHD in children and is an important example of the growing field of digital therapy and digital therapeutics," said Jeffrey Shuren, M.D., J.D., director of the FDA's Center for Devices and Radiological Health. "The FDA is committed to providing regulatory pathways that enable patients timely access to safe and effective innovative digital therapeutics."

ADHD is a common disorder that begins in childhood, affecting approximately four million children ages six to eleven. Symptoms include difficulty staying focused and paying attention, difficulty controlling behavior, and very high levels of activity. According to the Centers for Disease Control and Prevention, diagnosis of ADHD should be conducted by a trained health care professional and follow an evaluation of symptoms or pattern of symptoms, such as inattention, hyperactivity, and impulsivity that interfere with functioning or development.

My recommendation on all other online memory programs is to wait for more research and stick to human-to-human education. In-person teaching sends a message of caring and love that is very valued by students.

If brain training works, the field holds enormous promise to help people with cognitive impairments and to aid individuals who are recovering from cancer or perhaps even COVID-19. Some affirmation of the potential for cognitive training could be seen in the FDA's recent approval of a brain training game to treat ADHD. This is a field with great potential, but I want the designers to be researchers who understand more thorough implications. It is too early to know where this is all heading or the potential advantages.

You use working memory every day, in many situations: to read, write, plan, organize, follow a conversation, do mental math, or follow multistep directions. It helps you stay focused on, and engaged with, a task.

The following are examples of how poor working memory affects a student's daily life. This is how your child might feel at times:

- You want to add to a classroom conversation, but by the time the teacher calls on you, you forget what you wanted to say.
- You consistently lose your coat, cell phone, notebooks, or backpack.
- You get lost easily, even when you were just given directions.
- You have trouble following a conversation because you

missed or forgot what the other person has just said. Trying to catch everything causes gaps in what you hear.

- You have many unfinished projects or tasks because you become distracted and forget about the first project.
- You plan to do some work at home, but you forget to bring needed items with you.
- You have to reread a paragraph several times to retain the information.
- You miss deadlines because of your disorganization and inability to follow through on multistep directions.
- No matter what your child does, he or she needs working memory to accomplish many thinking tasks. Is the pace of a classroom setting the problem? If changing the pace can change the outcome, then that is a "no-brainer," right?

Working memory is essential at school. One study, done in the United Kingdom, looked at 3,000 grade-school and junior-high students and found that weak working memory was more indicative of struggles in school than was a low IQ. According to researchers, almost all the children with weak working memory scored low on reading comprehension and math tests.

RECAP: WORKING MEMORY

- As of 2020, there is great debate whether working memory can grow.
- Working memory is influenced by self-talk.
- Without sufficient working memory, information could be lost before you can combine it into a coherent, complete thought.
- Attention and memory go hand in hand. More attention, and you increase memory.
- I recommend www.BrainHQ.com and to improve memory and focus.
- The EndeavorRx device offers a non-drug option for improving symptoms associated with ADHD in children, which is FDA approved.

22

STRATEGIES FOR EFFICIENCY

Does your child see the process through or quit before they have reached their goal? Have they learned how to manage their time? Do they use resources? Do they depend on others or never use others around them? Is there something they can do to speed up what they should know to proceed?

Life is busy, and there is only so much time. Wasted time is lost forever. If your child has academic catch-up work to accomplish, the biggest challenge is: Where do you carve out time to make that happen? What is the most effective approach in the least amount of time? Or how long will it take to catch your child up to grade level? Are they remembering what they mastered in the previous session? Circling back to the last topic mastered and rechecking it the next time helps you answer that question. After a few weeks, you get a sense of how much reteaching is needed for mastering a concept. Students remember best what they learn first and last. Taking many short breaks is a great plan for this reason. You are creating many firsts and lasts.

There is no way to turn back time. Many adults waste time. Does your child have a habit of wasting time as a recreational activity? This may just be a negative behavior pattern to plan on changing. A behavior habit is changed with a certain approach we can discuss. The first step to breaking a bad habit is an awareness of that habit. Begin to use a timer and challenge yourself and your child to find fifteen minutes to an hour timeframes when you can insert a routine of working on the items identified in your Action Item list from Chapter 4. This can be time your child values as devoted attention to just them. Decide how they can avoid wasting time the way they usually do. If it is video games, set a timer and limit the time or frequency of usage. If the habit is to watch too much TV, plan the most important shows to them and leave the channel surfing for a while. Whatever it is, plan a solution. Then help them stick to it. You can then also plan time to work on academic skills. You can call it their "practice" or call it their "brain time," whatever term matches your child's motivation to improve and feels like a fit.

Next, after awareness, is finding triggers and planning an alternative plan. You want to use cues in your life, like a calendar, a cell phone calendar reminder, or plans like, "Every time after soccer practice, we work for a thirty-minute strategy." Something systematic to form a new routine to replace the wasting time habit. Then do not give up. If you fall off the pattern, model not feeling bad. Be determined to restart. If you have to refine anything to help you succeed, then do so. The goal will happen. You will find time in the habit of learning how *not* to waste time.

If one or both parents in the home often waste time, then you may say, "We are going to both stop wasting time and accomplish personal goals." If improving spelling is one of your child's goals or fluency, then this book has given you some tips on how to properly practice this and you as a parent can say you need to read more and you will be trading TV for reading also. Go through it together, and both accomplish the effort. It is hard for parents to order a child to do what they are unwilling to do themselves. After twenty-one days, a new habit becomes an established habit. You can do this.

You can have secret rewards they are working to earn by their devotion to the goal, which I recommend. Remember, parents, time with you is often the reward that means the most to your child. If they have been asking you to take them somewhere or to do something with you, then offer that. Love is a primal need, and you can reward your child with it. Share an ice-cream cone or a hike or take them on a ski trip. Think of things they would love. Get creative, and even an overnight in a hotel to use the pool and spa is a fun treat for you both. You can also help your child by rewarding effort and time on task. The outcome is not the goal for a growth mindset, but the process. Working hard and being persistent are qualities in life that get you just about anything.

If your child is ADD or ADHD and struggles with focus and attention, then we want to use some specific strategies helpful for the unique brains that have this quality. Now, remember I am a fan of the advanced creativity and unique way these focus-challenged students function and see the world. This is not a bad thing; it is a type of unique brain. Many neuroscientists have written about the gifts of ADD and ADHD. Check it out. I think it is important for kids to understand some of the brain science behind their gifts and challenges. This will help them to better appreciate and strategize their way through difficulties. Here are some ideas to think about helping your child save wasted time: improving impulse control, improving physical exercise times to create times for study to follow, and improving attitude by working on a growth mindset (see Chapter 7). These are skills that often challenge an ADD or ADHD student, but there are always "workarounds."

Impulse control can be improved. But first, you and your child must believe that. Do some research yourself if your child needs "proof" or explain that the brain is very moldable and can learn new skills with effort and practice. One strategy is to outline behavior expectations for upcoming situations. What should their behavior look like, and what would help accomplish the task of finding time to work on learning skills? How long can your child focus knowing they will have a break? Can they focus for ten minutes, with a break walking around for two minutes? Or can they sustain fifteen minutes for a five-minute break? Give them time for creative thoughts and see if they can resist impulses for a desired amount of time. Slowly, see if they can increase that time with engagement. As the learning time increases, it serves a two-fold purpose: first to improve impulse control and second to improve executive function in small measurable increments. Celebrate as you go and realize this takes effort and is improving. Accept some impulsivity and reward improvement. And I cannot overemphasize the importance of exercise. Also, your child should have adequate time with their own thoughts and free time in their schedule to feel like some time is their own. It is more important to this type of brain than other thinking styles. Music is an avenue to focus on to accomplish focus and joy. Music lessons might be something untapped or something they want more of in trade for adding some academics, just an idea. Music instruction is supportive of increased focus, a win-win! Listening to music with no words, like meditation music, is also supportive for study mood setting.

Does your child see the process through or quit before they have reached their goal? Beginning something and finishing it is a life skill. It is about prioritizing something over other distractions or temptations. Talk about classifying what you and your child can discuss into three categories. What things are experiments (things you are trying and intend to stop if they are not working)? Call them that and allow these things to be "conditional" commitments. Commitments cannot be left unfinished. I used to tell my sons that if they joined a sports team, they must finish the season. Their team needed them, and they made a commitment to the team. I also used to make them commit to the seasonal jobs they took to earn money after they were fifteen in our hometown. These sometimes turned out to be "torture." But they saw it through. Their "torture" stories became excellent dinner entertainment and earned them some honor code for enduring some tough personalities or conditions. For example, we lived at 6,800 feet in the mountains. And teaching skiing to little kids who cry all day in a blizzard makes for an entertaining dinner story and a long day. Define commitment and then teach the concept. OK, ready, *break!*

Exercise is a given, and I know we have all heard the endless benefits of exercise. I heard a new one the other day from a physical therapist. She said to me, "Remember, motion is lotion to your body." That is a good one to remember. But if you project the connection in Chapter 9: "Primal Reflexes" with the mind-body connection learned there, you can see that some students may want to study while walking. Would moving while they learn be such a pleasure they do not otherwise get to experience? That is a great question for your child. Maybe they want to make a recording and listen to it while they walk.

Whatever your strategy, the point is, make one. Taking on the hopes of a struggling student and committing to work with them is a vital commitment. It is a commitment that should be honored. These students are fragile. They have probably motivated themselves many times, only to feel incapable in their weak area. You can galvanize them. You can help to make learning, for them, a positive thing.

RECAP: STRATEGIES FOR EFFICIENCY

- Life is busy, and there is only so much time.
- Wasted time is lost forever.
- If your child's issue is not being time efficient, then strategies for time management becomes a focus.
- Does your child have a habit of wasting time as a recreational activity?
- Beginning something and finishing it is a life skill.
- Accept some impulsivity and reward improvement.
- Be committed to improving how your child is aware of time and uses their time.
- Timed tests are an inevitable part of life and awareness of time is a skill to grow.

23

STRATEGIES FOR CLARITY

The process for learning begins with confusion and ends with overall understanding. Accept the process. It repeats! Students who have not experienced discomfort often struggle with confusion. This is a sign of their lack of resilience.

Emotions play a big role in learning. Frustration is a common emotion experienced by struggling students, and it can be painful. Perhaps this prompted you to buy this book. Maybe your child is not coping well, and answers have not arrived with other efforts. Emotions are understandable, but they must be regulated to sustain learning. Learning may upset or overwhelm your child at times. Take it as a clue for a time-out and a teaching moment to approach that topic a bit softer next time. The emotions are somewhat justified to honor the past, but we need to leave them in the past to make progress and not make the process longer than need be.

Emotional regulation is easy to say but hard to do. It is an executive function skill that is important to learn and control. Explain to your child that when you are emotional, your thoughts are not as rational as when you are calm. Learning is not possible when you are excited. You can encourage your child to increase their appropriate emotional responses by sharing their feelings with you, whether positive or negative. Emphasize the need to do this calmly. This allows the child to express himself and get some comfort in being understood. And the learning activity is not derailed.

Another strategy to help with emotional regulation is to "recognize" just before an emotion becomes too intense. You can try deep breathing to a count of five, inhaling and then exhaling five times. This is known as the Five-Five-Five strategy. It is calming and helps with emotions. You can place yourself somewhere that makes you calm and happy to assist in the distraction. Do this with a child of any age. It is a dependable and effective strategy to give them control.

Yet another strategy for managing emotion is to imagine your feelings are like clouds. Now, watch them drift away in your mind. As you practice this imagery, you will find your mind drifting with random thoughts. This is good. Allow that to happen. This is using a strength of the ADD or ADHD brain to their advantage. Others will have to learn to be as good at that skill.

Physical activity produces brain chemicals to improve your mood. Create some intense bursts of energy to get those endorphins flowing and improve your emotional state. Stay calm. Never put yourself down with negative self-talk. Strategize your way through the confusion to get to consummate understanding. You can help your student create new mantras of self-talk to suggest what you are trying to produce: *I will not get upset when I stumble reading. Instead, I will take a deep breath, and try to be curious about that word and then begin the sentence again.* I am thinking of several students over the years who would get so upset at fluency errors. That is what was most important to them, but in the process, they did not learn what made them stumble in the first place. A mistake is a learning opportunity, and if you are reacting emotionally, you miss that chance, waste time, and upset yourself. Use your parental magic on this one and make it a long-term conversation. Check in and discuss how your kids are doing. Dissect incidents. The discussions can end with, "How could I have avoided feeling all those negative things?"

You can do a body scan and see if your emotions are in check. If you have feelings that are getting in the way, talk about them. Allow your child to tell you and acknowledge the feeling. Maybe it is fear, anxiety, envy, hope. Whatever it is, listen to them and help them put it aside for the sake of learning. Remind them, "There is no need to feel that now. We are learning." Learning should feel calm and curious. There should be an element of creativity to help explore ideas. Reward effort and help your child associate a positive feeling to any confusion. Often students need to use a reference of strategies. For a math word problem, that list would look like this: draw a picture, draw a diagram, find words that mean math operations in the problem, or write an equation as an example.

If you assume that you understand too early, then you find yourself unprepared. Some students avoid the process of learning. Once they grasp one element of the learning they say, "I get it!" and try to be done. This is a difficult habit to break. Show students that listening and refining their understanding is what is expected. Do not stop at the first instance of something that makes sense. This is something to look for as your student learns something difficult for them.

Look at your child's process for working through confusion. This needs to be taught, like any other skill. It is difficult to project the many personalities students may have and predict what they adopted due to their experiences.

You can take it as it comes. Begin with simple problems and move on to more complex ones. Review the skills and strategies and help them learn the difficult versions of the problems with confidence. Whether this is graduated levels of comprehension questions, math equations, or fraction problems, be patient and persistent. Utilize this graduated technique because it is reliable. It assures your student that things are predictable, and they have the hope of success. You are helping to build this up.

When they grasp a concept, allow them to practice it several more times. This lets them purposely create the success they are seeking. You can back up as far as you like, letting them create the success they need to ensure they will want to continue learning.

If the child believes he will fail, he becomes unwilling to attempt the effort. The psychology of this is mentioned in the idea of learned helplessness. It is very real and can be debilitating. Create success and take baby steps of complexity. This grows confidence. No more surprises for a while until you build some resilience.

Learning is the process of moving from utter confusion to total understanding. I make this point in this chapter because it is an underlying skill to make sure your child can judge properly and repeat. It will take time and patience. You need to continually reference where they are in the process. Help them gauge a better understanding of how to keep working through the details of learning.

Imagine placing learning on a scale of one to ten with one being total confusion and ten being total understanding. Ask your child, "Where do you think you are?" They might say, "A five." And the conversation begins. You may say, "No, you are at a nine." Just one more thing! Whatever is the case, you can show them how to check that they have finished with their task.

Struggling students feel anxious to be done with any given task that feels over their head. The learning is painful because they feel so unsure of themselves. That is how knowledge above your independent level feels. The new learning has nothing to attach to and will not be retained. It is too hard. You need to do this process with a lesson that is at their independent level. This could be just above their present skill level and aiming for the skill level you intend. As I said before, take small steps and develop their confidence.

Your student will accomplish what they believe they will. Teaching this expectation and perseverance is typical for students who have struggled.

You ask me how long it should take. I say it is proportional to the severity of the frustrations they have had. It is also proportional to the length of their frustrated learning. I spoke of a client in the reading chapter who was a non-reader in fourth grade. He is almost grade level now as an eighth grader.

It has been a four-year journey due to the severity of his learning disability and how angry and humiliated he felt in school his whole life. He would only be able to sustain learning until he felt angry. He was not annoyed with me. He was resentful that he was different from the other kids and that the work seemed super hard.

When we talk now, anger is rare. But it still shows up on days he is tired or hungry. This is normal because some things are hard. We are finishing the task now after four years of working to manage emotions. I drew a hard line and ended sessions early if necessary. I insisted he became polite and calm before continuing. A break is fine, and walking or jumping on a trampoline helped a lot. This boy broke his hand once. He hit a table while upset in a learning moment. The cast is off, and he was reminded for six weeks not to lose his temper. Such outbursts are rare now, and we have strategies that help him.

Plan for struggle and let your child tell you what might help them. Some kids may say, "I need a hug." Some kids say, "I need five minutes alone." Some kids may say that they need to pet the dog or cat. Watching fish swim is calming. I used a goldfish to make a study place calm and appropriate for a young first grader. I have a fish in my laundry room, for my enjoyment folding clothes, and for the cat to watch. Whatever works! Good job, parents.

RECAP: STRATEGIES FOR CLARITY

- Emotions play a big role in learning.
- Emotional regulation is easy to say and hard to do.
- Emotion is a component of executive function and needs to be developed with intentional effort.
- Struggling students are anxious to be done with any given task that is over their head.
- You can help your student to create new mantras of self-talk that suggest what you are trying to create.
- A mistake is a learning opportunity, and if you are emotionally reacting, your student misses that chance.
- Your student will accomplish what they believe they will.
- The learning is painful because struggling students feels so unsure of themselves.
- Spend energy helping your child recognize just before an emotion becomes too intense. Help him make a different choice as a goal.
- Look at your child's process for working through confusion.
- Spending time analyzing your child's process when confused is the key to changing them in the right direction.

FINAL THOUGHTS TO CONSIDER

24

LANGUAGE PROCESSING ISSUES

When a reading problem is involved that is hampering learning, often students are tested by a school psychologist to further learn about how the student's brain is processing information and to discern their general skill levels for math and literacy. Sometimes a diagnosis of language processing delays is found.

There are two types of language disorders: expressive and receptive. People with expressive language disorders have trouble expressing their thoughts. Those with receptive language disorders struggle to understand what others are saying or to follow a conversation. It's also possible to suffer from a combination of expressive and receptive language disorders.

Language disorders are most often developmental like other learning challenges. Developmental, in this case, means that the condition is a severe, chronic disability of an individual who has a mental or physical impairment by the age of twenty-two. This disability is likely to continue indefinitely and results in substantial functional limitations in three or more areas of major life activity. However, either language processing disorder can also start to manifest as a result of a neurological illness or a traumatic event affecting the brain, such as a stroke or a head injury. When language disorders are caused by an injury to the brain, they're referred to as aphasia.

This processing diagnosis is, generally, described as a "severe, chronic, and permanent disability." The adjective *developmental* is not to be confused with the noun *development.* Development is the process of developing growth-directed change while developmental is a trainee flight controller. This definition is why schools lower their expectations of students with this diagnosis, expecting less and giving "accommodations" that aim to make the "product" of the curriculum of that grade manageable for the student.

I feel differently about this diagnosis as I can find ways to make improvements in their skills. How I do that is beyond the scope of this chapter, and quite complex. I take a varied approach based on specific types of errors helping them to achieve literacy concordance with their skills. This often yields remarkable improvements. My work is often in conjunction with a speech pathologist. Together we make a great team on the student's behalf to rebuild literacy with new strategies and orthographic knowledge.

There are many ways a language processing disorder can present. In general, language processing issues can be sorted into to two distinct categories. Someone with an expressive language disorder will have a limited vocabulary for their age and struggle to learn new vocabulary. A clue to this condition is that often they will use a lot of filler words like *um* or use *stuff* and *things* instead of more specific words. It is common for them to confuse verb tenses or repeat phrases when telling a story or answering a question. They may frequently say or construct sentences with words that don't work together properly. Sometimes they have trouble learning new words, with a low retention rate. Some students will struggle to find the words they need to express themselves.

The student is aware they need to communicate better but often feels very frustrated by their inability to communicate thoughts. These all describe the expressive language disorder. I have a student who comes to mind. He has a significant expressive language processing disorder, and he struggles with accurately annunciating his words. He spoke at lightning speed, so his style of speaking was hidden in the speed with which he spoke. This charming young man also has significant difficulty spelling accurately with many invented spellings showing his lack of orthographic rules. His reading ability and engagement was quite high for his challenges. Well, I found that his spelling conventions or orthographic knowledge needed quite a bit of reteaching and after about a year of weekly teaching, he has rebuilt his understanding of basically second- through fifth-grade spelling.

He now speaks slower because we have learned how to say the parts of words properly. We also have retaught it all with excellent retention. One problem has revealed itself as the least teachable thing for his processing issue, and that is the location of an "l" in a word with two syllables or more. It is interesting that one skill is the toughest after learning about sixty lessons from long vowel patterns to syllable juncture rules. Since this issue is pretty consistent, we have practiced some techniques that help him. Now, he is aware of it and we have built several strategies around how he compensates for this challenge and by next year, I anticipate his future teachers will not know he was once so challenged. He may never spell perfectly, but he is functional now and amazingly confident. He does not avoid his reading or writing assignments now. He embraces them and is proud to show his grandmother and parents his progress.

What makes this story even more interesting is that his grandmother is a retired secondary English teacher. She has worked with him his whole life, and she was unable to address his issues. She made a testimonial video for me and expressed so eloquently in her own words that she doesn't know if it is a "well-kept secret but English teachers have *no* idea of how to fix a reading problem." Parents often think that English teachers are able to help a reading problem, but that is far from the truth. English teachers are literature experts, and they know how to teach the *product* of teaching English from grades six through twelve.

Elementary teachers are the reading specialists. They have been taught how to teach reading, but their training does not include what to do when a student struggles after they have used all the normally effective teaching methods. That is where a reading specialist comes into the picture. We have a master's degree in learning how to remediate a reading problem, and we also know how to teach content area reading skills. Reading is only one area of literacy. Reading specialists know how to address comprehension issues, vocabulary issues, and other details involved with language processing.

The other type of language processing diagnosis is called receptive language disorder. Someone with a receptive language disorder might seem disinterested in conversations or social situations because they are not following what they are hearing and seeing. They have difficulty following directions and often misunderstand what is asked and answer or act inappropriately. They have difficulty getting jokes and may seem shy or withdrawn in their behavior.

Now, if you combine both descriptions, there are brains who have both types of learning challenges. If someone exhibits symptoms from both lists, it's possible he or she has a combination expressive/receptive language disorder. Now that must be worse, or unteachable then? Well, no. All students are teachable.

Let me give you an example of a student who has made great strides thus far and exhibits a very severe expressive and receptive language disorder. Her brain is very unique and very teachable. She is an otherwise engaged student, whose literacy was four years behind as a sixth grader. She was comprehending at a first-grade level and reading at a fourth-grade level. She did not know what she was reading but was able to pretend to be fluent most of the time. She has a low vocabulary and can say many common words accurately, yet she has no idea of their meaning. She was trying to hide in plain sight in the classroom with valiant effort. She would copy sentences to attempt to answer when she was unable to construct a sentence on her own. She uses prepositional phrases incorrectly and has trouble with subject/ verb agreement as well as the use of pronouns. She would begin most sentences she attempted to write with the word so.

As a seventh grader, she is earning a C in an honors-level English class but has extended time to practice. She has hidden so long that she and I have had many emotions as she learns how her brain needs to learn. The joy now is much earned from her resistance and angst along the way, but that is typical. She has avoided the shame of feeling stupid in class during her whole education. I eliminated science and social studies temporarily to focus on her literacy skills. However, we *are* engaging in remediation content using those subjects. Recently, she researched and wrote a paper on black holes in the universe, a passionate interest of hers. We also read about our constitutional and founding fathers along with historical biographies on Amelia Earhart and past presidents and first ladies. The last one was Eleanor Roosevelt. She enjoys these much more because they are being delivered to her at her independent level, and she is actually *understanding* and *enjoying* reading. She has moved her comprehension level to sixth-grade and her writing to third-grade competencies. We are not finished, but we are well on her way. She has found her academic integrity, which she totally traded to survive. She has also found her belief that doing the work can be possible for her. She thought that *faking it* was her only option, and no teacher ever helped her the way I am.

Because of her struggles in English, her teachers did not want her to be in pre-algebra as a seventh grader but rather the course below that one which is a skills-review class preparing for pre-algebra next year. She showed her readiness last year and because of her reading disability, it is typical to override the student's desire for the math rigor (and in her case the place to hang her academic esteem she desires so desperately) and give them less rigor. I have a policy to allow students to try what they believe they can do. And sure enough, she is proving everyone wrong and succeeding. She will then try algebra in eighth grade and she will take geometry in ninth. She is so proud of her A+ in pre-algebra this year. Her self-esteem is reassured with her ability to be strong in math and she is aware of her progress which is further fueling her work ethic.

This polished and sweet girl presents so intelligently, and she is a very hard worker. Her goal is to attend Cambridge or Oxford University in England. Well, I am not going to burst her dream because she is so willing to work hard for it. She loves to write creative stories even though she struggles with basic sentence structure and spelling. We are making huge strides, and she is persevering with learning despite working harder at it than most students. She has learned how to write a simple sentence and compound sentences now. We agree that we are not going to write complex sentences yet. It is a celebration she knows the difference! We can achieve writing objectives by using these two basic structures for her grade level right now. She is learning much slower than most students do, but so what? We are accelerating and as her spelling improves, I am seeing the typical progress associated with that, so I am very pleased. We are working on her vocabulary development and attending to maintaining vocabulary understanding as she reads. This is new to her, and she is getting better with practice. Every other educator in her life, both at public and private schools, saw her diagnosis and reduced their expectation of her. No one had a plan to help her catch up on the things she missed.

She is a wonderful example of my desire to change the way American education deals with students who are behind. She is teachable; she just does not learn in a typical manner. Her diagnosis is not a reason she cannot learn; instead, it is a reason our current system did not work for her. Other methodologies do work, and yes, they take longer to teach, but it is her foundational skill. Should that not be paramount for her future at the expense of other educational experiences? We need to shift our thinking from what is systematic, to what is realistic to do for children, who come in a variety of thinking strengths and weaknesses.

It is hard for me to see solutions which could be implemented, not being implemented. I am also sure that with prudent redistribution of existing funds, we could do a much better job. There is wasted money in education. No one wants to hear that. But there is, and it is something that taxpayers need to be spoken to about with straight talk. In the meantime, parents, please know that children with developmental language processing disorders are teachable. You need to find a reading specialist who also believes that to work with your child.

Anyone else is hindered by the antiquated label of a "severe, chronic, and permanent disability" implication of the adjective "developmental" in front of the diagnosis. This was a snapshot of performance and we as a society want to give a limiting label to children whose brains are much more complex than the test they took which is pronouncing this debilitating inability to learn. I can tell you that humans are born to learn, and it is our responsibility to find out how to do that best. We can do better. I have proven it to myself over and over.

Parents, hope comes with realizing that progress is progress, and once you measure the pace you are able to achieve, then you are able to predict when you will get there.

RECAP: LANGUAGE PROCESSING ISSUES

- There are two types of language disorders: expressive and receptive.
- People with expressive language disorders have trouble expressing their thoughts.
- Begin with expanding vocabulary for an expressive language-challenged student.
- A student with receptive language disorder might seem disinterested in school learning settings, and maybe also in social situations because they are not following what they are hearing and seeing.
- "Developmental" means that the condition is a severe, chronic, and behind expected skill levels for their age.
- This definition is why schools generally lower their expectations of students with this diagnosis.
- I disagree with this definition, because I have proven this statement false too many times with students, their parents, and myself.
- The brain is plastic, and we know better now with proven research.
- Learning uniquely is true for all of us.
- Humans are the most diverse mammals on the planet, and that applies to thinking too.
- Thinking differently is actually normal.
- Every person on the planet has the job of learning how to drive their brain in a way that works for them.
- Be open to unique solutions.
- Lose the labels and change the strategies as a way to get started helping your child.

25

DRASTIC TIMES CALL FOR DRASTIC MEASURES

Should my child be held back? Do I need to change schools? When should I consider homeschooling? Should I alter my child's curriculum? How do I tell when the situation is dire and requires making a change? I can give some general advice to try to guide this scary decision many parents deny or avoid. Sometimes drastic times call for drastic measures.

The first situation to discuss which deserves drastic measures is when a student feels threatened: physically, socially, or emotionally. If there has been an event and the threat was carried out, then that is another more serious matter. But the threat, as perceived by the child, is what I am trying to define. This makes learning the brain's lowest priority, and sending the child back into the threat is not a solution. I would argue that a student returning to a threatening situation over and over will cause fear, anxiety, and a very negative association to learning where the threat is associated. The association the brain will make between the experience and the subject will be there and something to overcome. Why take that detour to progress when it is avoidable?

I am an advocate of making sure that the basic essential need of safety is present for learning. Even if that means there is no safe option other than homeschooling in the short term, so be it. Safety is number one. And that can be accomplished with a functioning school administration with a written progressive discipline plan which removes threats so the rest can learn. That is the harsh reality of education. You need to hold the line and sometimes that expulsion is the catalyst for the change that student needs as well. It is the lack of action that speaks volumes to all the parties involved. Think about it: by nothing happening, the bullied student feels alone, unsupported, and fearful. The bully feels in control and able to decide when to cause harm. The administration where this is happening has to take a hard look at how this escalated to this level without consequence. Students who understand the progressive discipline plan that is publicly and fairly applied will adhere to the expectations. I have seen it over and over. When I supervised student teachers in many schools it was always apparent how strong a progressive discipline plan was by walking around on campus. It was also apparent when I volunteered to be on WASC accreditation committees visiting schools for a three-day evaluation. It is observable and palpable in the behaviors and interactions of the students. My school had a very strict supportive code of conduct built into its culture, including our whole-school Friday performances. This was a whole-school gathering where we would share learning projects, do plays and skits, and have musical performances and choir performances. We all ended the week with a smile and respect for our diversity and the beauty of that. We always had a packed house, and we became a family where all were accepted. It is possible. Any school that offers excuses is saying to you they have not figured it out, and you need to move your child. Safety is top priority and a dealbreaker.

When you have a child who is being bullied and all avenues have been taken with regard to the school administration, and teachers are involved, but the problem persists, a change is mandatory. If it is a public school and you live in a community with multiple schools, you may be able to obtain a variance as a solution for all.

There are those in small communities who really cannot escape their limited school options. One client from a rural farm family comes to mind. They came to me with two sisters who had experienced some bullying and were struggling to keep passing grades. I ended up recommending changing schools due to some teacher inadequacies and ultimately because the leadership of the school was not an educator. His concept of how to handle students struggling was not effective or respectful to their potential. Finally, the parents chose to change schools and were already going to the private Catholic school which they thought would work out best, but it turns out it did not. And moving is not possible when you are dairy farmers. But the family found a solution after we all agreed to take a break and focus on their needs when they opened their mind to another religious school in the area, just not Catholic. The move turned out to suit their needs much better than any alternative, and the family has been doing well since an eighteen-month academic intervention. With this client, we used a reliable online learning platform in the interim and gave them pointed remediation to teach missing math, literacy skills, and study strategies. We achieved grade-level skills in this time, with no peers to worry about judging them, teasing them, or gossiping about them in their small-town grapevine. Since then, the two sisters have flourished in a different private religious school, and now know how to achieve learning with their unique brains. They have not needed intervention since. I keep getting positive reports of achievements and wonderful progress. It changed the whole family culture. No longer were evenings spent in fights, arguments, and stressful interactions. It became calmer, more loving, supportive, and fun. Pretty beautiful transformation. This is why I love my job. It radiates to the family when a child's learning struggles are attended to. Good grades and great attitudes have been achieved with a hard look at what each of their daughters needed. This case needed two changes in schooling until the fit was established for long-term independence.

It helps when you understand how the grade-based system works. Each year is a product, and that product is a step up from the previous year in expectations. This book has taught you how to think of your child's grade, compare it to their yearly progress, and see where they are with regard to that expectation. When a student has reading comprehension levels between two and three years or more below the grade level, asking them to participate productively in the learning is not productive. It is too far above their independent level, that they would constantly need to read and understand the tasks asked of them. This is seen all too often, unfortunately. Teachers cope by verbalizing every learning point to be tested, along with various other "accommodations" made to these students. What is sad, is they need something completely different than what they are receiving. Education currently is not designed to give them what I, as a reading specialist, would approve as appropriate for their learning. But this is no replacement for actual learning. I have other ideas which I tested at my school that would require an education paradigm shift, but in the meantime, I feel that a proactive response to this predicament would be a short-term intervention. First, the student needs to back up and learn what was missed. I cannot begin to explain the nuances of designing this, but a detailed assessment by a literacy specialist can do a good job at guiding this process to bring concordance to the skills. That is the trick with literacy. There are many details and for it to move along with each year of learning, it must all be in concordance or together. Often you see that students present with very unique sets of missing literacy issues, maybe in their orthographic knowledge, or phonemes, or vocabulary, or fluency. It can be complicated or simple, or anything in between. All are repairable, even those with dyslexic tendencies. This label is a large umbrella word that covers so many issues, it is not a useful label. It means reading is being processed in a very inefficient part of the brain, hence the errors and delays. You can change where reading is processed in the brain with certain teaching techniques, and yes, it is possible to function and learn through a dyslexic reading problem.

Since I brought it up, it is a great time to tell you the story of a dyslexic boy I met in January of his fourth-grade year. He was a nonreader. He knew a handful of two and three letter words when I met him. He had handwriting that was illegible. He was a master of avoidance behaviors in his Montessori school. His parents were losing faith that he would develop his reading skills. I have been working with him for four years now and he is in eighth grade. I have moved him into traditional charter school public education, and we have taught him how to print and do applied research specifically for dyslexic children with incredible results. He is now reading at seventh-grade level, and he is learning comprehensive vocabulary words middle schoolers should know. He is still receiving spelling instruction, and he is in grade-level pre-algebra. We are working on writing, comprehension, and math strategies that work around his language processing issues and working memory issues. He has learned so many school skills and strategies, and managing his emotions is among the most challenging for him. He is a lovely person who was shamed into so much fear and anger at the perception that he was not capable which has taken me proving it to him to believe we can change the outcome for him in school. We are on track to close the final gap for him to enter high school. This is a huge transformation from a completely nonfunctioning student to one who is ready to fly on his own. Yes, this one took four years, but it was more extensive than most with everything to learn, and I mean everything. But what a pleasure to accomplish this challenge for me. Every brain has its needs and preferences. This year, he is only doing math and language arts, but we are reading science and social studies passages, learning typing, watching teen news weekly, and doing extra vocabulary, grammar, and writing practice. This makes for a very busy week and full-time learning on what he specifically needs to be ready for in high school. This would not have been possible if I were not able to be in charge of his remaining fourth-grade year. His teacher was so happy to have some help and direction with his learning. And then in fifth and sixth grade he was immersed in grade-level work with extra time. We sacrificed learning content for traditional school expectations: learning how to test and learning how to study. I am excited to see what he will make of his life being taught how to be a learner and now feeling capable. His case is extreme, and it called for drastic measures. But on the other side now, his parents are grateful for the route out of his problem. They were not offered one from anyone else. Every other educator offers "accommodations," which is not a plan to catch him up. This is my plan to offer American education in my next book.

When considering the problem of being two to three years behind in math skills, this is not as simple for me to discuss. The product of expectations going up each year is also true for math. But math is dependent on logical brain development, number sense, working memory, long-term memorization skills, math vocabulary, and reading skills for word problems. It is a lot. If you are below grade level the reasons are many.

Dysgraphia is an inability to properly interpret diagrams like graphs or geometric diagrams. This is a perception processing issue that involves the visual process and can be permanent or part of a fixable vision issue. As, I said, it is complex. So how low your child is in math is a consideration, but it may take a math specialist to identify how best to bring productivity to the student. I have worked with many students over the years who were completely calculator dependent with few computational skills or inability to recall math facts. This is not a stopping block to higher-level mathematics. I have taught number sense and estimation skills to students with this issue many times, and the process is different for each student. The important thing is focusing on the vocabulary and concept development along the way and teaching strategies of thinking. Being slow is fine and sometimes becoming fast is not possible. It is not a dealbreaker.

Levels of math are not as simple in middle school. The only time that is not exactly true is in middle-school math. The math curriculum is pretty "flat" during sixth- and seventh-grade math classes. It is an opportune time to prepare those students who did not master concepts in elementary school's computational and number sense learning for the algebraic mathematics of high school. Even geometry is algebra based along with some inductive reasoning with the proofs and then formulaic volume and surface area expectations. The vocabulary in math is often an issue along with the skills expected, and these years often serve to reteach and reinforce the extensive math vocabulary expected from students. Sometimes it is not catching up students but preparing them for what is coming when math issues are in middle school. Every stage of math issue requires foresight and strategy to help your child with whatever their issues are to be ready for what is coming.

The naming of math classes purposely makes this middle-school math area hard to discern sometimes, with reasons that may vary, and it makes it sometimes hard to know about middle school math choices and the ramifications down the road with high school curriculum. Pre-algebra is a course often offered in seventh grade and is currently considered grade level. Then Algebra 1 offered in eighth grade is next in line and also grade level now. Twenty years ago, or more, Algebra 1 was grade level in ninth grade, but not many places anymore. If you can be in geometry in ninth grade as a freshman, then you can be in Algebra 2 as a tenth grader. This allows you to study and prepare for the SAT or ACT in eleventh grade because you have had the math covered on that test in your tenth-grade year. Your brain has the time to become comfortable with these ideas, and precalculus in eleventh grade reviews all of Algebra 2 in the fall with uglier numbers and just a few new ideas, which also helps the college-bound student wanting to score well on these entrance exams. This advantage was chosen for students based on what math class they took in seventh and eighth grade. I would rather expose students to these ideas and give them every opportunity to rise up to being college bound or competitive for the trades. It is my goal for every student because there are very few students who cannot be there with proper preparation and teaching. You can "accommodate" students into many excuses and low achievement. There is a time when excuses are just that, and the result becomes a low self-esteem, aiming low and staying safe. That is all too common to observe in any school in America.

You may think that I am too soft – oh no, quite the contrary. High expectations are my calling card and limiting beliefs about a student's past performance predicting the future is just ignorant. I have case study after case study and a decade of data to prove otherwise.

Math is one area that splits up students entering into ninth grade. Students enter Algebra 1 commonly, but most districts enter freshman in geometry. The important thing is that the foundation is there. Every math teacher agrees on that premise, and parents get that concept with math. The intervention prior to high school makes the smooth transition to college math expectations if that is your goal.

"The four-year degree is the new high school diploma." Many jobs require a degree to apply, and this might be changing, but the truth is, our society needs many specialists that require education. Our technological society needs scientists, engineers, designers, and programmers. Disciplines are crossing over with engineering and medicine, as a great example. We need specialists who need training, and this requires being teachable and possessing the ability to learn. Education directly correlates with a majority of people's income earning power. The media loves to focus on the exceptions. What is your backup plan? That is a great question for the sponsored ski racer hoping to win Olympic medals and be rich. Or the gamer who keeps telling you he is good enough to compete and get paid to play. Or the person who wants to try something artistic. Gosh, it could be great but that could also be a hobby if you need to find an income that is dependable.

I am a big fan of art so no throwing stones here. My school gave every student private music lessons, a foreign language, and an art class every week. We also had PE four days per week for kindergarten through fifth grade. The kids came to school for those reasons, and we squeezed efficient pointed education in-between all the fun and it was amazing how many students learned to love school. And no, my school was not a majority of at-risk learners. I would say we had athletes who needed flexibility and second homeowners who wanted small class sizes and effective education. The arts play a huge role in developing minds, as does physical movement. These are paramount actually, but the math and literacy skills are paramount too.

My favorite creative solution to mention here is to remove science and social studies from a student in first through eighth grade who is struggling in both math and language arts. This way, I double the time and energy I can devote to learning math and literacy skills. This has been a key decision when the student is desperately behind, and a motivated parent can homeschool their child for a year with this focus and see if that gap can be closed. It is worth a try if school is negatively impacting their sense of self.

Learning how to learn is the idea and the ultimate goal of education, making that the priority. Social concerns are the least of my worries as they are superficial, and ego based. If you teach your children social concerns are the most important thing, then what lesson is that? You need to pretend to have friends at a great personal cost? No, thank you. Friends are friends no matter your journey. That is a life lesson, too.

When your child dreads school on a daily basis, you need to address this problem for and with your child immediately. If you see your child's personality disappearing because of school and school stress, that is a call to action. If your child is getting bullied and you have tried all avenues to address this at school and there's no improvement, remove your child. The price they will pay is too large to their sense of self. If your child is having panic attacks over testing or becoming physically ill from anxiety, make a change. Drastic times look like these scenarios. Your child's drastic scenario may look completely different, but you are their parent. I believe that parents have a sense of what their child needs, and if that intuition you have is going off, believe yourself. Be the leader your child needs you to be, and do not listen to anyone not connected to your child's pain. You are their protector and assigned to help them prepare for their life.

It is all about the journey. Stop focusing on the prize and enjoy each step of the journey. Persistence is a life lesson and with practice and study comes learning.

RECAP: DRASTIC TIMES CALL FOR DRASTIC MEASURES

- You and your child are both involved in the decision.
- Providing a new school to repeat a grade may feel emotionally safe for a new beginning.
- Providing a homeschool year may resolve the problems by focusing on "catching up" and then re-entering the next year.
- You can reevaluate after a best effort year attempts to catch up. A professional is recommended for this process.
- I have found that there are creative ways to solve these situations that can be filled with love and travel or peacefulness.
- In a fast-paced world, to take the time to slow down and focus on repairing and rebuilding what is needed, is a positive character lesson.
- Adversity can be viewed as opportunity to accomplish something very rewarding.
- It is all about attitude, and parents set the stage.
- View challenge as an opportunity and enjoy the journey.

26

YOU CAN DO THIS

Parents are their child's first educators. Parents' roles as their child's educator are more important than any other responsibility you may have. Your child is depending on you to help them have the skills to succeed. Your child's learning success will be directly proportional to the topics in this book. Of that, I am sure. How well a parent has done preparing their child for learning is often the question.

When did the American family begin to rely so heavily on the education system? Most learnings were taught at home when education was formed in America. The one-room schoolhouse was a place to learn to read, write, and compute. Work ethic and perseverance were taught at home.

A parent whose child is not succeeding in school feels frustrated at the educators involved because they have not found the solution. Teachers feel frustrated with receiving students who are not prepared for learning. This is true at every level. When a student is assigned to you and they are not prepared to be learning what is mandated to teach, you can see the frustration on the teacher's side. Both criticize the other and feel some level of angst. That is human and normal.

Parents might not be aware of what would best help their child succeed in school. I wrote this book to help parents who ultimately have the responsibility and power to make a difference for their child. Whether they hire a professional to intervene, or they carve out the time to implement what they learned themselves, both are difficult and have a price of time, commitment, and attention to detail.

Teamwork makes the dream work. By working together and sharing some of the necessary growth goals with your child's teacher, you can collaborate. Most teachers are very willing to help supplement a parent filling in gaps. Use your teacher's expertise to help and seek district reading specialists, math specialists, and counselors' aid to help you deal with content and emotional challenges beyond the scope of this book. I have tried to touch on everything a parent can feasibly do and to foster conversations between parents and their children to lead them to the goal of improving their academic experience.

Finding experienced educators who share the vision in this book to be in your child's life should be a goal. If an educator thinks that your child has little potential and treats them as such, I would not endorse that placement. You need optimism in a teacher for growth. You need an educator willing to collaborate with you and maybe a team of experts you get involved in. You need an educator who connects with your child and makes them feel worthy and worthwhile, someone whose personality supports your child's brave self and encourages effort and curiosity.

Above all, find how your child can feel emotional safety as they address learning that challenges them. Maybe a year of homeschool will allow the privacy and rigor that is exactly for your child. Be ready to think out of the box to find a solution to end the discrepancy between your child's skills and their next year's grade level.

My goal is for all children to have basic math and literacy skills to navigate the educational, artistic, and work interests to live a fulfilled life. Solving learning problems requires a thorough approach to the child and their approach to learning, thinking, and self-perception of skills. Ask yourself, do I want to do this work, or who will help me on this journey? What educational resources can you call upon to discuss what areas you feel need to be addressed for your child? Use them. What obstacles do they need to overcome in achieving this process? My goal is for every child to be able to pursue the knowledge they seek and participate in the formation of their future.

I want to remind you of the importance of executive function in your reading process combining all aspects of literacy to work in harmony. Also, time management, planning, and essential organizational skills also require executive function skills. Managing impulses along with emotions also requires executive function skills. Designing proper study plans that increase learning requires planning and implementing strategies, which is reliant on executive function.

Look through the checklist you have formed for your child or each of your children. Have you narrowed down the issues that are holding them back? Have you found new avenues to explore? Do you have a plan of what to bring to your next teacher meeting, 504 Plan, or teacher conference? You can do this.

Your child depends on you. Prioritize catching up and ending the struggle. A big effort now will pay dividends into the future. Make learning fun and memorable by involving the senses. Enjoy the relationship that is formed when your child's learning process is respected, addressed, and nurtured. They do not know how to ask for help, but their behavior shows their emotions. Struggling students are often angry, withdrawn, or rebellious. How is their anger or feeling badly about their academic performance playing out given their personality? The Color Code test will help you understand what motivates your child. The idea of beginning at the first level of struggle is a general rule in math and literacy issues. Reach out for help in the areas you feel most intimidated. That is just fine. But now you know what the needs are, and you can decide how best to navigate your child's transformation into their potential, aiming for the idea of concordance. All skills at the same level functioning together is ideal. Bring the lowest skills up and then address them all to the same levels and you will find the learning then flows on its own. By levels I am meaning grade levels are a fair aim for all skills and behaviors.

I believe in you and encourage you to listen to your instincts and intuition and use sound resources along the way. I believe in you because a parent is motivated by the strongest love on the planet. I wish you and your child the very best on your journey. You got this!

ACKNOWLEDGMENTS

This book has been a long time in the making. I would like to acknowledge Angela Lauria and The Incubator team for helping accomplish my goal of writing a book which has been over a decade in the making. I do not think I would have the experience to learn as much as I have without the support of my volunteer Board of Directors at Custom Learning Academy (CLA) from 2005-2015. This board served to support me during the trials and establishment of a school in a community that reached across the United States with our clients being Lake Tahoe second homeowners often from many faraway places. It is during those years where I was able to focus on the topics in this book and really make a difference in students' achievement.

First, I want to acknowledge Tom Griffin, PhD, Education Attorney, who served as Board President of CLA for ten years. He was there to inform schools of the validity of our credits transferred whenever questioned. He was there to help advocate for our students to participate on the local public athletic teams associated with the high school and help me present proposals to the necessary boards to form an agreement. We advocated for that as a "rural exclusion" and negotiated an amenable arrangement that functioned smoothly for all of our students. We needed the legal support at times and other times we relied on his vast knowledge of school reform and our design to address individual student academic needs. He and I worked as a team to produce the data of effectiveness our yearly ITBS testing validated. Thank you, Tom, for your friendship and passion to serve students. Students are the customers in our line of work, he always reminded me. And thank you to his wife Susie for all the support behind the scenes.

Next I would like to thank Jill Ramar, MBA. Jill also served for ten years supporting the school with her parent point of view and her excellent communication skills to our school newspaper and marketing efforts. Jill's ability to use creativity and critical thinking skills was always an asset during any board meeting where growth issues or challenges presented themselves. Jill encouraged our yearly Magic Show, which was a fun family town event that profited the school and often recruited new students. Jill's support always helped us move forward and polished our brand. You were a client for a short time while we also learned from your son about vision stress. This common problem is a passion of yours because you were personally a witness to the power of fixing this correctable problem. Thank you so much for believing in the potential of children and modeling it with your own children.

Last but not least is Ermelinda Cashell. Thank you Ermelinda for bringing business support from your experience with your family's business experience. You brought a wealth of knowledge and confidence in the areas of cash flow management and financial structural support. This was a key element to my confidence to have the opportunity to offer a unique school to focus on student achievement. Your parental viewpoint of the athlete and college-bound student also supported my values of how excellence can be achieved by creativity. We incorporated very creative calendars of learning to minimize school stress impacting your daughter's ski racing competitions and training cycles. Her accomplishments in both academics and ski racing were unprecedented on the local teams. She has gone on to impressive college pursuits to include a year at the Sorbonne in Paris, and the pursuit of a medical career, the last I checked. You are an example of an engaged parent who supported and respected their child into a successful, confident adult. Thank you to Rob for allowing both of your time to be impacted on a regular basis for the ten years Ermelinda generously volunteered. Thank you both for your generous years of service and support.

Outside of my board members, I must acknowledge Dr. Meggin McIntosh. She was the professor who motivated me to enroll in my literacy graduate program and exposed me to the prolific topic of neuroscience as it applies to learning, which has captivated my curiosity for the last twenty-two years. I appreciate Meggin for her initial inspiration but when I needed a coach for myself in 2013, she was there to help me discover what my true calling and inspiration was for after my school closed. That is how my current company, Academic Transformations, was formed, with Meggin's help. She helped me realize my true mission on the planet with her professional guidance. I am a rare person to find my calling in life and be fulfilled every day because of it. I owe this all to Meggin, and I will forever appreciate you for being in my life.

ABOUT THE AUTHOR

Lisa Crosby is a mother of three sons and is a unique educator who began her career as a public high school math teacher for fifteen years, where she was on the opening staff of two new public high schools. Lisa and her husband raised their three sons in Truckee, California. Lisa enjoys recreation in the Sierra Nevada Mountains in all seasons with her Samoyed dogs. Lisa is passionate about education, her family, her dogs, which she uses as therapy dogs with those who could benefit, and travel. She volunteers with her dogs at senior centers and hospitals, visiting patients and residents.

Lisa is a literacy specialist and math teacher through calculus, who specializes in math and test anxiety. She is also a physics and physical science teacher who has a background in mechanical engineering. Lisa has studied neuroscience as it applies to learning as a component of her master's degree and attends yearly neuroscience conferences, following and learning about current research in neuroscience and brain development.

Lisa founded and was the executive director and principal of a nonprofit private K-grade twelve college prep school which began in 2005 named Custom Learning Academy (CLA). CLA put neuroscience into practice and succeeded with ten years of unprecedented testing data through 2015. Her oldest son accomplished all his high school math classes at CLA, and her second and third sons graduated from her school accomplishing fifteen AP classes each. She earned full accreditation in 2007 and was NCAA approved for the athletes aiming for college sports. CLA was a forward-thinking, tech savvy school that offered college prep rigor, while remediating all background gaps in math and literacy along the way to produce confident students ready for their future. Her unique approach to education emphasized social-emotional safety and respected the individuality of each student with a customized approach and small class sizes.

Most recently, Lisa is the founder and president of Academic Transformations in Reno, Nevada. Academic Transformations provides Learning Coaches for remediating struggling students of any age. Lisa has extensive experience with those coping with dyslexia, ADD/ ADHD, or anxiety in their educational pursuits. Additionally, Lisa is an Education Advocate and Public Speaker. Academic Transformations serves clients all over the continental US. Lisa most enjoys giving hope and success to students and families, whose lives transform with her work.

www.AcademicTransformations.com

Difference Press is the exclusive publishing arm of The Author Incubator, an educational company for entrepreneurs – including life coaches, healers, consultants, and community leaders – looking for a comprehensive solution to get their books written, published, and promoted. Its founder, Dr. Angela Lauria, has been bringing to life the literary ventures of hundreds of authors-in-transformation since 1994.

A boutique-style self-publishing service for clients of The Author Incubator, Difference Press boasts a fair and easy-to-understand profit structure, low-priced author copies, and author-friendly contract terms. Most importantly, all of our #incubatedauthors maintain ownership of their copyright at all times.

LET'S START A MOVEMENT WITH YOUR MESSAGE

In a market where hundreds of thousands of books are published every year and are never heard from again, The Author Incubator is different. Not only do all Difference Press books reach Amazon bestseller status, but all of our authors are actively changing lives and making a difference.

Since launching in 2013, we've served over 500 authors who came to us with an idea for a book and were able to write it and get it self-published in less than 6 months. In addition, more than 100 of those books were picked up by traditional publishers and are now available in bookstores. We do this by selecting the highest quality and highest potential applicants for our future programs.

Our program doesn't only teach you how to write a book – our team of coaches, developmental editors, copy editors, art directors, and marketing experts incubate you from having a book idea to being a published, bestselling author, ensuring that the book you create can actually make a difference in the world. Then we give you the training you need to use your book to make the difference in the world, or to create a business out of serving your readers.

ARE YOU READY TO MAKE A DIFFERENCE?

You've seen other people make a difference with a book. Now it's your turn. If you are ready to stop watching and start taking massive action, go to http://theauthorincubator.com/apply/.

"Yes, I'm ready!"

OTHER BOOKS BY DIFFERENCE PRESS

Unleash Your Power Through Reiki: The Guide to This Energetic Healing Art by Allison L. Brown

Be Strong, Be Wise: 5 Easy Steps to Discussing Sexual Ethics with Teens by Amy R. Carpenter

BOSS LADY Real Estate Agent: Show up, Stand out, and Rule the Market (Like a Girl) by Stephanie Jones

Turn Back Your Biological Clock: Your Ultimate Guide to Better Health and Longevity by Duncan McCollum, D.C.

Unconventional Healing: The Ultimate Guide to Overcoming Fibromyalgia Symptoms by Nicole Nguyen Van Binh

The Fearless Entrepreneur: Break through the Corporate Mindset and Start Your Dream Business by Clarisa Romero

Clinician Retention Strategies: The Healthcare Executive's Guide to Leading through the Storm and Keeping Your Vital Staff by Dr. Karen Wade

Stop Worrying about Bladder Leaks: The Guide to Overcoming Urinary Incontinence by Shelia Craig Whiteman PT, DPT, CLT

A Jesus I Can Follow: Do I Leave the Church or Do I Stay? by Sue Williams

Building Relationships that Last: The Guide to Mutually Fulfilling Love by Freda Wilson

Thank you for your commitment to reading this book. I know you now have direction to help your child and engage with their teachers in productive ways. I love you for seeking to be there for your child in every way possible. Bravo and big hug to you!

There is hope for every child, and my hope is that you are inspired to guide your child into a confident student with a growth mindset. Understanding the essential foundations explained in the chapters of this book further serves to guide decisions in education for your child in the future based on what you have learned about them. Knowing the principles discussed that are essential for learning also applies to education changes you are asked to vote on.

To thank you, I have two secret gifts for you. First, I have a quarterly newsletter where I share useful information for parents to support their children in education. Sign up with your email at www.AcademicTransformations.com/newsletter.

Second, if you go to this secret back page of my website: www.AcademicTransformations.com/TheStrugglingStudent/more and enter STUDENTSUCCESS, you will find a series of videos from me to you. Get a cup of coffee and sit down with me to overview any of the topic chapters you may want to know more about. Go to the chapters you identified for your child to hear more of the tips and advice I would give my clients, friends, and family. Come and share a cup of coffee with me. I would love to help you further.